Centerville Library
Washington-Centerville Public Library
Centerville, Ohio

DISCARD

W9-CNG-183

Centerville Library
Washington-Centerville Public Library
Centerville, Ohio

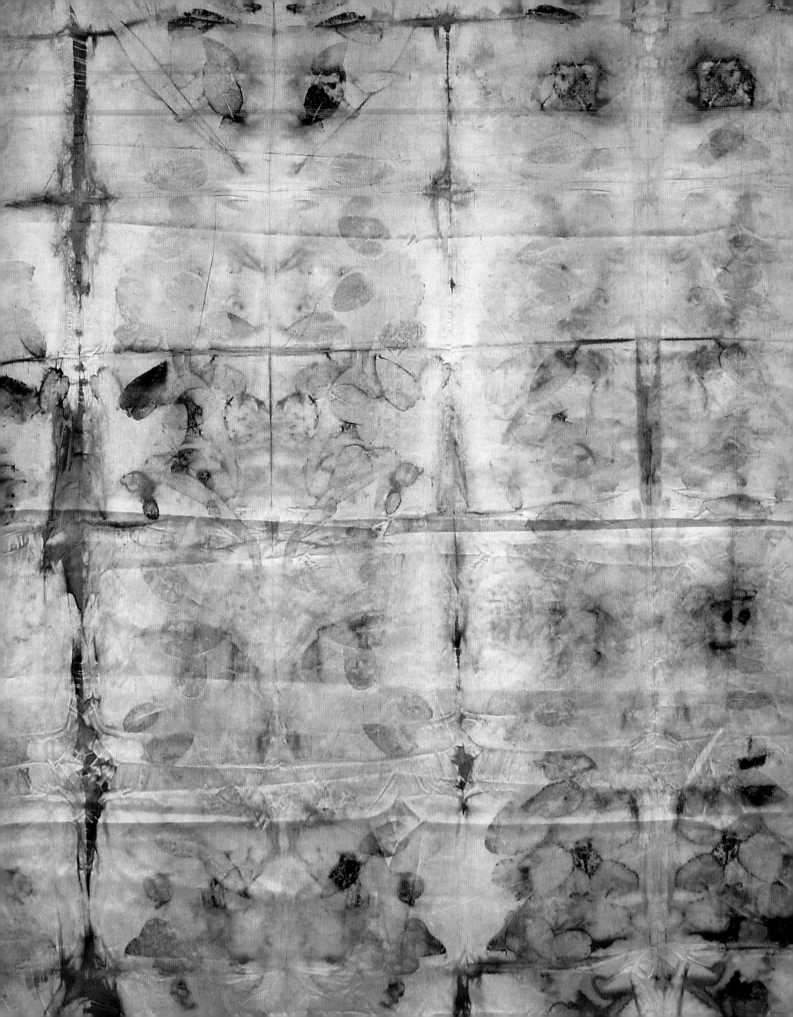

ECO COLOUR

for my parents

ECO COLOUR

botanical dyes for beautiful textiles

INDIA FLINT

INTERWEAVE
interweavestore.com

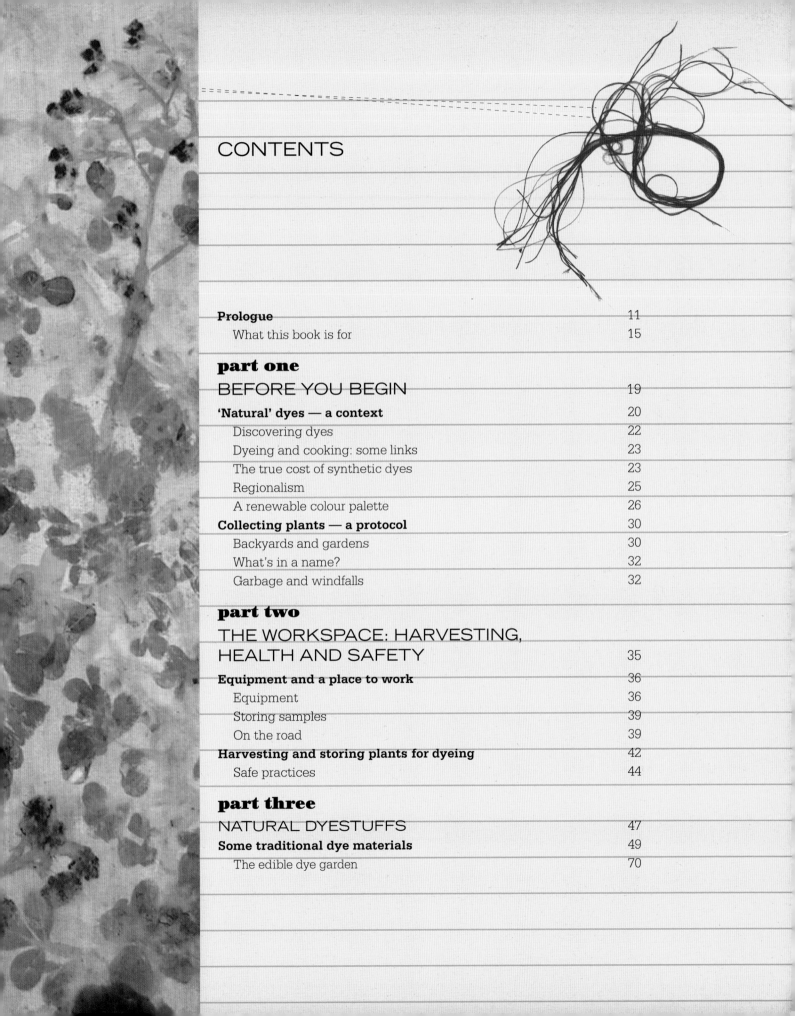

CONTENTS

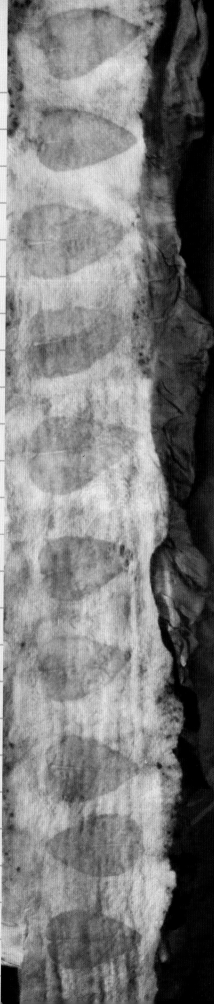

part seven

SOME OTHER CONSIDERATIONS 201

part eight

REFERENCES 225

Above: The author as a child. Above right: The author's grandmother, Bertha Pilskalns. Top right: Details of 'sommergarten' faerie dress felted of wool, flax and silk, and printed with leaves from various *Rosa*, *Philadelphus* and *Fragaria* species.

PROLOGUE

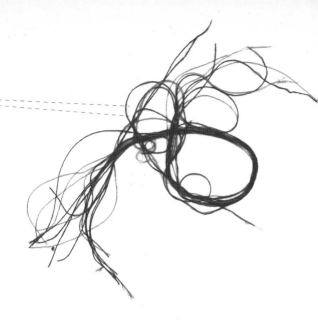

When I was a very small child, I had the great good fortune to be cared for by my maternal grandmother while my mother pursued studies in art. Little did I realise how influential her guidance would prove and that I would eventually make a living using the simple techniques she taught me all those years ago.

Grandmother sewed all her clothes on an old portable hand-cranked Singer sewing machine, purchased in 1927 and lugged by her through war-torn Europe on the flight from Latvia in 1944. Using this machine, she made stylish clothing for her daughters from tattered rags during the famine years. Particularly memorable is a nightgown (sadly, later lost in a bushfire) fabricated from a linen sheet hand-woven by my great-grandmother from home-grown and home-spun flax. This was worn in succession by my aunt, my mother and eventually me. Later in Australia, the sturdy Singer was used to sew curtains and pillowcases for the little house she worked so hard to buy. The same sewing machine kept me sane many years later, when I was living on the outskirts of the Andamooka opal fields in the far north of South Australia, in a house independent of the power grid.

As well as growing vegetables and flowers, making jams and baking delicious bread, my grandmother also made (by hand) feather pillows for each of her grandchildren. This involved an arduous journey by public transport to the slaughter-house to collect the bloodied feathers. These were tied in a cloth bag, scalded and thoroughly rinsed and dried before Grandmother (sitting in a closed room with her long hair tied up in a duster) stuffed the feathers into the ticking cases and stitched them up firmly. That was more than forty years ago. I still lay my head to rest every night on the pillow I watched her sew. It makes for good dreams.

But withal it was the magic she created in the dye-pot that impressed me most. When her blouses and cardigans became faded with age, she would over-dye them with colours extracted from onion skins, or left-over tea or

calendula flowers from the garden. While she would boil her cloth and add cooking salt as a mordant (not necessarily practices I will recommend in this book), the very idea of making colour from the garden was completely enchanting for me.

My mother, too, played a fundamental role in nurturing what would become my passion, as in addition to instructing me in the art of botanical observation and illustration, it was she who took charge of dyeing the eggs for the Easter celebrations every year. In the Latvian tradition, fresh hen eggs are wrapped in layers of plant material, beginning with tiny green strawberry leaves and other pretty herbs from the garden, and finishing with a good layer of dark brown onion skins. The bundled eggs are placed in a saucepan with water, brought to the boil, simmered for ten minutes and allowed to cool. Unwrapping each egg is always a delight as delicate patterns are revealed, each one unique. Experimenting with the egg-dyeing traditions using eucalyptus leaves on cloth led me to the discovery of the eco-print in 1999.

My father complemented this practical knowledge by instilling in me the love of wild nature, trees and forests. My first forest outing took place when I was only three weeks old, tucked into his old haversack (so I have been told) with a blanket and dozing happily as my parents climbed the Cathedral Range in Victoria.

As well as marvellous parents, I was also blessed with splendid great-aunts. Tante Ilse, a master bookbinder who lived near the Pilsensee in Bavaria, showed me the technique of making delicate leaf-prints to decorate the endpapers of books. Tante Rose was a passionate gardener who taught me the importance of binary nomenclature in plant identification, and Tante Milda made amazing wines and liqueurs from a wide array of berries, flowers and roots.

My paternal grandparents (mathematicians by profession) spent their weekends pottering about a small-holding in Vermont, harvesting edible plants from the wild and cultivating a complementary range of vegetables. Here I learned to keep a look out for black bears when gathering raspberries, and discovered for myself the staining properties of elderberries.

This book is thus a confluence of not one but several lifetimes' experiences, and a distillation of many learned skills. The text is by no means exhaustive, nor is it intended to be prescriptive. Rather it should function as a guidebook to an ongoing and colourful journey of exploration through the flora of the world, and as a series of signposts to other sources of knowledge. It has been a very long time in the brewing.

Below: A Latvian meadow — rich with promise for the dyer.

Plants lend their beautiful fragrance to the dyed cloth.

what this book is for

While commercial users of natural dyes demand industry standards, uniformity of dye material and colour-swatch conformity to agreed benchmarks, this book has been written in the hope of offering a more adventurous path to plant colour. Modern life surrounds us with a constant cocktail of toxins. They are in the food we eat, the cosmetics we apply, the household cleaning agents we use. They are given off by the upholstery in our cars, homes and offices, by building materials and even by our clothes.

Synthetic textiles and synthetic dyes are silent contributors to ill health. Many commercially dyed textiles still shed colour after many rinses. Some may not have been rinsed properly at all, to ensure that they are at their most brilliant and enticing at the point of sale. Brightly coloured garments usually have a care label recommending laundering prior to first use, and often the rinsing water will show a great deal of colour. Unfortunately the very act of washing loads the fabric with yet another set of toxins from the detergent. Even so-called natural dyes that have been fixed or enhanced with toxic mordants will inevitably disperse unattached molecules of indeterminate matter.

If a plastic PET water bottle (made of polyethylene terephthalate) cannot safely be re-used more than a few times before it begins to break down and releases phthalates into its contents, how can the wearing of polyester fabrics possibly be safe? Each time that easy-care synthetic polo shirt is flung into a washing machine the laundering process is making a further contribution towards the breakdown of the textile so that millions of tiny fibres find their way onto the skin, our largest and most easily accessible organ. It's not a pretty thought.

To reduce the toxic load in our bodies, it is obviously necessary to clean up our act, starting with the home by trying to reduce or eliminate noxious substances where we can. Assess the paints, solvents, glues, insecticides, cosmetics and cleaning aids you use and aim for those that will do the least damage. Read the list of ingredients on the labels and arm yourself with one of the many decoding books available. If in doubt, search the internet for further information.

This book should equip readers with the skills and information to extract dyes from a range of natural sources, make decisions as to the appropriate methods to apply to specific situations, analyse substances for their potential as mordants and apply a range of print dye techniques. They will also be able to implement safe work practice in the home and studio.

The instructions and suggestions offered here may not always lead
to permanent colours. On the other hand, you will have the satisfaction
of being an explorer in your own backyard, searching out hitherto
undiscovered potential. If a colour doesn't last forever, the cloth can simply
be dyed again. After all, our bodies change with time as well; our skins
wrinkle and our hair goes grey. Faded cloth is far more easily restored!

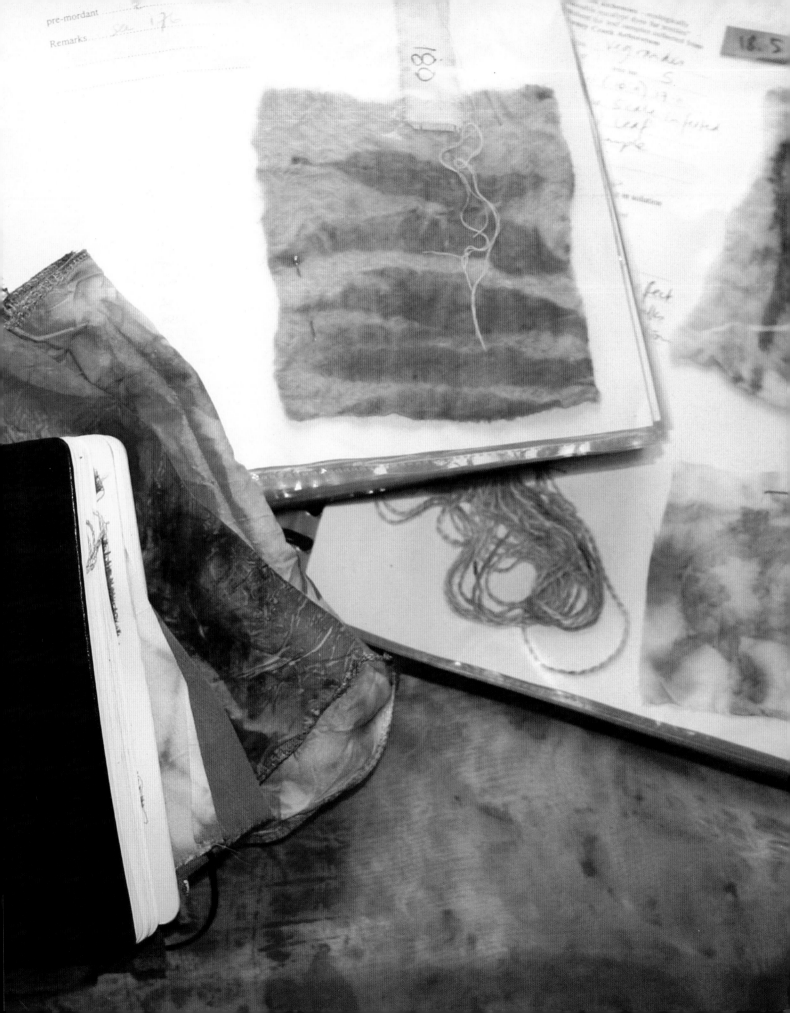

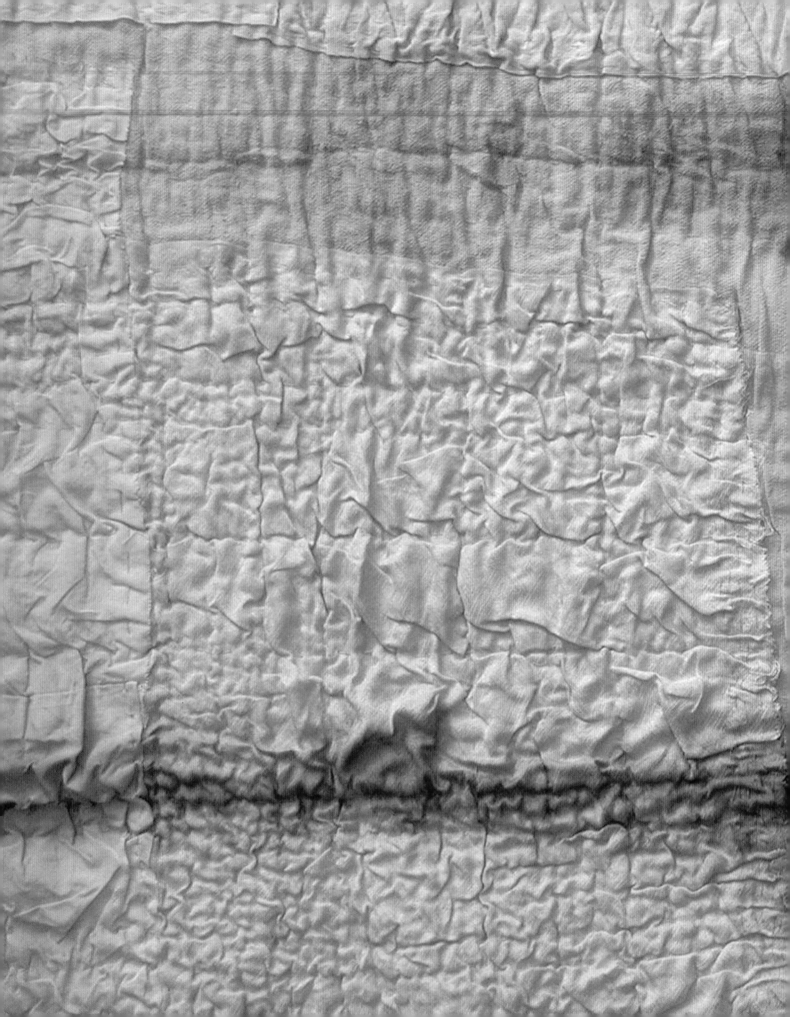

part one

BEFORE YOU BEGIN

'NATURAL' DYES —
A CONTEXT

From early times, humans have wanted to enhance their lives with colours; whether worn as jewellery, smeared onto bodies and walls in the form of paint, etched into the skin as tattoos or applied variously to clothing as embroidery, stains or whole-dyed cloth. Colour was a means of denoting social status and a deterrent to evil spirits as much as it was simply a source of pleasure. Dyes and stains were extracted from a diverse range of sources, including molluscs, lichens, insects, minerals, peat bogs and plants.

It is important, however, not to use the terms 'natural' and 'chemical' dyes to try to separate environmental sources from the synthesised, as the word 'chemical' quite simply describes everything. We are all made up of chemicals, as is our entire world in which the natural phenomena can be described using the sciences of chemistry, physics and mathematics. I prefer to use the terms 'natural' and 'synthetic' when describing dyes (even though pedants may suggest that a plant extract is synthesised from a plant). This avoids the misunderstandings that otherwise arise when dyes are referred to as 'chemical'.

The descriptor 'Tyrian purple' comes to us from the Mediterranean region, where dyers working along the coasts coloured their cloth with a photo-sensitive substance found in the hypobranchial glands of a range of molluscs, most notably those of the genus *Murex*. As the yellowish substance was exposed to sunlight, it changed to a rich violet colour. Millions of these small creatures were sacrificed to satisfy the rich and elite of the day. Roman emperors, for example, were distinguished by their purple togas, giving rise to the phrase 'born to the purple'. As the mollusc population diminished, so people searched for other sources of this sumptuous colour, discovering similar shades to be had through the ammonia-based processing of certain lichens. Initially, the murex dyes were adulterated with red-purple lichen extracts to stretch resources, but this practice eventually gave way to full lichen-based dyeing for the violet

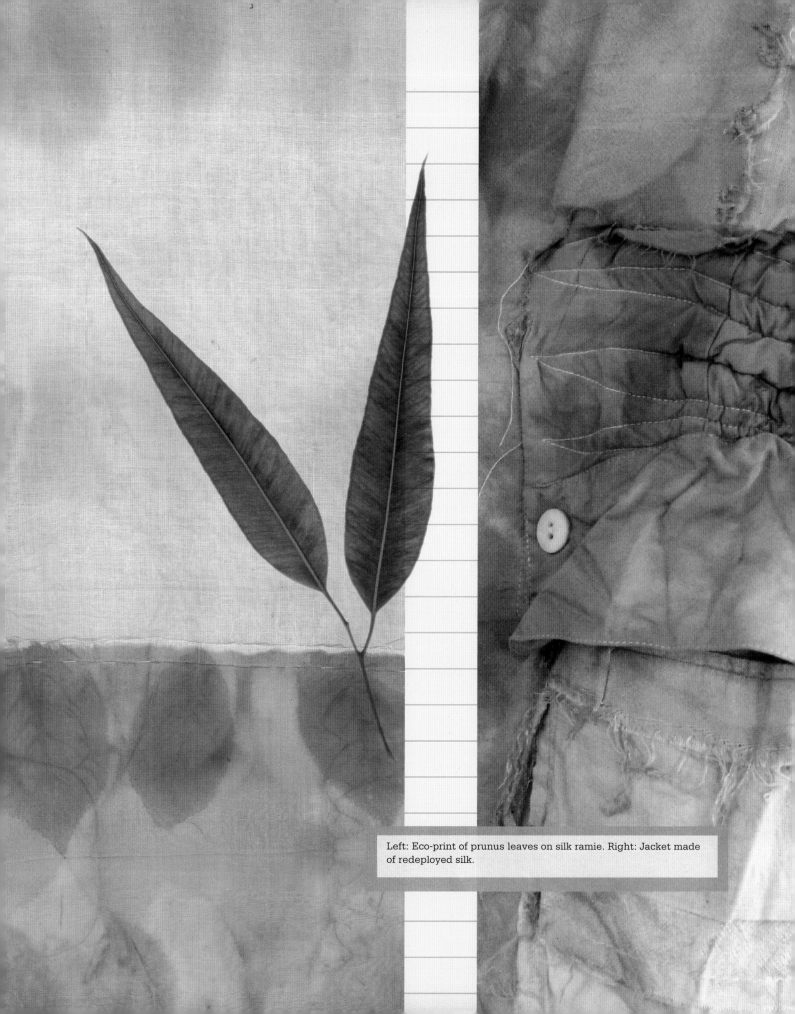

Left: Eco-print of prunus leaves on silk ramie. Right: Jacket made of redeployed silk.

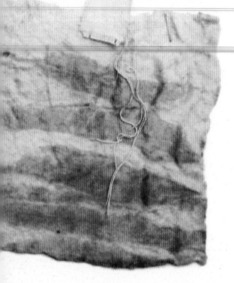

shades. The famed Harris tweeds of Scotland were dyed using lichens for reds, purples and browns, other endemic plants for yellows, greens and gold, and fermented woad (*Isatis tinctoria*) to make blue.

In parts of Scandinavia, the traditional thick woollen skirts of regional costumes were dyed by extended immersion in peat bogs. The process sometimes took up to two years, as the cloth was immersed in the bog, left to soak and occasionally aired, possibly to encourage oxidisation. The acidic nature of the bog would have acted as a wool conditioner, helping to soften the coarse fibres as the cloth turned from a warm golden brown to (eventually) a rich black. Eucalypt-stained rivers such as those on Kangaroo Island in the state of South Australia might offer similar possibilities.

But dyes made from plants are not limited to extracts from leaves. Bark, buds, flowers, fruit (including berries), seeds and roots from the one species can sometimes give quite different colours. Variations in methods of extraction and application can extend the palette further.

discovering dyes

There are many stories about the discovery of blue, but my favourite was told to me when I was quite young, I think by my grandmother. In the story there is a woman with a young baby who must leave her village and travel to a far place. She walks through the woods for days and nights and eventually comes to the edge of the trees, where she makes a small fire to cook a meal. While the food is warming, she wraps her nursling in fresh leaves and covers the child with her soft woollen shawl. When she has eaten, the child has been fed and the fire has died down, she spreads the warm ashes to make a soft bed for them both and together they lie down to sleep. In the morning she awakes to find that the combination of the dampness produced by the baby, the leaves in which it has been wrapped and the alkaline ashes of their bed have stained the shawl in the blue of the heavens. Perhaps that baby had been wrapped in woad leaves.

In Japan, *ai-zome* indigo dyeing using *Polygonum tinctorium* is a cherished art. The brilliant blue dye is coaxed into being through a complex fermentation involving rice wine, ash and bran, and is used to strengthen and extend the life of textiles as well as to give colour. This traditional dye process is kind to cloth and has minimal impact on the ecology.

Rich reds were derived primarily from madder (*Rubia tinctoria*), which originated on the Indian subcontinent. The vibrant scarlet patterns in the jewel-like carpets of the Middle East were derived from this plant and relied on a complex and lengthy process known as Turkey Red. Even today the carpets dyed using traditional plant colours still eclipse those coloured with

tea-bags and totes

Old shirts make useful storage bags for plant materials; sew together along the bottom hem, then sew across the arms at the top of the sleeves and trim. Insert a clothes hanger into the top of the shirt and simply button up the front to close. Such plant bags are then easily stored hanging on a rod and, because air can freely circulate, tend not to develop mould.

The sleeve remnants can be transformed into 'tea-bags' for small amounts of plant matter. If the dyestuff is stitched into the sleeve end (long sleeves can be cut into two bags), then a lot of pressure can be applied to squeeze out colour without fear of the bag coming undone.

synthetic dyes, though the use of the latter might appear faster and simpler. Such plant dyes are used in Turkey's DOBAG project (DOBAG is a Turkish acronym that identifies the Natural Dye Research and Development Project).

dyeing and cooking: some links

I have observed over the years that dye techniques in different societies seem to be quite closely related to their culinary practices. For example, in Europe and Britain, where food was cooked in pots over heat, dyes were traditionally processed by boiling, and this is probably how many colours were discovered in the first place. Common salt (sodium chloride) was used to preserve and enhance food and is considered to be one of the earliest mordants.

Japanese cooking features numerous practices involving fermentation and brewing, for example in the making of soy sauce, teas and tofu. Some of these may have influenced the development of the indigo dyeing process for which Japanese textiles are famed. Japanese indigo dyeing requires careful nurturing of the indigo vat with combinations of bran, sake and ash. The contents of the vat are felt, smelled and tasted as they mature. On the other hand, the technique of soy-based mordants for cotton could conceivably have been discovered when the cloth used to strain tofu (soybean curd) was subsequently inadvertently immersed in a dye-bath.

Australian indigenous culture is founded on the use of stone and wood rather than metals; the cooking traditions centre largely on the fire pit, so the process of boiling food in metal vessels was not practised until after the European invasion. In traditional Australian indigenous textiles (and body adornment), pigments and dyes were ground to pastes and applied directly to the object being decorated. This could perhaps explain why the dyes peculiar to the eucalypt (endemic to that southern island continent) were not used by Australia's first people.

the true cost of synthetic dyes

Before William Henry Perkin accidentally discovered that first synthetic dye (aniline purple) while trying to synthesise quinine in 1856, the colours applied to cloth came almost exclusively from nature. Although these were collectively and somewhat romantically described by the term 'natural dyes,' some of the extraction and application processes used were far from nature and certainly not harmless. The use of toxic chemicals as dye adjuncts (see pages 88–89) had unhealthy and ongoing consequences for both the dye practitioner and the environment.

natural blues

Woad (*Isatis tinctoria*, above) provided blue for European dyers for at least five millennia. France in particular was famed for woad production well into the Middle Ages; however, the industry gradually declined with the introduction of the more intense blue indigo in the form of *Indigofera tinctoria* from the Indian subcontinent. To achieve the blue colour, the dyer needed to ferment the plant material in the presence of an alkali — quite similar conditions to those that conspired in our faerie-tale opposite. Simple boiling of woad leaves produces another colour entirely, namely maroon (on protein fibres and on cellulose fibres that have been pre-mordanted using soy).

Delightful terminology including 'aqua fortis', 'orpiment' and 'oil of vitriol' referred to, respectively, nitric acid, arsenic tri-sulphide and concentrated sulphuric acid. Illustrations of eighteenth-century dye workshops showing vapours rising from open vats and liquids swishing underfoot encourage the speculation that a significant percentage of dyers of that era would have enjoyed a shortened life expectancy. Even today many dye workers are still compromised by dangerous conditions; in India, children are sent to rinse dyed cloth in ponds and streams and are encouraged to romp in the water with the dye-soaked cloth.

While popular opinion has it that Perkins is the father of synthetic dyes, Prussian blue — the colour that resulted when ferrous salts were combined with potassium ferro-cyanide (discovered in the mid 1700s) — hardly seems a 'natural' dye. Even William Morris, who drove the nineteenth-century Arts and Crafts movement in defiance of the introduction of synthetics and so fervently promoted natural dyes, did not consider the environmental consequences of large-scale dyeing and the effects on local waterways, and probably did as much to undermine the perception of natural dyes as he did to promote them.

The comparatively speedy colour results offered by the availability of synthetic dyes, however, made them very popular indeed. Purchase of a container of powder must have seemed so much easier than growing, harvesting and processing with the appropriate mordant (in the case of adjective dyes, which are those that require the addition of a mordant in order to bond with the fibre or to achieve a particular colour). The cost to the environment and to collective cultural knowledge has, however, been staggering. Within a few generations, the recipes for colour that had been handed down for centuries were largely forgotten; many were lost completely. Rivers and streams suffered, as did the factory workers who synthesised the dyes. The textiles also suffered, as some of the dyes used contained harsh components that made fibres brittle and thus led to early breakdown. I once bought a piece of fifty-year-old black cotton gingham at a country auction. The cloth had been stored since purchase in an old suitcase and had not been washed since leaving the mill. As one of my children was keen to have a garment made from it, I tossed it into the washing machine for the usual pre-sewing wash, only to find that all of the black threads in the weave totally disintegrated while the white (un-dyed) remained intact. The black dye had completely eaten away the thread.

In more recent times, even domestic textile dyeing using plant materials usually implied the use of additive chemical mordants. These mordants range from relatively harmless compounds such as alum (potassium aluminium sulphate), table salt (sodium chloride) and vinegar (diluted acetic acid) to dangerous and potentially lethal substances such as chrome (potassium dichromate), tin (stannous chloride), copper (copper sulphate) and iron (ferrous sulphate).

During a brief journey to India in 2006, I visited the village of Pochampally. Here the use of natural dyes to colour yarn for ikat weaving is gradually being re-introduced — for the simple reason that the ground-water has been completely poisoned by synthetic dye residues seeping through the soil, and people realised too late that these substances made them sick. Water for drinking must now be trucked in from Hyderabad (about two hours away by road) and it is unlikely the well water will become safe to drink again. Unfortunately some villagers are still persisting with synthetic dyes to get such colours as turquoise, using toxic mixes without masks or gloves, their hands permanently stained brilliant blue. Wastes were still being disposed of by pouring them onto the ground. The next vital step in the project will be to ensure that all adjunct mordants used to fix the natural dyes are also of low environmental impact. Given the 'quick magic' offered by the addition of metallic salts to plant dye processes, it is unlikely this will happen soon.

The salts of chrome, tin, copper and iron are not only potentially injurious to the health of dye makers, they also present serious ecological difficulties in terms of safe post-dyeing disposal. For the individual, disposing of metallic salt wastes remaining after domestic or small-scale workshop dyeing poses a problem, requiring evaporation pits to reduce the residue to a manageable sludge, thus minimising the volume of material for disposal. Unfortunately, the question of safe disposal of this toxic sludge is not one that has as yet been resolved satisfactorily, nor can it possibly be safe to wear cloth that has been soaked in a substance such as potassium dichromate (it is a known carcinogen). For this reason, this book encompasses only ecologically sustainable plant dye methods using renewable resources and attempts to take the path of doing the least harm to the dyer, the end user (of the object) and the environment.

regionalism

The other significant idea underpinning this book is that of 'regionalism'. I work as a freelance costumier, writer and designer specialising in hand-worked slow fashion, redeploying salvaged materials where possible, but also utilising renewable resources as required. I exclusively use plant dyes to colour my work, harvesting them from trees, shrubs and flowers grown on the family farm, supplemented by the collection of roadside weeds. No toxic chemical adjuncts are used in generating or fixing colours.

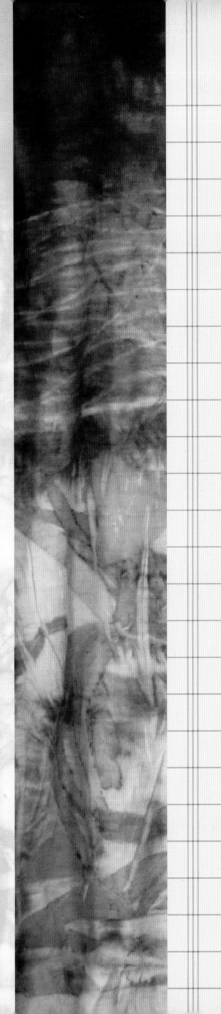

When asking, 'Why work regionally?', consider the following examples. Bizarrely, oranges irrigated with valuable water from the Murray River in South Australia are fed to sheep or simply picked and dumped in landfills, while supermarket shelves are loaded with identical product from the United States. Cherries are flown to Australia from California and offered at prices which, when the cost of a human airfare for the equivalent weight is deducted, would leave the farm-gate price in the negative. We ludicrously import water in glass bottles from Europe while exporting ours in the form of cotton and rice. Instead of eating locally grown food in season, Australian consumers demand supplies of strawberries and tomatoes all year round.

Similar foolishness is seen in the 'natural' dye world, where many dyes are made from plants harvested from fragile environments and shipped over great distances. It is all a matter of balance. Careful thought will determine whether it is more ecologically sustainable for an Australian manufacturer to use organically grown cotton sourced locally or silk sourced from China with the inherent transport costs. The debate is not a simple one. Organic cotton initially seems the soft option, but how does the value of the water used to grow the cotton compare with the environmental impact of transporting the silk over such a distance? What processes will be applied to the cotton on its way to the point of sale? On the other hand, are the conditions for the silk workers fair, and what might be the wastes? Each option has its merits; each also has an extensive environmental footprint. Clearly there are no easy answers.

When purchasing imported dyestuffs, a responsible dyer will insist on product from ethical sustainable producers.

a renewable colour palette

Dyes from plants are a renewable resource, whereas synthetic dyes derived from petrochemicals or fossil sources, such as coal, are not. Literally every plant in the world will have some sort of colour to offer the dyer. There are at least as many subtly different hues as there are plant species in the world, and an infinite range of colours and shades to be had.

Even a small group of plants may yield a rich diversity of colour, as hues will vary depending on the season, the geographical and climatic location of the substrate (including temperature and precipitation), the chemical burden of the air (think metropolitan, industrial, suburban or rural) and the quality of the soil. Whether material is used fresh or allowed to dry first, picked from the plant or collected as fallen matter, green in spring or rich with autumn colour are but a few other factors. The method of processing (hot, cold, fast, slow) introduces yet more possibilities; the use and types

India Flint
"Arcadian alchemies – ecologically
sustainable eucalypt dyes for textiles"
worksheet for leaf samples collected from
Currency Creek Arboretum

eucalyptus *macrocarpa* ssp

row ...16... tree no. ...2.1...

date ...3·11 (10·11) 17·11...

material collected ...dried leaves...

....

....

....

sample process ~~steaming~~
⟨simmering in solution⟩

dye vessel   stainless steel
        copper
        iron
        ⟨aluminium⟩

pre-mordant ....

Remarks ....

of mordant and the quality and pH of the water used in the dye-bath are also factors in determining colour outcomes. Some plants, such as the perennial *Wachendorfia thyrsiflora*, will give quite different colours from roots (red and green), leaves (tan) and flowers (yellow and orange). Multiply the different chemical compositions of the plants by the number of process variants discussed in this book and it will soon become clear that a lifetime could be spent dyeing without ever running out of new possibilities.

The internet is full of advertisements adjuring the uninformed to purchase exotic dyestuffs without thought as to the potential consequences. While there are, of course, ethical fair traders, their numbers are relatively few, and many natural dyes sold commercially are inappropriately harvested from ecologically fragile regions, depleting local stocks and endangering traditional practices. Those little packets of logwood chips sold as dye by craft suppliers may seem quite innocuous; consider, however, that these chips come from the heartwood and can only be produced by sacrificing the whole tree. The clear-felling of whole forests in order to generate dyes to colour cloth, when similar hues might be achieved from plants sourced closer to home, is deplorable.

Every culture has its own dye traditions, handed down through generations, reflecting local flora, geology and climate and informed by medicine, history, botany, economy and sometimes even religious practice.

Appliquéd, embroidered and resist-dyed redeployed silk and cotton singlet.

EXPLOITATION IN THE LOGWOOD AND INDIGO TRADES

Discovered by the Spanish on the Yucatan Peninsula, logwood (Haematoxylon campechianum) became so popular that vast areas of natural tropical vegetation were cleared to establish commercial plantations on the islands of Haiti and Jamaica. Logwood from Central America was included in the treasures pirated on the high seas of the Atlantic. The British exploited their own colony Honduras for the sake of this dyestuff and proceeded to exact a substantial tax from cutters. Though it makes a brilliant purple dye, the colour fades quite quickly on exposure to sunlight, so one rather wonders what the fuss was all about.

The production of indigo has a 5,000-year history in India, and both blue-dyed textiles and wads of the dye eventually found their way to Europe along the Silk Road in medieval times. European customers were much impressed with indigo blue, as it was considerably deeper and richer than that of woad. To protect the local woad industry, various impediments were placed in the way of indigo's use in dye houses. Labelled by some as the 'Devil's Dye', for a long time it was only permitted as an adjunct to woad. Eventually woad production declined and indigo took over.

When the British occupied the east coast of North America they found the climate to be conducive to growing indigo and it was hoped that this closer source might be more economical than that supplied by overland trade. Indigo was established near Charleston, South Carolina, by an enterprising sixteen-year-old, Eliza Lucas, who was left in charge of the family plantation while her father, George, served as Governor of Antigua. Eventually, through extraordinary perseverance, a viable dyestuff was indeed extracted ... and later used to dye the coats of those who fought in the Wars of Independence, thus distinguishing them from the British Redcoats.

With Independence came the demise of the potential British exploitation of North America. Clive of India leapt into the gap, so to speak, conquering Bengal in 1757 and so gaining large tracts of fertile land and establishing the exploitive activities of the East India Company. Importing European 'managers', they required farmers in Bengal to produce a certain quantity of indigo each year, inducing their co-operation by offering a small payment in advance, to be offset against the value of the crop and to deliver their refined harvest to specified factories. There, the measures were determined by those in charge and said farmers inevitably underpaid, as they were sometimes offered only one-eighth of the market value of the dye.

After deductions (which included the expenses associated with registering the agreement papers, the cost of seed supplied and even transport charges) the grower might not only get nothing in hand but could actually end up indebted to the planter on account of the advance given to him. The debt would increase over the years and would be passed down from father to son, effectively binding the family to the planter. In addition, the enforced cultivation of indigo affected the production of food. These were times of great hardship, of beatings and intimidation.

To cut a long and complex story short, in the mid 1800s the brothers Biswas, who had had enough of the situation, managed to persuade the growers in their village to 'passively rebel' by not growing any indigo at all. Despite the village being razed by fire in retaliation, the rebellion eventually spread to other villages and the growing of indigo in Bengal ceased by the 1860s. The British then moved their activities to Bihar, creating similar misery among the peasantry, with the result that in 1917 Mahatma Gandhi visited Champaran (in the region) to hold an enquiry into peasant exploitation. His quiet but polite refusal to leave the district when his activities came to the attention of the authorities is considered by many to be his first act of peaceful civil disobedience, leading thirty years later to the end of British rule in India.

At the end of the nineteenth century, Indian indigo production was undermined by the development of synthetic indigo dyes and what might have become a useful independently managed industry sank into temporary oblivion. In the 1980s the growing of indigo began gradually to be resurrected and today India is once again a source of beautiful blue.

Far left: *Indigofera tinctoria* growing at Hacienda San Juan Buenavista near the Pacific Ocean, in El Salvador. Left: Cakes of indigo extract drying in the sun. Below: Indigo test strips.

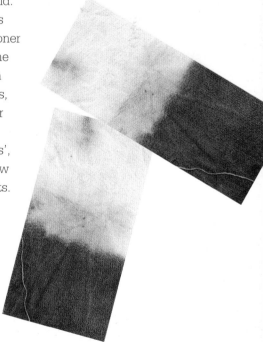

Indigo sample —
concertina fold + clamp

Throughout history, dyes have been valuable trade commodities and in many cases have led to horrific exploitations both of people and of the environment, as occurred in the indigo and logwood trades (see page 28).

Today, fragile bio-regions are still imperilled by the thoughtless harvesting and exporting of often rare plants. In recent years, a certain global soft-drink company's decision to flavour their sweet aerated liquids with vanilla beans had a serious impact on the vanilla industry, creating unprecedented demand for this precious plant product. It is our responsibility as dye practitioners — even those at a very small scale — to consider very carefully just how our actions are likely to affect our world.

The purpose of this book is to attempt to offer some guidance in terms of harvesting, storage, processing and application for the textile practitioner wishing to develop a locally flavoured palette for colouring their cloth. The beauty of natural dyes lies in the multitudes of possible variations. When using such haphazard and relatively spontaneous materials as plant dyes, standardisation is not the goal. The object of the game is to produce ever more beautiful colours and patterns and to celebrate the diversity that comes with a regionally based practice situated in a context of 'slowness', where time is literally of the essence. Slow dyeing, like slow food and slow fashion, requires more time and effort, but generates extraordinary results.

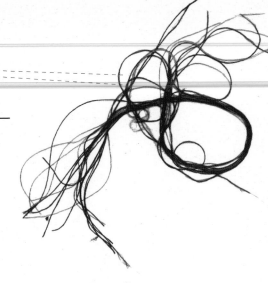

COLLECTING PLANTS —
A PROTOCOL

*Given the vast range of plants to choose from, where do we begin?
Whether the colour is worth the effort is a matter for individual judgement
based on a number of factors. When searching for plants to experiment
with in the dye-pot, availability (abundance or rarity) and potential
inherent toxicity are but two things to consider. Start by thinking locally.
The term 'non-exploitive harvesting' encapsulates the concept perfectly.*

Why import a dye to make a brown when so many shades are likely to be
available nearby? In Australia, for example, the abundance of eucalypts
and acacias leaves no justification for importing, say, cutch (a brown
dyestuff). Just as 'slow cooking' is regaining in popularity, so too should
we return to 'slow dyeing', using locally available dyestuffs harvested and
processed with due care for the environment.

backyards and gardens

It is always preferable to begin with the plants from your garden. There
are many clues as to whether a plant may show promise in the dye-pot; for
example, leaves with a sharp scent denote the presence of aromatic oils
and frequently also acids, often a reliable indicator that dye precursors
(substances that change by reacting to heat or to the presence of catalysts
in the form of co-mordants to generate colour) as well as visible colour
may be present. Staining on pavements, where leaves have fallen on
concrete and left their printed images, is another promising indicator.
Don't be afraid to approach tree-pruning crews working along roadsides.

If you haven't a garden of your own or that of a friend or neighbour that
you can harvest from, consider what is abundant on publicly accessible land
(roadsides) in your region. A good rule when gathering material in public
places is to harvest known weeds. Assess the weeds and pest plants armed
with your local government authority's noxious plant list. Generally, such
documents will have good descriptions and often clear illustrations of
prescribed weeds to help in identification.

The garden provides a plethora of useful materials for dyeing.

Oven bags are most useful if many small samples requiring heat are being processed together. Simply place the fibre in the oven bag with the dye and scrunch the top lightly together with a rubber band, ensuring air can escape as the bag is heated.

The bags can either be clipped using a bulldog clip against the side of a dye-pot to be heated while another larger batch is being processed, or stacked in a steamer basket over boiling water.

Remember the bags will expand as they are heated, so if they are sealed tightly they will have a tendency to pop! Oven bags can also be used to protect work that is enjoying slow dyeing in the warmth provided by the compost heap. If the colour influence of the heap is not required, package work in an oven bag to prevent attack by micro-fauna.

Oven bags can be recycled several times and when eventually punctured can still be used to wrap work before eventual disposal.

what's in a name?

Look for clues in the species name — *tinctoria* or *tinctorum* indicates that the plant has traditionally been used in dyeing. The Linnaean system is that where genus is followed by species (and sometimes sub-species); the former states the plant family and the latter offers a descriptor. This system — sometimes also somewhat erroneously known as the Latin names for plants — forms the accepted structure for the binary nomenclature of plants. Binary nomenclature is not limited to Latin, though, and draws on Greek as well as on the names of the original finders and classifiers. This system of organisation, or taxonomy, is universally understood where European languages (including English) are spoken. While the obvious species name is *tinctoria/tinctorum*, there are many others that are also helpful indicators. *Nigra/niger* (black), *luteum/lutea* (gold or yellow), *sanguinea/sanguineum* (bloodlike), *caeruleum/caerulea* (blue), *purpurea/purpureum* (púrple), *rubra/rubrum* (red), *viridis* (green) and so forth are among the many codifiers that can help us in our selection. *Officinale* indicates the plant was traditionally used in medicine. Given that traditional medicinal herbs can contain a range of aromatic, acid or alkaloid chemicals, it's a safe bet they'll also give rewards in the dye-pot.

garbage and windfalls

Approach your green grocer for 'green garbage'. Onion skins, carrot tops, wilted spinach, beetroot leaves and off-cuts of red cabbage are all good sources of colour. Negotiate with your local council for green waste pruned from parks and gardens. Florists are often pleased to offload spent flowers and greenery, as it saves them the expense of disposal. Green waste en route from kitchen to compost can make a happy detour through a dye-pot. North American textile artist Christopher Leitch has built a whole practice around compost-dyeing silk with rotting vegetable matter.

Never, ever, collect a plant from the wild that you cannot identify — at the very least, by its common name, and more preferably by genus and species. The plant you are looking at may be rare or endangered. This rule applies particularly to lichens and fungi, which may have minuscule features that can be difficult for the inexperienced to distinguish. Lichens (actually fungi and algae growing in symbiosis) are often exceedingly slow growing (sometimes as little as 1 millimetre per annum), and both groups include many species that have not yet been formally identified. They should on no account be taken from the wild. If you are determined to work with lichens, then approach the wardens of cemeteries and graveyards

where lichens are regularly scrubbed from headstones; they may grant permission for careful removal of lichens from inscriptions using a gentle implement such as a wooden spatula. Otherwise their slow rate of growth and recovery, coupled with the fact that similar colours can be derived from sustainable sources, makes their collection inexcusable.

If in any doubt at all, remember the admonishment given by Aragorn in Tolkien's *The Lord of the Rings* and '... have a care! Cut no living wood.'[1]

Windfalls are another splendid source of dye material. Often whole branches or plants are found broken after severe storms. This is the time to be collecting. However, windfalls from protected plants should be left in situ (for ecological as well as legal reasons) and it is worth familiarising yourself with local government regulations. Permission to collect windfalls is always needed in botanic gardens, where strict protocols apply.

Should you wish to collect fungi for dyeing, be sure to equip yourself with a comprehensive guidebook. While there are indeed a great many fungi that contain dyes, many of these may also be toxic. More importantly, many fungi species have not yet been identified at all. Their properties would therefore be unknown. Once again the rule is 'no identification — no picking'.

Having narrowed the field using these various parameters and identified a selection of plants, we can further edit the range by applying a few assessment techniques.

As mentioned earlier, the presence of a sharp scent is a valuable indicator. Rubbing a leaf between finger and thumb or across the surface of a piece of cloth can also help to determine dye potential: if a leaf crushed into cloth makes a visible stain, it is also quite likely the plant will yield a dye of some sort. The amusing contradiction here is that often the substances that give colour in a dye-bath may be colourless or even invisible before processing. The eucalypts are an outstanding example of such reticent colour.

Above, from left: *Lavandula angustifolia* imparts a delicious scent to wool along with a lemon yellow colour; Vintage kimono silkfelt scarf (shown finished on page 219) rolled around *Eucalyptus cinerea* leaves for eco-printing; Soursob (*Oxalis pes-caprae*) yields dyes as well as being a useful mordant.

COLLECTING PLANTS

33

1 TOLKIEN J.R.R., 1954 (reprinted 1985) *The Lord of the Rings*, Unwin Paperbacks, London p 462

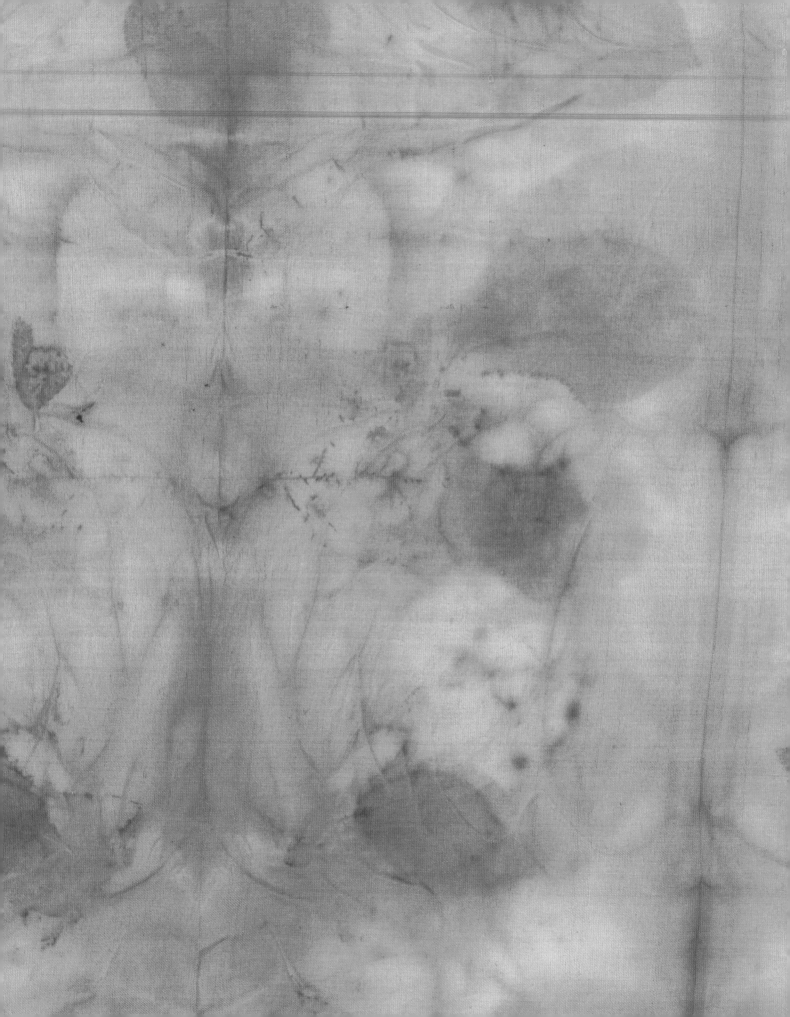

part two

THE WORKSPACE: HARVESTING, HEALTH AND SAFETY

EQUIPMENT AND A PLACE TO WORK

It is, of course, most desirable to have a separate well-ventilated workspace outfitted with lots of shelving, hot and cold running water, a sink and a heating device. For many this remains dream territory, in which case the home kitchen or the back verandah will have to do. Some sort of work surface and a drainage area are desirable, as is shelving for the jars of solar-dye-in-progress and mordant brews.

Most of my dye work takes place in a former blacksmith's shop on the family farm, over an open fire around which are stacked countless pots and tins. It provides a handy ash source as well. No fires are lit in summer because it is usually hot indoors anyway and the risk of bushfires from escaping chimney sparks makes it somewhat hazardous; dyeing in those months is restricted to heating pots of eucalyptus on the gas stove in the farmhouse kitchen, supplemented by solar and bundle dyeing.

equipment

Most of the traditional recipe books specify large stainless-steel saucepans as the ideal dye vessel, but remember that this sort of equipment is really only necessary when dyeing large pieces that require even colour and precisely repeatable results.

Acquiring equipment for the type of practice outlined in this book is cheap and simple. Charity shops, garage sales, kerbside collection days and Virgoan friends with passions for discarding surplus pots are all goldmines for the committed dyer. Collect vessels made of iron, copper, brass, tin, aluminium and stainless steel. Domestic cooking pots of any size are always useful. Aluminium pots can obviate the need for an alum co-mordant, while iron pots are far kinder to fibre than the addition of iron salts. Old-fashioned aluminium steamer baskets are wonderful not only for steaming but also as resists and as small travelling colanders.

Should you find small pots that leak, simply use them as co-mordants by placing them in a larger pot together with the dye liquid, or wrap your

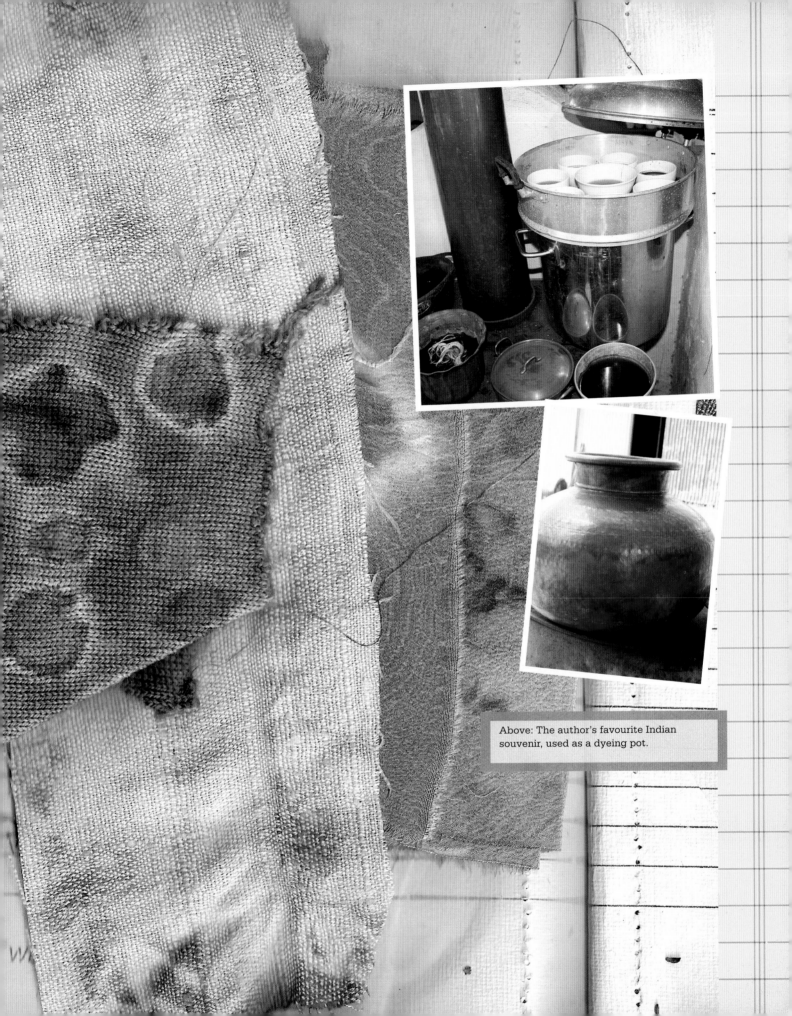

Above: The author's favourite Indian souvenir, used as a dyeing pot.

Scraps of onion-dyed silk cloth rolled into balls ready for knitting.

bundles around them for long-term benefits. The car-parks and footpaths outside pubs and bars are veritable treasure troves of bottle-tops and ring-pulls. Dedicated scavengers will think nothing of picking up rusty paperclips and hairpins, knowing they will make lovely marks on cloth. Keep a box for odd scrap metals and gather them whenever you can. These can be valuable adjuncts to dye-baths as well as interesting resists.

storing samples

Keep a notebook and stitch in small swatches of dyed fabrics to remind you of what the notes are actually about. Digital cameras are extremely useful for documentation, as you can establish extensive files on computer without chewing up acres of trees for printing. I use both, as there is nothing quite as satisfying as leafing through a well-stuffed notebook.

Large cloth samples can be neatly stored using cheap trouser-pressing clothes hangers. You can get quite a lot on one hanger and it makes them much easier to sort through. Be aware that moths can cause problems; the only natural defence against them that is truly effective is using a camphorwood chest as a repellent.

on the road

The beauty of making dyes with plants is that one doesn't really need extensive or expensive equipment. Certainly if a cauldron is available it will be most useful; nevertheless, colour can if desired be applied to cloth without the need for any dye-pots at all. When wandering the world I take a few favourite treasures with me, including a tiny teapot (with built-in strainer), an ancient hand-made Japanese hammer, a small supply of fabric samples (which will of course be supplemented on the way) and a plentiful supply of snap-lock bags. On the way I collect small pieces of metal from roadsides and building sites to use as resists and mordants. Inevitably they come home in my suitcase as travel souvenirs. When travelling by air I also take a supply of fabric shreds to roll into string while watching the in-flight movies. Once at my destination, I use the string to tie up small bundles. I mordant cotton scraps with the teabags so thoughtfully supplied by hotels once they have passed through my teacup. Those funny little containers of UHT milk constitute another handy mordant. The reticulated water service offers fresh avenues for experimentation at each new stop, as do the waters of rivers, streams, puddles and oceans encountered on the journey. Truly dedicated dyers can work anywhere.

the tea-test method

Crumble the material to be assessed into an old teacup or a small white porcelain bowl and pour on boiling water. Allow to steep for ten minutes or so. If the liquid becomes coloured in such a short space of time, it is likely the material has potential for dyeing.

Try this method with fresh or dry leaves, shredded bark, crushed seeds and squashed berries.

USEFUL EQUIPMENT

| A selection of pots in all sizes and of various metals, including brass, copper, aluminium, iron, stainless steel, old metal teapots and used catering-size food tins

| Tongs

| A couple of good stirring or poking sticks

| Strainers (cheap plastic ones are fine; also visit charity shops for old metal ones)

| Rubber gloves (the big insulated plumbing types are best, as they will protect hands from hot solutions) — fold the cuffs back to prevent liquids running on to your arms

| A few buckets for rinsing and carrying stuff about

| An assortment of pegs and clips for compressing fabric

| Wood blocks, tin lids, old CDs, odd-shaped metal fragments, round river pebbles, cotton reels, bottle caps and marbles to use as resists

| Glass jars for solar dyeing and making mordant solutions

| Snap-lock bags; although not exactly eco-friendly, these are very handy for collecting samples and flowers for freezing and for storing small dye-lots and remnants. Rinse, dry and re-use them for as long as you can to reduce their environmental impact

| A heat source — gas, an open fire or an electric ring are the usual options. The Avani Textile Co-operative in the Himalaya use solar energy to pre-heat their water. In Mongolia, parabolic mirror systems focus solar radiation to supply the energy needed to quickly boil water

| A drying rack

| Cardboard boxes and cloth bags or pillowcases for storing dried plant material — in climates where storing seasonally harvested materials may attract insects and mould, it may be preferable to store finely crushed materials in large glass jars or metal storage containers instead

| Notebook and pencil for keeping track of methods and results

| Labels for jars and bottles so you can identify and date samples

| Supply of masks to wear when dealing with anything dusty or mouldy

| Stout shoes with closed toes to protect the feet

| A smock or apron if you are fussy about your clothes

Some readers may question the use of wood to fuel my cooking fires. The timber used is gathered from windfalls on our paddocks. If left to rot it would emit just as much carbon as it does when burned. Given that at least half of our windfalls remain on the paddocks to provide homes for small creatures and that we have an ongoing tree-planting program I consider the use of wood as fuel justified.

Ideally dye-pots would be solar heated, as they are in the Avani handcraft project in the Himalaya (see www.avani-kumaon.org for more information).

Used tea-bags can be recycled to provide dyestuffs.

HARVESTING AND STORING PLANTS FOR DYEING

As you are gradually overtaken by the passion for making plant dyes, it becomes increasingly difficult to resist gathering all the stuff that 'might have potential' which falls across your path. My own house is full of odd bags of dried leaves, bunches of windfalls and baskets of this, that and the other. Add to this the need to harvest various plants in flower before they brown and wither, to collect berries before the sparrows attack the elderberry bushes and to see just what one can do with those wilted lily flowers, and it is easy to appreciate life can and does frequently descend into utter chaos.

The only real order that exists is in my freezer, where each of the six drawers is filled with snap-lock bags of flowers and berries awaiting processing. While freezer storage is certainly somewhat indulgent in terms of energy use, it is nonetheless an essential step in processing certain plant materials. What follows here is advice of the 'do as I would under perfect conditions' sort, as opposed to the 'do as I do' variety. I take comfort in the discreet notice 'Dull Women Have Immaculate Homes' affixed to the wall in my kitchen.

This is what I would really like to do.

When collecting windfalls, pile the branches onto a tarpaulin or an old sheet and allow them to dry. When the leaves become crisp, step and jump about on the pile to reduce it and break it up. Generally the leaves and small twigs will fall off, so the larger branched parts can be removed and the little bits put in a bag for storage. Cloth bags such as old flour bags are best, as the contents are less likely to grow mould. Alternatively, cardboard boxes make good storage. Those with a passion for order may like to label the storage container with the contents, date and locality of collection (this information can be helpful when trying to repeat a favoured colour).

Prunings from the garden can be bunched together and hung to dry in a cool shady spot. When dry, either leave them hanging or follow the stripping process for windfalls.

Magic maple leaves give beautiful colours, as do the little winged seeds.

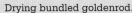

Drying bundled goldenrod.

Flowers can be dried in bunches or separated from their stalks and dried on a mesh rack. Blue and purple flowers give the best colour if they are stored frozen in a small container such as a recycled yoghurt pot or snap-lock bag.

Seeds, nuts and bark can be stored in mesh bags salvaged from the greengrocers. Very small quantities of dried plant material can be stuffed into an old stocking or an abandoned sock, provided the sock itself will not add a synthetic colour stain to the mix. The stocking or sock can then be used as a kind of tea-bag in the dye process.

When collecting autumn leaves for cold-bundling, layer them in an old telephone book to flatten them. The leaves are best used wilted so they are still flexible enough not to shatter when wrapped in a bundle.

safe practices

It is vital to keep the pots and pans used for food separate from those used for dyes. Even though most of the assistants described in this book are of little or low toxicity, some of the plants used can kill if ingested, and just as the pots can release small molecules of matter in reaction to a dye substance, they can also absorb minimal amounts. Some poisons are in fact cumulative, meaning they can build up in the body over time. Safe is so much better than sorry, so keep dye work and food well apart. The only exception to this rule is in the case of the plants recommended in the text as being completely safe to ingest and therefore harmless as food dyes (see pages 70–71). Even then potential allergies must be taken into account.

This also means being disciplined about consuming food and drink while working with dyes. The simple rule is just don't do it. I once worked briefly at a South Australian university, where to my horror I discovered that the staff kept their tea and coffee supplies in the noxious chemicals store-room off the textiles studio. This normally double-locked room was filled with a nauseating smell from the cocktail of chemical vapours from the substances stored there, yet people innocently helped themselves to sugar from the open bowl stored in a small compartment in the room and were surprised that I was appalled. The sugar was visually indistinguishable from any of the other white crystalline substances stored in that space. In addition, sugar is a hygroscopic substance, meaning it absorbs moisture (including chemical vapours) from the atmosphere around it. I still shudder at the thought of anyone actually consuming the stuff.

Boronia denticulata flowers gathered in a small plastic bag.

occupational health and safety rules

- Many of the substances traditionally employed in both synthetic and plant-based dyeing are highly toxic. Even innocuous-seeming plants, such as jonquils, can be fatal if ingested.

- Have a dedicated set of pots that are used only for plant dyes. Avoid processing plant dyes in your kitchen unless you are quite certain the plant is not toxic. The vapours of even non-toxic plants can lead to discomfort for sensitive individuals, so make sure the workplace is well ventilated.

- Wear the appropriate clothing and footwear when working with dyes and hot liquids. Shoes must be fully enclosed; no sandals or thongs (flip-flops). Clothing needs to be practical and without dangly bits that are likely to cause trouble with dye-pots.

- Food and drink must not be consumed while working with any dyes.

- Remember that skin is a highly receptive protein fibre. Avoid putting bare hands into a dye bath unless you are quite sure the bath is cool, and the plant is a non-poisonous species to which you are not allergic.

- Keep all mordant substances — even if they are theoretically non-toxic — in a safe place out of reach of children or animals.

- Make sure to wear a mask when dealing with any mouldy substances to avoid breathing in spores.

NATURAL DYESTUFFS

part three

India Flint

"**Arcadian alchemies** – ecologically sustainable eucalypt dyes for textiles" worksheet for leaf samples collected from **Currency Creek Arboretum**

eucalyptus...... suggrandis ssp suggrandis

row........ 17 .....tree no........ 3 ....

date... 3. 11 (10.11) 17.11 ....

material collected... fresh green leaves

....

....

....

sample process (steaming) simmering in solution

dye vessel
    stainless steel
    copper
    iron
    (aluminium)

pre-mordant ....

Remarks..

....

....

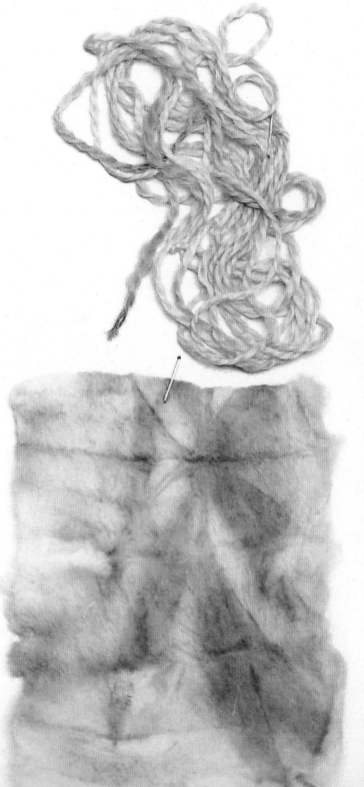
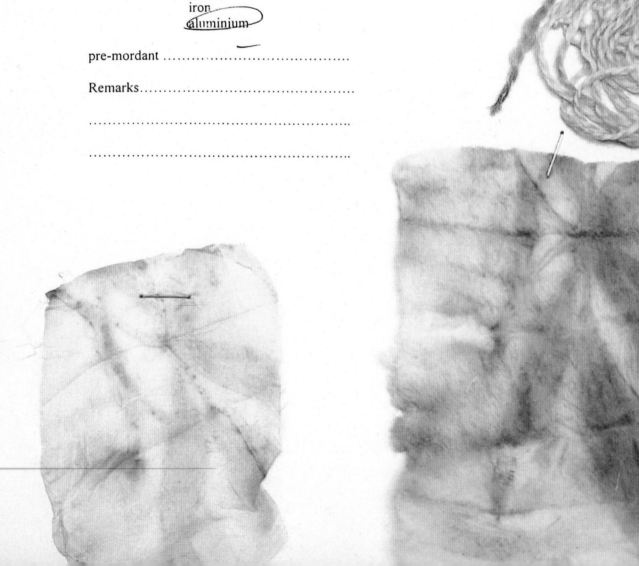

SOME TRADITIONAL
DYE MATERIALS

The list provided on the following pages illustrates the broad range of dye materials traditionally used worldwide for colouring cloth. While these were mostly plants, the list also includes fauna in the form of molluscs and insects. Where I have been able to establish the plant (or fauna) part used, it has been noted; however, the traditional recipes for each, with the associated conventional mordants, may be sourced (if desired) by the reader both from the internet and from the many books listed in the bibliography, as the task of describing each individual recipe comprehensively would require a tome of encyclopaedic proportions and thus lies beyond the scope of this book.

Given that all plants may offer slightly different shades dependent on the season of harvest, climate, soil conditions, growing location and age, prescriptive instructions could be taken as site specific. Unless distilled water is specified to make up the standard dye bath, the results produced in locations other than the home region are likely to be at least slightly different from the original sample. Water varies widely around the globe, not only in quality but also in what soluble substances it contains. These dissolved salts and minerals will determine the colour outcomes and possibly also the durability of the colour.

Most of the plants on the list were used with some sort of mordant. Where a chrome mordant was added, the colour outcome was likely to be yellow no matter what plant was used because the yellow colour actually came from the chrome salts (which are a bright orange in dry powdered form). My theory is that the plant material simply provided the acids necessary for the colour to bond with the substrate (cloth) being dyed. In other words, the plant was acting as the mordant for the colour from the metallic salt of chrome. The adjunct mordants for specific colours do tend to conform to a pattern. Reds and pinks usually involved tin (or an alkali in the case of *Carthamus* or *Coreopsis*); blacks are linked with iron; yellows, if not with chrome, then with alum; greens with copper, iron or alum. In the case of blue from any of the indigo-producing species, colour extraction and application were the result of complex processes involving fermentation under alkaline conditions. The blues from berries and flowers are highly likely to involve the addition of an alkali such as alum or ash. Using dye-pots made from copper, brass, aluminium or iron coupled with extended time in the dye-bath will be far safer than using potentially toxic adjunct mordants. Alternatively, experiment with the plants on the list by processing them in a non-reactive vessel (such as Pyrex, ceramic, stainless steel or enamel) in the presence of fragments of the appropriate metal.

Given the limitations of language (I only read three well, and although binary plant nomenclature could be compared to a form of Esperanto as a universal language of gardeners, it is nonetheless difficult to make out in script other than those used by European languages) and the scarcity of documented sources for many countries, we can safely speculate that the list only represents the very tip of the dye-plant iceberg. The 'Plants for a Future' website (www.pfaf.org) lists no fewer than 1,171 further species. The reading list at the conclusion of this book provides a further resource.

The inventory can, however, be used as a valuable assistant to plant selection, as the plants listed here have been in use because they consistently produce predictable results as well as exhibiting wash- and light-fastness. Our ancestors will have based their selection on plants that rewarded their efforts rather than those which faded quickly.

Remember, though, that far more possibilities exist than have yet been essayed, and whole forests full of unidentified plants are still to be explored, not only in terms of colour. Tragically, many of them are being cleared, and plants full of potential (medicinal as well as colourful) are thus disappearing untried from our world. Bear in mind, too, that with the advent of synthetic dyes in the nineteenth century, many plant dye techniques were forgotten as the dyes of 'instant gratification' were eagerly adopted and the keepers of dye knowledge died without being asked to hand down their recipes.

In the list, the binary nomenclature precedes the vernacular. The reader will no doubt appreciate the importance of the former given the frequent overlapping and repetitions in the latter. Some plants occur in a number of colour sections, as the application of a range of mordants and processes to different parts of the plant (leaves, bark, wood, berries and seeds) as well as the use of cloth of different fibres may generate a range of hues. Where the genus is followed by 'sp' I have either been unable to determine the particular species used or, as in the case of *Acacia* and *Eucalyptus*, there are simply too many to list. I must confess that while I have experimented with a number of plants listed here I certainly haven't tested them all. Time and plant availability have been against me!

	TAXONOMIC NAME	COMMON NAME	PART(S) USED
BLACKS AND GREYS	*Amaranthus spinosus*	Spiny amaranth	ash
	Aporosa dioica	—	leaves
	Baccaurea sapida	Leteku	bark, leaves and fruits
	Betula spp.	Birch	bark, roots
	Bischofia javanica	Urium	bark and leaves
	Colquhounia coccinea	Hom	whole plant
	Corylus chinensis	Hazel	bark
	Diospyros mollis	Ebony	fruit
	Eucalyptus spp.	Eucalypts	leaves and bark
	Eurya japonica	Eurya	leaves
	Flemingia macrophylla	—	leaves and bark
	Haematoxylon campechianum	Logwood	heartwood
	Ilex embelioides	—	bark
	Juglans cinerea	Butternut	roots and husk from nuts
	Juglans nigra	Black walnut	roots and husk from nuts
	Litchi chinensis	Litchi	fruit husks
	Lycopus europaeus	Gypsywort	leaves
	Nerium indicum	—	roots and bark
	Pinus wallichiana	Tongschi	bark
	Polemonium caeruleum	Jacob's ladder	leaves and stems
	Psidium guajava	Guava	leaves
	Punica granatum	Pomegranate	skins of fruit, tip cuttings
	Pyrus pashia	Semo	fruits
	Quercus infectoria	Oak	gallnuts
	Quercus ithaburensis	Walloon oak	acorn caps
	Sapium sebiferum	Chinese tallow tree	leaves
	Solanum indicum	Bekhuri	half-ripe fruits
	Sphagnum spp.	Peat	peatbog (in situ)
	Syzygium cumini	Barjamuk	bark and fruits
	Triadica sebifera	Chinese tallow tree	leaves
	Verbascum thapsiforme	Mullein	leaves

	TAXONOMIC NAME	COMMON NAME	PART(S) USED
PURPLES — FLORA	*Aloe vaombe*	Vaombe	foliage
	Antidesma ghaesembilla	Yangu/blackcurrant	berries
	Arrabidaea chica	Pucham	leaves
	Beilschmiedia tawa	Tawa	berries
	Berberis darwinii	Darwin's berberis	berries
	Betula spp.	Birch	bark, roots
	Caesalpinia sappan	Brazilwood/Sappan	flowers
	Chrozophora tinctoria	Dyer's croton/dyer's litmus	flowers, fruit and sap
	Cladonia pyxidata	Cudbear lichen	whole organism
	Corymbia (syn. *Eucalyptus citriodora*)	—	leaves
	Dermocybe splendida	Fungus	stems
	Desmodium multiflorum	—	flower
	Eucalyptus globulus	—	leaves
	Fagus sylvatica f. *purpurea*	Copper beech	leaves
	Haematoxylon campechianum	Logwood	heartwood
	Helianthus annuus	Sunflower	seed hulls
	Lithospermum erythrorhizon	Purple root (gromwell)	root
	Lithospermum euchromon	Purple root	root
	Melastoma malabathricum	Ke-Seng	fruits
	Myrtus bullata	Ramarama	berries
	Nothopanax arboreum	Whauwhaupaku	berries
	Ochrolechia tartaria	Cudbear lichen	whole organism
	Phormium tenax	Harakeke	dried seed pods
	Ribes nigrum	Blackcurrant	berries
	Ribes odoratum	Buffalo currant	berries
	Roccella tinctoria	Orchil lichen/litmus	whole organism
	Sambucus canadensis	American elderberry	fruit
	Sambucus nigra	Elderberry	berries
	Umbilicaria pustulata	Cudbear lichen	whole organism
	Urceolaria calcarea	Cudbear lichen	whole organism
PURPLES — FAUNA	*Dactylopius* spp. (formerly known as *Coccus* spp.)	Cochineal/grana	whole insect
	Eriococcus spp.	—	whole insect
	Kermes biblicus	—	whole insect
	Kermes spatulatus	—	whole insect
	Murex brandaris	Mollusc	hypobranchial glandular extract
	Murex trunculus	Mollusc	hypobranchial glandular extract
	Purpura haemastoma	Mollusc	hypobranchial glandular extract

	TAXONOMIC NAME	COMMON NAME	PART(S) USED
BLUES	Acer rubrum	Red maple	bark
	Baphicacanthus cusia	Indian indigo	leaves
	Baptisia australis	False indigo	leaves
	Baptisia leucantha	False indigo	leaves
	Baptisia tinctoria	Wild indigo	leaves
	Berberis darwinii	Darwin's berberis	berries
	Chrozophora tinctoria	Dyer's croton/dyer's litmus	flowers, fruit, sap
	Clerodendron trichotomum	Kusagi	berries
	Clitorea mariana	Aparajita	flowers
	Entada pursaetha	Ghilla	young pods
	Indigofera arrecta	African indigo	leaves
	Indigofera australis	Australian indigo	leaves
	Indigofera micheliana	Indigo	leaves
	Indigofera suffruticosa	Indigo	leaves
	Indigofera sumatrana	Indigo	leaves
	Indigofera tinctoria	Indigo	leaves
	Isatis tinctoria	Woad	leaves
	Ligustrum lucidum	Privet	berries
	Lonchocarpus cyanescens	Yoruba indigo	leaves
	Marsdenia tinctoria	Indigo	leaves
	Nerium tinctorium	Indian indigo	leaves
	Persicaria tinctoria	Dyer's knotweed	leaves
	Phaius tankervilliae	—	leaves and flowers
	Pharbitis nil	Morning glory	leaves
	Polygonum hydropiper	Chlum-gon	whole plant
	Polygonum tinctorium	Japanese indigo	leaves
	Punica granatum	Pomegranate	flower and fruits
	Ribes nigrum	Blackcurrant	berries
	Ribes odoratum	Buffalo currant	berries
	Solanum nigrum	Blackberry nightshade	berries
	Strobilanthes flaccidifolius	Chinese rain bell	leaves
	Tephrosia candida	Bilokhoni	leaves
	Terminalia chebula	Hilikha	root and bark
	Vaccinium spp.	Huckleberries	fruit
	Wrightia tinctoria	Pala indigo	leaves

	TAXONOMIC NAME	COMMON NAME	PART(S) USED
GREENS	Achillea millefolium	Yarrow	leaves
	Anthracophyllum archeri	Fungus	whole organism
	Andropogon virginicus	Broomsedge	stalks and leaves
	Angelica sylvestris	Angelica	leaves and shoots
	Anigozanthos flavidus	Green kangaroo paw	flowers
	Apium graveolens	Celery	leaves
	Arctostaphylos uva-ursi	Bärentraube	dried berries
	Artemisia japonica	Yomogi	leaves and stalks
	Baptisia australis	False indigo	leaves
	Buddleia davidii	Buddleia	purple flowers
	Calendula officinalis	Marigold	flowers
	Capsicum annuum	Red capsicum (pepper)	leaves
	Cheiranthus cheiri	Wallflower	leaves and flowers
	Clematis spp.	Clematis	leaves
	Coços nucifera	Coconut	juice and sap
	Convallaria majalis	Lily of the valley	leaves
	Daldinia concentrica	Fungi	whole organism
	Diospyros kaki	Japanese persimmon	leaves
	Elaeocarpus dentatus	Hinau	bark
	Eucalyptus spp.	Eucalypts	leaves
	Foeniculum vulgare	Fennel	foliage
	Genista tinctoria	Dyer's broom	leaves and soft stalks
	Ginkgo biloba	Ginkgo	leaves
	Hedera helix	Ivy	leaves
	Hypericum perforatum	St John's wort	flowers
	Hypericum tetrapterum	St Peter's wort	flowers
	Juniperus spp.	Junipers	berries
	Laurus nobilis	Bay laurel	leaves
	Leptospermum scoparium	Manuka	leaves, twigs, flowers
	Maclura pomifera	Osage orange	heartwood, bark
	Mahonia japonica	Mahonia	bark
	Medicago sativa	Alfalfa	leaves and stalks
	Nepeta cataria	Catmint	leaves and stalks
	Nephelium lappaceum	Rambutan	shoots
	Passiflora edulis	Passionflower	leaves, fruit skins
	Podocarpus hallii	Totara	bark
	Podocarpus totara	Totara	bark
	Prunus japonica	Korean cherry	leaves
	Psidium guajava	Guava	fruit, juice

	TAXONOMIC NAME	COMMON NAME	PART(S) USED
GREENS (CONT)	*Pteridium esculentum*	Bracken fern	fronds
	Punica granatum	Pomegranate/granado/anar	skin of fruit
	Rhododendron spp.	Rhododendron	leaves
	Rosmarinus officinalis	Rosemary	leaves
	Rudbeckia hirta	Black-eyed Susan	flowers
	Sambucus nigra	Elder	leaves
	Sapium baccatum	Seleng	leaves
	Scabiosa columbaria	Scabious	flowers
	Solidago canadensis	Goldenrod	leaves
	Tagetes patula	Marigold	flowers
	Taraxacum officinale	Dandelion	flowers
	Urtica dioica	Nettle	leaves
	Urtica urens	Small nettle	leaves
YELLOWS AND GOLDS	*Achillea millefolium*	Yarrow	leaves
	Allium cepa	Onions	skins
	Alnus firma	Alder	leaves, bark
	Anacyclus clavatus	Daisy	flowers
	Anchusa virginiana	—	roots
	Anthemis chia	Chamomile species	flowers
	Anthemis tinctoria	Dyer's chamomile	flowers
	Anthemis tomentosa	Chamomile	flowers
	Arctium lappa	Burdock	root
	Artemisia absinthium	Wormwood	leaves
	Artocarpus heterophyllus	Jackfruit	wood shavings
	Berberis vulgaris	Barberry tree	roots
	Betula lutea	Golden birch	bark, leaves
	Burasaia madagascariensis	Tambarasaha	roots
	Butea monosperma	Tesu/palash	flowers
	Caesalpinia sappan	Brazilwood/Sappan (Asia)	leaves
	Calendula officinalis	Marigold	flowers
	Callistemma chinensis	Chinese aster	flowers
	Carica papaya	Pawpaw	fruits
	Carthamus tinctorius	Safflower/saffron thistle	flowers
	Carya tomentosa	Hickory	bark
	Chelidonium majus	Schöllkraut	leaves and stalks
	Chlorophora tinctoria	Fustic	chips
	Chrysanthemum coronarium	Chrysanthemum	flowers
	Chrysanthemum discolor	Chrysanthemum	flowers

	TAXONOMIC NAME	COMMON NAME	PART(S) USED
YELLOWS AND GOLDS (CONT)	Cleome serrulata	Beeweed	flowers and leaves
	Coreopsis tinctoria	Coreopsis	flowers
	Crocus sativus	Saffron	stamens
	Cudrania cochinchinensis	Pulikaint	leaves and seeds
	Cudrania javanensis	Javanese wood	heartwood
	Curcuma domestica	Turmeric	root
	Curcuma longa	Turmeric	root
	Cytisus scoparius	Broom	flowers, young stems
	Datisca cannabina	False hemp	leaves and stalks
	Delphinium semibarbatum	Persian larkspur	flowers, leaves, stems
	Digitalis ferruginea	Foxglove	leaves and stems
	Digitalis lanata	Foxglove	leaves and stems
	Digitalis purpurea	Foxglove	leaves and stems
	Eucalyptus spp.	Eucalypts	leaves, flowers
	Eupatorium cannabinum	Hemp agrimony	leaves
	Euphorbia spp.	Spurge	leaves and flowers
	Ficus altissima	Gadgubar	stem cuttings
	Ficus gasparriniana	Ru-kha	roots
	Fraxinus americana	White ash	bark
	Garcinia hanburyi	Gamboge	resin
	Gardenia jasminoides	Gardenia	leaves and flowers
	Genista tinctoria	Dyer's broom	flowers
	Helianthus annuus	Sunflower	petals
	Helichrysum spp.	Everlasting daisy (yellow) species	flowers
	Hicoria tomentosa	Hickory	bark
	Hypericum empetrifolium	St John's wort	flowers
	Hypericum perforatum	St John's wort	flowers
	Hypericum tetrapterum	St Peter's wort	flowers
	Illicium griffithii	Lissi	seeds, bark and leaves
	Inula viscosa	—	flowers, leaves, stems
	Kalmia latifolia	Mountain laurel	leaves
	Leptospermum scoparium	Manuka	flowers
	Lilium tigrinum	Tiger lily	flowers and stamens
	Liriodendron tulipifera	Tulip tree	leaves
	Maclura pomifera	Osage orange	bark, heartwood
	Mahonia japonica	Mahonia	leaves
	Malus domestica	Apple	leaves
	Mangifera laurina	Mango	bark, leaves

	TAXONOMIC NAME	COMMON NAME	PART(S) USED
YELLOWS AND GOLDS (CONT)	*Matricaria chamomilla*	True chamomile	flowers
	Michelia montana	Pansopa	bark and flower
	Miscanthus tinctorius	Karyasu (grass)	foliage
	Morus tinctoria	Dyer's mulberry	wood chips
	Myrica rubra	Barberry	fruit, leaves
	Nyctanthes arbor-tristis	Night jasmine	flowers
	Persicaria maculosa	Redshank	leaves and shoots
	Phellodenron amurense	Kihada	inner bark
	Polygonum persicaria	Smartweed/arsemart	leaves and stalks
	Populus nigra	Lombardy poplar	leaves
	Prunus persica	Peach	leaves and bark
	Punica granatum	Pomegranate/granado/anar	skin of fruit (fresh)
	Quercus ithaburensis	Walloon oak	acorn caps
	Quercus prinus	Chestnut oak	bark
	Quercus velutina	Quercitron oak	bark
	Reseda luteola/lutea	Dyer's weld	leaves
	Rhamnus infectoria	Persian berries	fruits
	Rhamnus tinctoria	Persian berries	fruit
	Rheum rhaponticum	Rhubarb	leaves, stems, roots
	Rhododendron kaempferi	Wild azalea	leaves
	Rhododendron spp.	Rhododendron	leaves
	Rhus coriaria	Sicilian sumac	leaves, shoots and bark
	Rhus cotinus	Fustic	stems and trunk
	Rhus glabra	Sumac	berries
	Rubus fruticosus	Blackberry	new shoots, leaves
	Rudbeckia hirta	Black-eyed Susan	flowers
	Rumex acetosa	Sorrel	leaves
	Rumex crispus	Dock	leaves
	Rumex sanguineus	Dock	leaves
	Rosmarinus officinalis	Rosemary	leaves
	Salix babylonica	Weeping willow	leaves
	Salvia officinalis	Sage	leaves
	Salvia triloba	Three-leafed sage	stems and leaves
	Sassafras albidum	Sassafras	bark
	Scabiosa columbaria	Scabious	flowers
	Serratula tinctoria	Saw wort	leaves
	Solidago canadensis	Goldenrod	leaves
	Solidago virgaurea	Goldenrod	leaves

	TAXONOMIC NAME	COMMON NAME	PART(S) USED
YELLOWS AND GOLDS (CONT)	*Sophora tetraptera*	Khowai	flowers
	Spartium junceum	—	flowers and young shoots
	Symplocos paniculata	Parehangne	bark
	Tagetes patula	Marigold	flowers
	Tanacetum vulgare	Tansy	flowers
	Taraxacum officinale	Dandelion	flowers
	Thermopsis rhombifolia	Buffalo bean	flowers
	Thymus spp.	Thyme	leaves
	Tripleurospermum maritimum	Scentless chamomile	flowers
	Ulex parviflorus	Gorse/furze	flowers
	Urtica urens	Small nettle	leaves
	Verbascum thapsiforme	Mullein	flowers
	Vitex agnus-castus	Chaste tree	leaves and young shoots
	Vitex lucens	Puriri	bark, berries
	Vitis vinifera	Wine grapevine	leaves
	Weinmannia racemosa	Kamahi	bark
	Xanthium strumarium	Cockleburr	whole plant
ORANGES	*Betula pendula*	Silver birch	leaves, bark
	Bixa orellana	Annatto/achiote	seeds
	Buddleja globosa	Buddleia	flowers
	Coreopsis tinctoria	Coreopsis	flowers
	Cortinarius basirubescens	Fungi	whole organism
	Cotinus coggygria	Smoke tree	bark
	Crocus sativus	Saffron crocus	stamens
	Danais latisepala	Bongo	roots
	Dermocybe splendida	Fungus	stems
	Eucalyptus spp.	Eucalypts	leaves
	Gymnopilus austrosapineus	Fungus	whole organism
	Helianthus tuberosus	Jerusalem artichoke	flowers and leaves
	Lawsonia inermis	Henna	leaves
	Mahonia japonica	Mahonia	leaves
	Mallotus philippinensis	Asian lotus tree	seeds
	Nyctanthes arbor-tristis	Night jasmine	flowers
	Piptoporous australiensis	Fungus	whole organism
	Pycnoporus coccineus	Fungus	whole organism
	Rhododendron japonicum	Rhododendron	flowers
	Rhus cotinus	Fustic	stems and trunk

	TAXONOMIC NAME	COMMON NAME	PART(S) USED
ORANGES (CONT)	*Rumex hymenosepalus*	Tanner's dock	roots
	Spiraea japonica	Maybush	leaves and stems
	Tagetes erecta	Marigold	flowers
	Taraxacum officinale	Dandelion	roots
	Taxus baccata	Yew	heartwood
	Woodfordia fruticosa	Chot-tingba	flowers
REDS — FLORA	*Alkanna tinctoria*	Alkanet/dyer's bugloss	roots
	Allium spp.	Onions	skins
	Anchusa tinctoria	Chinese forget-me-not	roots
	Anigozanthos flavidus	Green kangaroo paw	roots
	Baphia nitida	Camwood/barwood	heartwood
	Betula spp.	Birch	roots
	Bischofia javanica	Bishopwood	bark
	Bixa orellana	Annatto/achiote	seeds
	Caesalpinia echinata	Brazilwood (Brazil)	heartwood
	Caesalpinia sappan	'Brazilwood'/Sappan (Asia)	heartwood
	Carthamus tinctorius	Safflower/saffron thistle	flowers
	Chrozophora tinctoria	Dyer's croton/dyer's litmus	flowers, fruit and sap
	Coprosma australis	Raurekau	bark
	Cortinarius semisanguineus	Fungus	whole organism
	Daphne papyracea	Shugu-sheng	bark and fruit
	Dermocybe splendida	Fungus	stems
	Enchylaena tomentosa var. *tomentosa*	Ruby saltbush	berries
	Ficus gasparriniana	Ru-kha	roots
	Galium boreale	Bedstraw	roots
	Galium mollugo	Bedstraw	roots
	Galium verum	Lady's bedstraw	roots
	Geranium thunbergii	Cranesbill	flowers, roots
	Hibiscus spp.	Hibiscus	flowers
	Haemodorum coccineum	Scarlet bloodroot	roots
	Haematoxylon brasiletto	Nicaragua wood/hypernick	heartwood
	Hypericum perforatum	St John's wort	flowers
	Hypericum tetrapterum	St Peter's wort	flowers
	Labourdonnaisia madagascariensis	Nato	bark
	Lawsonia inermis	Henna	leaves
	Mallotus japonicus	Mallotus	flowers

	TAXONOMIC NAME	COMMON NAME	PART(S) USED
REDS — FLORA (CONT)	*Malus domestica*	Apple	bark
	Miliusa roxburghiana	Bong-kha	bark and ripe fruits
	Morinda citrifolia	Indian mulberry	root bark
	Morinda coreia	—	root bark
	Morinda persicifolia	—	root bark
	Oldenlandia umbellata	Chayroot	root bark
	Phytolacca decandra	Pokeberry	berries
	Pterocarpus indicus	Indian padauk	wood shavings
	Pterocarpus santalinus	Red sandalwood	heartwood
	Relbunium spp.	South American Madder	roots
	Rivina humilis	Bloodberry	fruit
	Rosa canina	Dog rose	hips
	Rosa eglanteria	Eglantine	hips
	Rubia akane	Japanese madder	root
	Rubia cardifolia	Asian madder species	root
	Rubia cordifolia	Mungeet	root
	Rubia davisiana	Turkish madder species	root
	Rubia rotundifolia	Middle-Eastern madder species	root
	Rubia sikkimensis	Naga madder	whole plant
	Rubia tinctorum	Madder	root
	Rubus fruticosus,	Blackberry	new shoots, berries
	Ruta graveolens	Rue	leaves, flowers
	Sanguinaria canadensis	Bloodroot	root
	Schefflera digitata	Pate	ripe berries
	Schinopsis balansae	Quebracho	heartwood
	Schinopsis lorentzii	Quebracho	heartwood
	Shepherdia canadensis	Russett buffalo berry	fruit
	Tectona grandis	Teak	mature leaves
REDS — FAUNA	*Coccus fragariae*	—	whole insect (dried bodies of females)
	Coccus uvae-ursi	—	whole insect (dried bodies of females)
	Dactylopius coccus (formerly known as *Coccus cacti*)	Cochineal/grana	whole insect
	Eriococcus spp.	—	whole insect
	Kermes biblicus	Kermes	egg cases
	Kermes spatulatus	Kermes	egg cases
	Kermes vermilio	Kermes	egg cases
	Laccifer lacca	Gum-lac	resin secreted by insect

	TAXONOMIC NAME	COMMON NAME	PART(S) USED
REDS — FAUNA (CONT)	*Margarodes polonicus*	Polish kermes	whole insect
	Porphyrophorus polonicus	Polish kermes	whole insect
	Tachardia lacca	Indian lac	resin secreted by insect
PINKS — FLORA	*Althea rosea*	Hollyhock	flowers
	Beta vulgaris	Beetroot	root
	Calluna vulgaris	Heather	leaves and flower buds
	Carthamus tinctorius	Safflower/saffron thistle	flowers
	Cedrela toona	Indian mahogany	bark
	Ceriops roxburghiana	Mangrove	bark
	Chenopodium capitatum	Strawberry blite	fruit
	Coreopsis tinctoria	Coreopsis	flowers
	Cortinarius basirubescens	Fungus	whole organism
	Diospyros peregrina	—	fruit
	Eucalyptus ficifolia	Red flowering gum	flowers
	Fuchsia excorticata	Kotukutuku	bark
	Ginkgo biloba	Ginkgo	bark
	Hedera helix	Ivy	berries
	Humulus japonicus	Hops	flowers
	Mespilus germanica	Medlar	bark
	Nothofagus obliqua	Southern beech	bark
	Phormium tenax	Harakeke	leaves
	Photinia robusta	—	leaves
	Quercus rubra	Red oak	autumn leaves
	Rosa canina	Dog rose	hips
	Rosa eglanteria	Eglantine	hips
	Rubia tinctoria	Madder	root
	Salix nigra	Black willow	bark
	Shepherdia canadensis	Russet buffalo berry	fruit
	Weinmannia sylvicola	Towai	leaves, twigs
PINKS — FAUNA	*Coccus fragariae*	—	whole insect (dried bodies of females)
	Coccus uvae-ursi	—	whole insect (dried bodies of females)
	Dactylopius coccus (formerly known as *Coccus cacti*)	Cochineal/grana	whole insect
	Eriococcus spp.	—	whole insect
	Kermes biblicus	Kermes	egg cases

	TAXONOMIC NAME	COMMON NAME	PART(S) USED
PINKS — FAUNA (CONT)	*Kermes spatulatus*	Kermes	egg cases
	Kermes vermilio	Kermes	egg cases
	Laccifer lacca	Gum-lac	resin secreted by insect
	Margarodes polonicus	Polish kermes	whole insect
	Porphyrophorus polonicus	Polish kermes	whole insect
	Tachardia lacca	Indian lac	resin secreted by insect
BROWNS	*Acacia catechu*	Catechu/cutch	heartwood and pods
	Acer platanoides	Norway maple	bark
	Allium spp.	Onions	skins
	Alnus jorullensis	Alder	bark
	Areca catechu	Bombay catechu/betel nut	nuts
	Camellia sinensis	Tea	leaves
	Carya illinoensis	Pecan	nut hulls (green)
	Carya laciniosa	Hickory	nut hulls (green)
	Castanea sativa	Sweet chestnut	bark
	Ceriops candolleana	Tingi	bark
	Coffea arabica	Coffee	grounds
	Coffea robusta	Coffee	grounds
	Coprosma australis	—	bark
	Cortinarius basirubescens	Fungus	whole organism
	Engelhardtia spicata	Corcorshing	bark
	Eucalyptus spp.	Eucalypts	leaves, bark, roots, kino
	Eucryphia cordifolia	—	bark
	Fallopia japonica	Japanese knotweed	leaves
	Garuga gamblei	Sibon asing	bark
	Haronga madagascariensis	Harongana	bark
	Juglans cinerea	Butternut	roots and nuts
	Juglans nigra	Black walnut	roots and nuts
	Juglans regia	English walnut	nut hulls (green)
	Lawsonia inermis	Henna	leaves
	Lobaria pulmonaria	Lichen	whole organism
	Malus sylvestris	Apple	bark
	Morinda citrifolia	Indian mulberry	root bark — dyed red first and then over-dyed
	Morinda coreia	—	root bark — dyed red first and then over-dyed

	TAXONOMIC NAME	COMMON NAME	PART(S) USED
BROWNS (CONT)	*Morus tinctoria*	Dyer's mulberry	leaves and bark
	Nyssa sylvatica	Tupelo	bark
	Peltophorum ferrugineum	Jambal	bark
	Phyllocladus trichomanoides	Tanekaha	bark
	Pisolithus spp.	Fungus	whole organism
	Prosopis alba	—	roots
	Punica granatum	Pomegranate	skin of fruit (dry — brown red)
	Quercus alba	White oak	bark, acorns, galls
	Rhamnus purshiana	Chittam	bark
	Rosa rugosa	Hamanasu	roots
	Salix caprea	Goat willow/pussy willow	bark
	Sassafras albidum	Sassafras	root bark
	Scleroderma areolatum	Fungus	whole organism
	Tectona grandis	Teak	young leaves and root bark
	Tsuga canadensis	Hemlock	bark
	Tsuga heterophylla	Western hemlock	bark
	Uncaria gambier	Gambier	leaves and twigs
	Viburnum tomentosum	Viburnum	leaves, bark
	Weinmannia sylvicola	Towai	bark

A BRIEF EXPLICATION OF SOME OF THE COLOUR-RELATED SPECIFIC EPITHETS USED IN BINARY NOMENCLATURE (APART FROM THE OBVIOUS TINCTORIA/TINCTORIUS, MEANING USED OR USEFUL FOR DYEING)

alba — white

atropurpurea — dark purple

aurea/aureus — golden

caeruleus — sky blue

caesia — bluish grey

cinerea/cinereus — ash-grey

citrinus — lemon yellow

coccinea/coccineus — scarlet

cruentus — blood red

cyanea — azure blue

erythronema — red filaments/stamens

ferrugineus — rust-coloured

flavidus — pale yellow

flavum — yellow

fulvus — yellow-brown

griseus — pearl grey

hepaticus — liver-coloured

laterita — dark brick red

luridus — dull yellow

lutea — yellow

melanoxylon — black wood

nigra — black

nigricans — black

phoeniceus — purple-red, scarlet

pictum — painted, coloured

prasinus — bright green

punicea — crimson-purple

purpurascens — becoming purple

purpurea — purple

rosea — rose-pink coloured

ruber — red

rubicunda — dark red, ruddy

rubiginosa — reddish brown, rust colour

rufus — reddish

sanguineus — blood red

violacea — violet-coloured

virens — green

viridiflorus — green-flowering

viridis/viridus — green

xanthonema — yellow filaments/stamens

SOME OF THE SCENT-RELATED SPECIFIC EPITHETS USED IN BINARY NOMENCLATURE (A STRONG SCENT OFTEN INDICATES A USE IN DYEING)

citriodora — lemon-scented

foetidus — strong-smelling, unpleasant

moschatus — musk-smelling

odora — having a smell

odorata — sweet-smelling

suaveolens — sweet-smelling

India Flint

"Arcadian alchemies – ecologically sustainable eucalypt dyes for textiles" worksheet for leaf samples collected from **Currency Creek Arboretum**

eucalyptus..... oxymitra

row...... 9 ....tree no..... 28

date........ 3.4 (4/5 · 11)

material collected..... green leaf

....

....

sample process ⟨steaming⟩

simmering in solution

dye vessel stainless steel

copper

iron

⟨aluminium⟩

pre-mordant ....

Remarks..

....

....

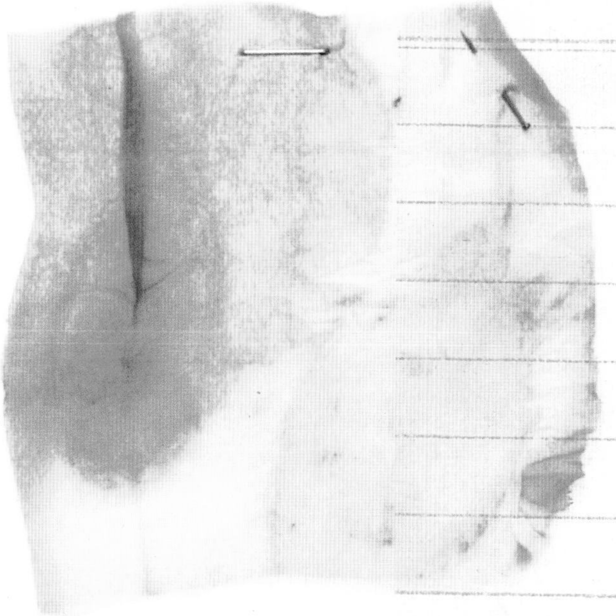

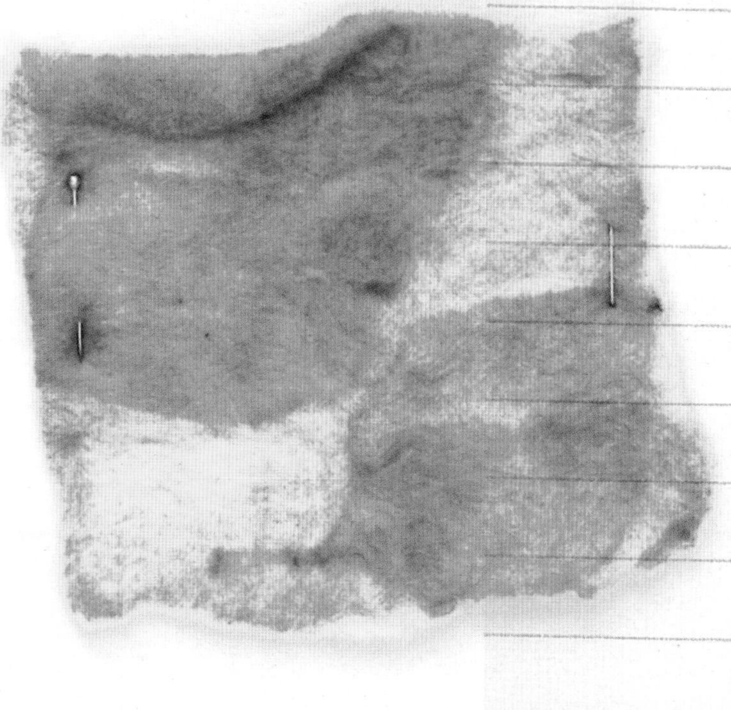

POISONOUS PLANTS

Many of the plants found in suburban gardens are poisonous to some degree and should certainly not be consumed. Exercise caution when processing plant dyes and make sure that your workspace is well ventilated in the event that you are using something which may be toxic. Even seemingly innocuous species, such as fruit trees, have poisonous parts: leaves from peach and plum trees contain cyanide, as do the inner soft almond-like kernels of the peach pits.

The bulbs, leaves and flowers of jonquils, daffodils and lily of the valley are poisonous. Essential oils from the narcissus family were reputed to have been used in Venice during the Middle Ages to drive the unsuspecting insane. The leaves of rhubarb are rich in oxalic acid, which, while useful as a mordant, is also a poison famous in urban myth as a possible means of disposing of a superfluous spouse.

The leaves and fruits (the latter rarely found in modern species) of the potato are toxic even though the tubers are most nourishing. Oddly enough, the fruits of the tomato plants, also members of the *Solanum* family, are good to eat; the leaves, however, are poisonous, as are those of the blackberry nightshade (*Solanum nigrum*), whose berries are an indigenous food in Australia.

The flowers and berries of elder trees (*Sambucus nigra*) are much prized for making both still and sparkling wines; all other parts of the plant, including the smoke from burning wood, are poisonous. Old English tradition has it that the tree is inhabited by a potentially malevolent spirit, of whom permission must be asked before the berries are taken. This threat of poisoning did not deter children in Latvia from making flutes from the branches, which are tube-like with a soft core that can be easily scraped out.

Buddleia shrubs are often planted to attract butterflies to a garden and are a source of dye. These, too, are noxious. When agapanthus flowers were used as decorations for a dessert plate by an apprentice at a famous South Australian restaurant in the 1980s, it caused something of a scandal. Not only are the flowers toxic, but the occasion on which the indiscretion occurred also happened to be the day that the restaurant critic of the main daily newspaper was taking his lunch there. Poinsettia (*Euphorbia pulcherrima*), beloved in Europe as indoor plants, secrete an alkaloid sap and shouldn't be nibbled on either.

The root of the beautiful but somewhat sinister monkshood, also known as wolfbane (*Aconitum napellus*), is rumoured to have a similar flavour to horseradish. I say 'rumoured' because the plant is deadly (and swiftly) poisonous and it is unlikely that victims would have had time to give considered flavour analyses in the short period between ingestion and (inevitable) demise.

The oleander (*Nerium* species), so popular in Mediterranean climates, is deadly when ingested. In addition, the sap may raise a nasty allergic rash.

These are but a few of the surprises that may be waiting in the domestic garden. Being able to identify the plant you are working with is vital. Common names lead to much confusion, so the importance of the knowledge of binary nomenclature cannot be sufficiently stressed. Simple mistakes such as confusing autumn crocus (*Colchicum autumnale*) with the saffron crocus (*Crocus sativus*) can lead to death if parts of the wrong plants are ingested.

The shy anemone (all species; pictured opposite) is another plant to keep out of the salad bowl if you are aiming to elude an early appointment with the reaper.

While one should avoid dyeing clothes and blankets for children and babies in known toxins, remember that once the dye has bonded to the cloth, and given that the dyed object has been well rinsed, very little 'shedding' of toxins should occur. The real danger is in the dye liquid, so use common sense and avoid ingestion, inhalation or immersion. See pages 222–223 for hints as to disposal of leftover dyestuffs.

Above: The lupin plant. Below and opposite: Lupin eco-printed fabric.

the edible dye garden

The list of plants that might be selected for a dye garden is rather long, as can be seen from the catalogue of traditional dyeplants contained elsewhere in this book (pages 51–63). One useful criterion when selecting plants would be whether or not they are edible, despite the fact that some food grows on toxic plants. This section describes dyeplants that can be eaten, whereas the section entitled 'Edible plant dyes for culinary magic' (page 72) deals specifically with plants as a source of colouring for food.

Rosemary makes a good yellow dye as well as providing delicious flavour to pasta sauces. Purple basil (*Ocimum basilicum* var. *purpureum*) makes a delightful eco-print. Purple sage can be beaten into cloth using the *hapa-zome* technique, making a lovely bronze leaf print. Violas make rich blue shades when used in the ice-flower dye technique and can be used in salads as well as for colouring icing a deep purple.

The roots of *Alkanna tinctoria* can be ground and mixed with water (or spirits) and the tincture used as red food colouring.

The leaves of most deciduous fruit trees can be used to make dyes, as can the bark. Pick the leaves fresh and allow to dry spread on a meshed frame in a cool dark place. Bark stripped from the off-cuts after annual pruning can be dried and stored for later use.

All aromatic herbs, especially those of the genus *Mentha*, can be used to make leaf prints, using both hot-bundling and *hapa-zome* techniques.

Opposite are listed a few plants that are mostly relatively safe to use in dyeing, given their parallel uses in the kitchen. Remember, though, that *Rheum raponticum* (rhubarb) leaves are poisonous (a leaf decoction mixed with crushed garlic can help to control aphids), *Prunus persica* (peach) leaves contain cyanide (don't be tempted to brew them for tea) and any greenery from a plant of the genus *Solanum* can provoke a very nasty tummy upset indeed if ingested.

Top: *Rosa centrifolia* sp. Above left: Dill plants (*Anethum graveolens*). Above right: Calendula flowers (*Calendula officinalis*).

EDIBLE DYEPLANTS

	TAXONOMIC NAME	COMMON NAME	PART(S) USED
BLACKS	*Juglans* spp.	Walnut varieties	Green hulls cooked in iron pot
PURPLES	*Morus nigra*	Mulberry	Berries used hot or cold (the degree of heat will affect the shade) with or without mordant
	Sambucus nigra	Elderberry	Berries, with or without alum mordant
	Viola spp.	Pansies	Petals used in ice-flower dye with ash or alum mordant
	Solanum tuberosum spp.	Potatoes	Purple congo potatoes have colourful skins. If cooked whole, the mash is purple as well. The skins can give colour to silk
BLUES	*Morus nigra*	Mulberry	Berries used hot or cold (heat will affect shade) with alum or ash mordant
	Viola spp.	Pansies	Flower petals with alum or ash mordant
GREENS	*Allium cepa*	Brown onion	Boiled decoction of skins together with scrap iron with or without urine
	Daucus carota	Carrot	Cooked tops (for deeper green, use iron pot)
	Tetragona expansa	New Zealand spinach	Flowers used cold with sodium carbonate mordant
	Viola odorata	Violet	Skins with or without alum mordant
YELLOWS	*Allium cepa*	Brown onion	Skins with or without alum mordant
	Calendula officinalis	Marigold	Flower petals
	Crocus sativus	Saffron crocus	Stamens
	Rheum raponticum	Rhubarb	Leaves simmered in water make a mordant as well as a dye
	Rosmarinus officinalis	Rosemary	Leaves with/without alum mordant
REDS	*Salvia officinalis*	Purple sage	Leaves with/without alum mordant
	Allium cepa	Spanish onion	Contact print from skins using hot- or cold-bundling with vinegar mordant
	Beta vulgaris	Beetroot	Root peelings with vinegar mordant
	Rubus spp.	Raspberries	Frozen berry dye
BROWNS	*Morus nigra*	Mulberry	Berries used hot or cold (heat will affect shade) with vinegar mordant
	Sambucus nigra	Elderberry	Berries with vinegar mordant
	Allium cepa	Spanish onion	Boiled decoction of skins, no mordant needed

Citruslimon

edible plant dyes for culinary magic

It is astonishing that Azo dyes (synthetic dyes containing the azo group of two nitrogen atoms connecting aromatic ring compounds; widely used in the textile, printing, paper manufacturing, pharmaceutical and food industries) are still permitted to be added to food in many countries (including Australia) when they have been proven to cause liver cancer and are banned in Europe. There are quite a few non-toxic plants that can be used to colour food as well as textiles. At Christmas time, our biscuits are iced with brilliant colours all safely sourced from the family garden where the only spray ever used is cooking-quality vegetable oil to deter scale on the lemon trees.

When making fancy cakes and celebratory biscuits it is certainly much more satisfying to use plant extracts to colour the decorations than to add drops of dubious synthetic substances to them.

Allium cepa ONION
An extract from the skins can be used to add colour to gravies; peeled hard-boiled eggs can be given amusing surface patterns.

Beta vulgaris BEETROOT
The juice makes a splendid colorant. The liquid in which tinned beetroot is preserved comes prepared with sugar, salt and vinegar (all known mordants). Pink mashed potato is popular with small children!

Calendula officinalis MARIGOLD FLOWER PETALS
These can be used to colour icing or to add a rich flavour to yeast dough for special bread.

Rosa spp. ROSE LEAVES
The green leaves of roses can be ground in a mortar and pestle and added to icing for a pretty green.

Viola odorata VIOLET
Tincture of flowers (in alcohol), or as a syrup.

Viola spp. PANSIES
Freeze the pansy petals, then tie into a small muslin bag, allow to thaw naturally and then squeeze the purple juice into a bowl of plain white icing. This makes a delightful purple, ideal for icing fancy cakes and biscuits. If a blue shade is required, add a minuscule amount (¼ teaspoon) of bicarbonate of soda (baking soda).

Above left: Vegetable patch with beetroot, coriander, parsley and onions — all good sources of dye. Above right: Pansies. Opposite: Biscuits iced using natural dyes.

part four

PREPARING, PROCESSING AND APPLYING DYES

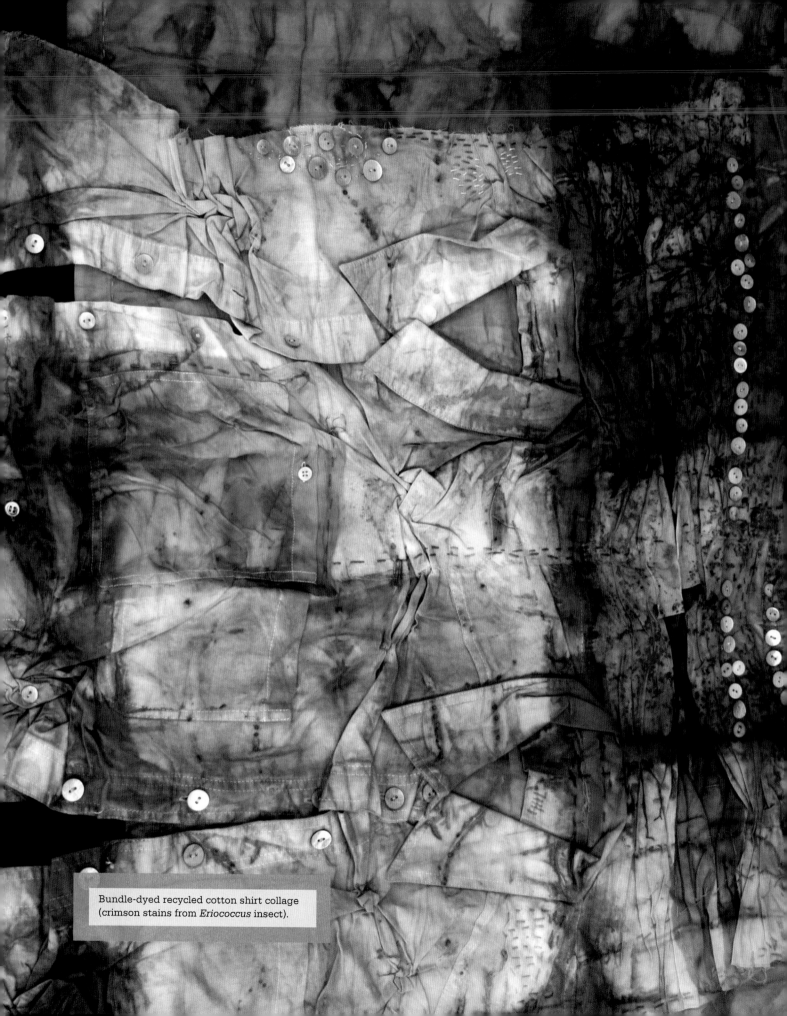

Bundle-dyed recycled cotton shirt collage
(crimson stains from *Eriococcus* insect).

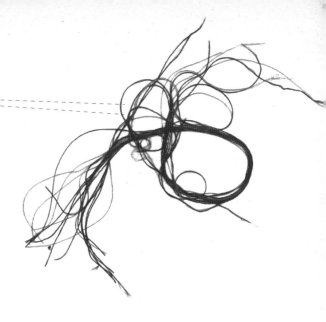

PREPARING TO DYE

*Different plants and plant parts require different treatments on the road
to the dye-pot. Think carefully about which approach you will use. For
example, blue and purple flowers, being quite delicate, will often simply
turn brown in a hot solution. Anyone who has ever admired the delightful
dried cornflowers in Lady Grey's tea blend before pouring on the boiling
water to make the brew will know that the blue colour vanishes in seconds.
So it stands to reason that such things as flowers require a cooler method.*

Blue flowers give the best results when the ice-flower technique (see
page 138) is used. Yellow flowers, on the other hand, seem to respond
quite well to hot processing (see page 106).

Eucalyptus flowers can be simply soaked in water at room temperature
for a couple of days, during which the liquid will absorb most of the colour
from them.

Tough plant parts, such as leathery leaves, barks and seeds, benefit
from soaking in water overnight before processing. Crushing, grinding or
macerating to expose as much surface area as possible to the dye-bath will
help the extraction of colour.

Consider whether you wish your cloth to be evenly dyed, in which case
you will require a pot that is sufficiently large to allow movement of the fibre
during processing. Should you wish the plant material to make patterns on
the cloth, think about eco-printing instead. If you do use a large pot, plan
to recycle the leftover liquid in another dye-bath.

treating the fibre before dyeing

It is traditional to thoroughly wash or scour all fibres before dyeing.
Certainly scouring greasy wool helps even take-up of colour, but violent
boiling of new cloth to remove factory-added starch seems extreme,
particularly as that starch may actually have helpful mordant properties.
Whether you bother with this stage depends very much on the sort of

Above: Some of the sheep on the family property 'Hope Springs': a Merino–Texel crossbred ewe (left) and an English Leicester, or Leicester Longwool (right). Background, this page: English Leicester fleece on the sheep.

Contract killing

That shatoosh is harvested by combing the Tibetan antelope, or chiru, is a myth. Three animals are slaughtered to harvest the fibre for one shawl and this bloody harvest has been illegal for the past thirty years. Despite this, the chiru population has declined from an estimated one million at the end of the last millennium to the point of near extinction less than ten years later.

dyeing you wish to practise. If evenly applied colour and consistent, repeatable results are what your heart desires, then scouring will be necessary. If on the other hand you are happy to be given a (possibly) new and beautiful surprise each time something emerges from the depths, leap in regardless. It is useful, however, to have an understanding of the different types of fibres available to help predict how they might respond to particular treatments.

animal fibres

For nearly 11,000 years, humankind has been enjoying the benefits to be had from animal fibres, even though the development through selective breeding of thick, soft, woolly sheep as we know them today was rather more recent. The animal fibres used in contemporary clothing and furnishing include wool (from sheep), cashmere and mohair (both from goats), shatoosh (allegedly combed from an endangered species of antelope), camel, llama, alpaca, yak, angora (rabbit) and horsehair (tails are used to weave cloth for upholstery). The soft undercoat from many dogs and cats spins and felts quite well, but is rarely used commercially. Silk is possibly the most luxurious animal fibre of all; it is hand-reeled from a cocoon spun by a fat mulberry-leaf-fed caterpillar exuding a liquid from its head. This liquid hardens on contact with air to become silk thread. The tensile strength of these filaments is stronger than steel thread of the equivalent diameter.

PREPARING WOOL

Greasy wool fresh from the sheep is probably best washed in a loosely woven bag of some sort. Mesh citrus bags and old pillowcases will do very nicely. On the other hand, if the wool has a lot of vegetable matter in it, it

dyeing discards

When re-using old garments in the dye-bath, remember that every wash the garment has been through will have a cumulative mordant effect. Most detergents contain washing soda (sodium carbonate) as well as a host of other ingredients, and even the most vigorous rinse will leave traces behind.

Quite often stains that were presumed to have been removed will suddenly reappear in a dye bath. Embroider around them and turn them into a design feature.

Inset, below: The brown ewe pictured opposite, when bred with an English Leicester ram, produced this spotty-fleeced sheep.

Inset, top right: English Leicesters on the family farm. Above: A Romney x Leicester ewe. Background: Eco-print on knit.

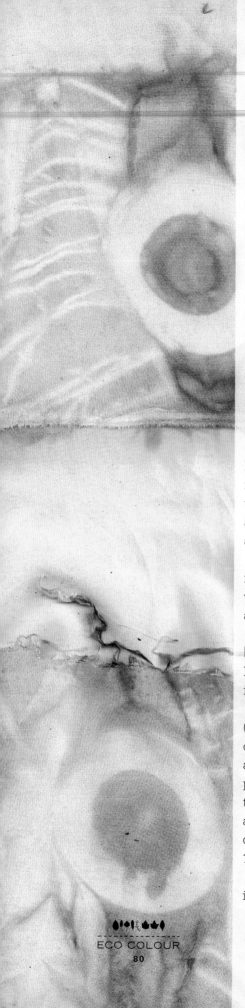

may be best to give it a first soak in a large washing bowl to allow seeds and other plant material to float to the surface and be scooped off. Wool-washing water (particularly that which has been used for rams' wool) is much prized in some countries as an adjunct mordant and is even sometimes used as the foundation solution for making natural indigo vats. Sheep wool is rich in nitrogen and most shearers will justifiably refuse to shear sheep that are even slightly damp, on the basis that ammonia fumes are being given off from the wool. This would indicate there is sufficient ammonia present in wool-washing water to have an effect on a dye-bath. Other substances present would include suint (sweat and lanolin), vegetable matter and dust.

The vital rule is to make sure the temperature of the wash bath and the subsequent rinse do not vary by more than 5° C (9° F). In the Middle Ages, the soapwort (*Saponaria officinalis*) was used as a wetting agent, while human urine was used in England's 'dark satanic mills' during the Industrial Revolution. More recently, industrial scouring was done by adding a quantity of ammonia or washing soda to a soap solution followed by bleaching with hydrogen peroxide (gradually more environmentally friendly methods involving fatty alcohol ethoxylates are being introduced — see www.woolontheweb.com.au for lots of interesting technical information about wool). These are, however, industrial extremes best avoided in an artisanal craft practice.

On the other hand, greasy unwashed wool can be successfully dyed both in a hot eucalyptus bath and using solar-dye techniques. There will be a variable take-up of dye along the fibre due to the natural coating behaving as both mordant and resist.

PREPARING SILK AND OTHER ANIMAL FIBRES

Mohair, alpaca, angora, camel and other animal fibres may all be treated in the same way as silk.

Silk fabrics, when purchased new, are sometimes coated with sericin (a protein isolated from the silkworm, and often included in the ingredients of hair and fabric conditioners — it is also what silk is actually made of, just as keratin is the protein that forms wool and hair) and feel quite stiff. The preparation of silk is called de-gumming and traditionally involved boiling the silk in a dilute solution of an olive-oil-based soap. Simmering the cloth in a weak solution of water and bicarbonate of soda (baking soda) for a couple of hours will also do the trick. Use a ratio of 5 g (⅙ oz) bicarbonate of soda to 100 g (3½ oz) silk in enough water to allow some movement of the fibre.

I never bother de-gumming silk, as the sericin is eventually removed in hot dye-baths anyway. Readers may like to experiment by folding

Dyeing silk with avocado pits produces
a surprising and striking russet colour.

fresh silk using shibori techniques, clamping or tying off and then 'de-gumming' the bundle. When the bundle has dried and been unfolded it can be immersed in a dye-bath. Depending on the source of the dye used there may well be visible colour differences across the scoured and unscoured areas of the cloth.

plant fibres

Familiar plant-based fibres include ramie (made from the fibre of the *Boehmeria nivea*, a close relative of the nettle), linen (from flax *Linum* spp.), cotton (*Gossypium* spp.), nettle (*Urtica* spp.), jute, sisal (from the agave cactus), raffia, pineapple, reed, banana and hemp. There are thousands of lesser-known varieties that are specific to individual regions. New fibres that look and feel like silk are being developed from bamboo, corn or maize, soy and milk proteins; research on such fibres began early in the last century but for various reasons the experiments faltered. Bamboo fibre is now marketed as Eko-Cashmere™, corn or maize fibre cleverly sold as NatureWorks™, soy as Soysilk™ and milk protein as Silk Latte™. The first two must be treated as for cellulose fibres, but soy and milk fibres are protein based and should be handled like their namesakes.

COTTON AND OTHER CELLULOSIC FIBRES

Cotton cloth is spun from the fluffy hairs that cushion the seeds on the boll of the cotton plant (of which the species *Gossypium hirsutum* is the most commonly grown). The growing of cotton requires huge amounts of pesticides as well as water for irrigation, and the processing produces so much dust that factory workers have been known to develop a kind of cotton-induced emphysema as well as a range of cancers. Organically grown cotton avoids the application of agricultural chemicals but is no less thirsty. (This is why I use redeployed cotton sourced from discarded clothing whenever possible.)

Linen is woven from flax, a blue-flowered plant of surprisingly delicate appearance. My own great-grandmother grew flax on the family farm in Latvia. The transformation from plant to thread required some quite intensive labour. Mature plants were uprooted and dried before being laid to soak in a pond for a few weeks. This process, where pond bacteria help to break down the fleshy part of the plant, is called retting. The fibres were then dried and beaten to separate out the fibre and make it more pliable. It was then drawn across a large spiked board called a hackle to align all the fibres before spinning. My ancestor then wove cloth for sheets and shirts for her family.

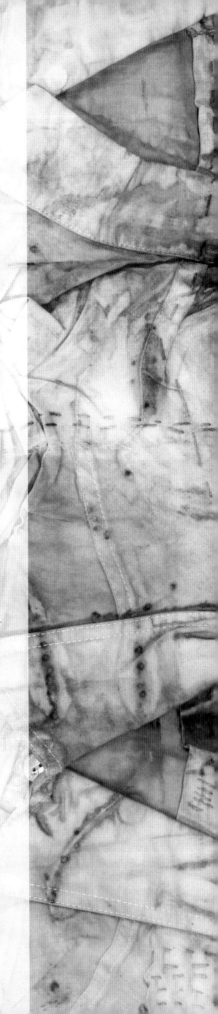

Nettle fibres — made famous in the faerie tale in which a princess must spend thirteen years in silence knitting nettle shirts to save her brothers — were treated in much the same way except that, being exceptionally strong, they require boiling in an alkaline solution to promote separation of the fibres. Once retted and beaten, the small irritating hairs no longer pose a problem and the fibre is beautifully soft and silky. Nettles are now being grown commercially for the textile industry in Italy. Nettle leaves are a good source of green dye, are delicious to eat when steamed and are also rich in iron; useful for bodily health as well as for mordant properties.

Ramie is an extremely strong fibre predominantly produced in China, where it can be harvested several times a year in high-rainfall areas. Like nettle and linen fabrics, ramie becomes progressively softer and more comfortable with use, as does hemp, produced from the cannabis plant. All parts of the hemp plant are very useful; the fibres can be used for thick ropes as well as to weave exquisitely fine cloth. The leaves make excellent green mulch (in addition to their psychotropic potential) and the seeds were traditionally ground to release oil as well as to make a paste similar in consistency to peanut butter. This paste was most nourishing and helped farming families in harsh northern climates survive bitter cold winters. According to my grandmother, the old people apparently also quite enjoyed smoking the leaves in their pipes in order to alleviate rheumatic aches and pains. The hemp that was traditionally grown for cloth and fibre is nowhere near as potent as the cultivars grown for the illicit drugs trade.

Banana fibres are a plentiful side-product from the growing of the fruit and can be used in papermaking as well as for the production of a shining cloth apparently much in demand for wedding dresses in parts of Asia.

PREPARATION

The usual preparation of new cotton cloth is to boil it for several hours in a solution of washing soda (sodium carbonate) and water to remove the starch with which the rolls are coated during the manufacturing process. After scouring, consider whether a mordant is needed. I prefer not to boil anything if it can be avoided, and in any case, depending on the constitution of the starch, it too might well have mordant properties. Rice starch, for example, is likely to be rich in protein and should therefore actually be an assistant to dyeing. It seems wasteful to wash it away.

1 Eucalyptus leaves, previously used in other dye processes. While they appear weary, there is still much potential for colour. **2** Leaves are laid on the cloth. **3** The cloth is rolled into a bundle. **4** The bundle after boiling. The rich colour has been picked up from the boiling solution. **5** Unrolling the work. **6** The colour of the prints — greens and golds as opposed to the reds which were previously extracted show that eucalyptus leaves may contain a range of available dye colour. **7** If desired, the crinkles in the fabric may be pressed while it is still damp. However, once allowed to dry, the fabric will retain this interesting texture.

Vinegar and copper mordant for greens.

Above: Osage oranges and she-oak seeds — useful mordants and resists. Below: Oxidised corrugated iron can assist with dyeing blacks.

MORDANTS

Somewhere back in the mists of time, when our ancestors were trying to decorate their body coverings by staining them with plant juices and minerals, they probably observed that when the two substances overlapped the staying power of the colour was improved. They would also have noted dramatic colour shifts where metals rubbed against plant-stained cloth. It may have dawned on some perceptive soul that the cloths used to soak up the ever-present dampness associated with infants had special affinity for plant dyes. Legend has it that the Romans discovered the benefits of applying alum to their textiles to fix colour and also improve general wearing and resilience. In short, early dyers began to realise the importance of adjuncts in the dyeing and colouring processes. We call these adjuncts 'mordants'.

Mordants can be loosely defined as substances that are added to the equation in order to fix or shift colour at some stage in the dye process. More exactly, they are substances that act as a bridge, or bond, between the molecules of the fibre being dyed, and the substance that is being used to dye it. (The word mordant comes from the Latin *mordère*, meaning 'to bite'). Similarly the linguistic relationship to German (probably from the Saxon) can be seen in the related *beitzmittel* (mordant) and the English word 'bites'. The study of language is fascinating and can show us that where links in name for substances or practices are closely related, communities are likely to have had a connection of some sort at the time of their development. Just as the German *weben* and weaving are close, we can assume that the major discoveries in textile and dye practice were made fairly early on in history and carried with people as they wandered, migrated, explored or traded.

    Mordants may be applied before, during or after dyeing. These processes are commonly called pre-mordanting, simultaneous or co-mordanting, and post-mordanting. There are infinite variations of colour that can be achieved depending on which mordant is applied and at what stage, not to mention what process and temperature have been selected to dye the chosen

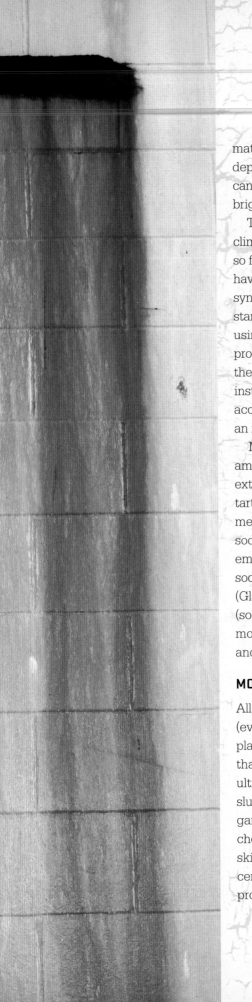

material. The final effect of a (sometimes extended) dye exploration will vary depending on the sorts of procedures that are implemented. Mordants can help to assure light- and wash-fastness, prevent colour bleeding and brighten or change some dye colours.

The results may vary according to the sequence of procedures, the climate in the region of harvest, the time of year, the water used and so forth. Some will be subtle, some dramatic. Mordants and dyes will have different effects depending on the fibres used (protein, cellulose or synthetic). The method of preparation of the fibre (wet/dry/scoured/greasy/starched, etc.) will also influence the end colour result. Be aware that if using a dye substance and a mordant together in one pot (the co-mordant process), sometimes colour can be wasted when the dye simply bonds to the mordant before either of them has attached to the fibre. In such instances the colour may be visible suspended in solution but is not accessible, as the dye and mordant may have amalgamated and formed an insoluble unattachable mix.

Mordant substances have traditionally included such compounds as ammonia, urea, acetic acid, tannic acid, sumac, gall nuts, various bark extracts, oleic acid, stearic acid, sulphuric acid, tartaric acid, cream of tartar (the last two are not one and the same) and Turkey Red oil; and metallic substances such as various combinations or soluble salts of sodium, chromium, aluminium, iron, copper, arsenic and tin. Sodium salts embrace the compounds sodium bicarbonate (bicarbonate of soda/baking soda), sodium carbonate (washing soda), hydrated sodium sulphate (Glauber's salts) and sodium hydroxide (caustic soda). Common salt (sodium chloride) has been a traditional mordant, but remember that in modern times table salt contains iodine in addition to the sodium chloride and this will affect results.

MORDANT TOXICITY

All but a handful of the above mordants are toxic when ingested (even cooking salt when taken in excess), and none of them, except the plant extracts, can be easily disposed of. While it has been suggested that waste solutions should be reduced in a covered evaporation pit, ultimately there is no safe method of disposing of the residual toxic sludge. It is worth considering that the rich and brilliantly coloured garments that we purchase 'off the rack' may well contain harmful chemical residues *that will be in constant contact with our skins*. As the skin is one of the most receptive and sensitive organs of the body, certainly allowing one's own 'permeable membrane' to be in prolonged proximity to potentially toxic substances seems foolhardy. It is simply a

Stormcast seaweed, such as this drying on calcium-rich rocks at Kaikoura, New Zealand, can be easily gathered for dyes.

matter of common sense that the use of mordants ought to be avoided completely where the finished product is intended for use by infants, for example, and if a mordant is absolutely necessary, some safe alternative substituted. Certainly if no mordants are used, disposal of spent solutions is not a problem.

On the other side of the argument, mordants often improve the fastness of the dye on the fibre; as well as the ongoing wash-fastness, they provide light- and perspiration-fastness. Strong perspiration has been known to actually permanently change the colours of some plant dyes. The choice of mordant is most important, as the different substances and even the sequence of their application will determine the final colour. While one can, of course, immerse a number of items pre-mordanted in a range of substances into one dye-bath, do be aware that minute particles of the mordant can be given off and contribute to an unpredictable cocktail. This only becomes a problem if one wants to have precisely replicable results — not necessarily the intent of this book.

Other substances traditionally used as mordants included soot, coal, blood, soil and mud, whether applied in their raw state or mixed with water, acids, alkalis or urine. In some parts of Asia, an extract of buffalo hide plays a role in dyeing. Seaweed was traditionally burned in the Hebrides to make a soda ash for use as an adjunct. The length of time the fibre is immersed in mordant is important, as is the time the sample is allowed to rest to cure or absorb the mordant before being dyed. In Japan, soy-mordanted cloth is allowed to cure for a year before being immersed in the dye-bath.

One of the least harmful of the traditional mordants is alum, usually in the form of potassium aluminium sulphate. This substance has had a place in domestic kitchens for years and was used in the pickling process for preserving salted cucumbers, as well as being an ingredient in baking powder together with bicarbonate of soda (baking soda). Admittedly this isn't necessarily a gold-plated recommendation, but it would certainly seem safe enough to put in a dye-pot given that the contents are not destined to be eaten. Disposal in domestic gardens isn't a problem, as compost heaps will actually welcome the addition of a slightly alkaline substance to counterbalance the high acidity introduced by piles of leaf litter, and most of the alum that was present in the solution will have bonded with the fibre being dyed.

In the interest of ecological sustainability and the ongoing health of the dyer, this book leaves most traditional mordants behind and goes in search of less harmful options.

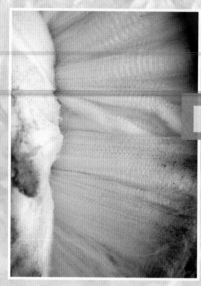

Fleece parting on a merino sheep.

wool

Dramatic differences may be noted between protein fibres (wool, silk, human hair and other animal fibres, including skin!) and plant fibres (cotton, linen/flax, ramie and so on) in terms of their responses to dyes. Although wool and silk are frequently bracketed under the label of 'protein fibres', there is a difference between these fibres too; while both are made of protein (the former keratin and the latter fibroin), and contain hydrogen, oxygen and carbon, wool also contains sulphur. The presence of sulphur causes wool to yellow under the influence of sunlight, makes it particularly attractive to moths and undoubtedly influences the end result of the dye process.

When metallic salt mordants are employed in the dye process, they attach themselves to the hydrogen bonds in the fibres, acting as electron receptors to assist in bonding the dye with the fibre. Concentrated use of mordants may have adverse effects on the molecular structure of the fibre; for example, experience shows that excessive use of alum (potassium aluminium sulphate) tends to make wool 'sticky', rendering it unsuitable for use in knitting, weaving and embroidery. It stands to reason that strong alkalis and strong acids will also damage the fibres, and while both wool and silk are resistant to weak acid solutions, as well as to weak alkalis, solutions with a pH of above 8 will destroy wool.

The traditional method of mordanting wool, involving a combination of alum and cream of tartar (also an ingredient in baking powder), is highly effective in assisting the brighter take-up of colour. Where eucalyptus-leaf dyes are used, however, the process is unnecessary.

Dissolve a teaspoon each of alum and cream of tartar in a little hot water and then mix with a bucket of lukewarm water (about 10 litres, or 2 gallons, in volume). Immerse about 500 g (1 pound) of pre-dampened wool (this also works well for mohair) in the mixture and work it about using rubber-gloved hands. Be careful; excessive working may lead to felting, as all the pre-requisite conditions for that ongoing and irreversible process are present! Allow to soak overnight, then gently squeeze out the excess moisture and hang the wool to dry in a shady place. Keep the liquid in the bucket; it can do service as an ongoing mordant bath if the alum and cream of tartar are replenished regularly. Choose an enamel or glass container for long-term use, as plastic buckets release assorted nasties into the solution and become quite slimy around the vessel walls.

cotton

The ash and soy method for mordanting cotton has been covered elsewhere in this book (see page 104). The more the method is repeated in sequence, the better the eventual take-up of dye. Another conventional mordant method for cellulose fibres involves a mixture of alum and washing soda (sodium carbonate). Two teaspoons of alum to one of washing soda will be enough to mordant 500 g (1 pound) of cloth. Dissolve each substance separately in a cup of hot water and add to a mordanting pot containing 10 litres (2 gallons) of water. Stir well, then add the fibre. Simmer for one hour, then allow to cool overnight. Spin out excess liquid and dye as required. Experiment by following up with tannin and soy treatments if desired, or substitute tannin for the alkali when boiling. This treatment works well also for hemp, linen and ramie. Ash-water (see page 145) can be substituted for the washing soda, bearing in mind that the strength of the solution cannot really be calibrated. One can, however, test the pH using a commercial kit.

Mordants particularly useful on cellulose fibres also include tea, sea water, ash-water, acorn milk, whey (from cheese production), skim milk, eggs, acacia barks and the variety of saps obtainable from thistles and *Euphorbia* species. Such saps can be painted or printed on to the substrate, which is then overdyed after the sap has dried.

silk

Silk has a particular affinity for plant dyes and only needs pre-mordanting if a particular colour outcome (for example, using alum as a pre-mordant for yellow coreopsis flowers to give pink on silk) is required. In Japan, silk is traditionally mordanted with soy. This is not absolutely essential to the dye process but does make the resulting colour a little deeper and brighter than it might otherwise have been.

looking for alternatives

Alternative mordants include urine, tins and lids from containers used to preserve food (the tins can be used as dye vessels, while the lids are dual-purpose resists and mordants), eggs, ash, soy milk, sea water, fermented fruit vinegars, the compost heap, oxidised wine, iron teas, (copper) coins, manure (sheep and cow), aqueous plant solutions and seed oils. There will, of course, be many more depending upon how many and which substances are combined. The possible blends are almost unlimited.

When examining plants for mordant possibilities, consider the genus and species names for clues to their potential properties. Just as *tinctoria* tells us

It has become fashionable in recent years to use ammonia-based household cleaning agents as mordants. While this can be justified if one is cleaning the house and uses the fabric that one is intending to dye to wipe up the spray, it becomes dangerous practice if the substance is used in combination with other mordants. Unexpected chemical reactions may occur and toxic vapours be given off. Cleaning agents should never be used when dyeing cloth that will be worn by babies and young children.

the plant was traditionally used for dyeing, and *officinalis* that it had medicinal applications, so too can we find guides to potential mordants. *Oxalis* would indicate oxalic acid, *salix* the presence of salicylic acid (or a closely related compound) and so forth.

tannin

Plants traditionally used in tanning will be of great benefit in the dyeing of cotton, hemp, linen and ramie. The application of a tannin mordant as a precursor to a protein mordant is common to many long-established dye traditions.

Some of the plants historically used in temperate regions were:

Dyer's sumac (*Cotinus coggygria*): not to be confused with the North American Sumac *Rhus typhina* or the Sicilian variety *Rhus coriaria*; don't be tempted to buy the packaged sumac from food specialists — it is not worth it! Fresh leaves are best, but be careful with *Rhus toxicus* as it can provoke severe allergies.

Oak (*Quercus* sp.): the bark, acorn cups and galls are all useful.

Spruce (*Picea* sp.): bark.

Pomegranate (*Punica granatum*): rind (fruit), bark (prunings).

Hemlock (*Tsuga canadensis*): bark.[2]

Chestnut (*Castanea sativa*): use the husks of the chestnut (eat the yummy bits inside!).

Myrobolan (*Myrobolanus chebula*): used as mordant in Kalamkari, a form of dyeing practised in India, which used myrobolan together with gall nut, milk, pomegranate rind and ruminant dung.

Bracken (*Pteridium esculentum*): adult leaves and stems are rich in tannin, formerly used to tan hides.

The wattle species *Acacia mearnsii* is presently cultivated in South Africa, Sri Lanka, Australia and Brazil as a commercial source of tannin, but it is not unique in its tannin-rich properties. All of the *Acacia* species contain tannin in the bark to varying degrees, and given the short lifespan of this genus (usually 8–20 years), residents of Australia, where the wattle is endemic, should have little trouble sourcing samples.

The seed pods are a rich source of colour as well as tannin and should be collected from the ground under the tree, where they will have been baked to a gorgeous chocolate brown by the sun. Cement paths on which the leaf litter and pods fall are invariably stained in haphazard dark-brown patterns.

Many tropical species, such as mangroves (*Rhizophora*) and quebracho (*Schinopsis balansae*, *Schinopsis lorentzii*), are harvested from the wild for commercial tannins. Avoid purchasing such products, as such harvesting promotes wholesale destruction of habitat.

Looking into our own backyards, we can find *Rumex* species (dock and sorrel) almost universal on weed

2 Incidentally, this is not the Hemlock drunk by Socrates; that was *Conium maculatum*.

lists around the globe. Dry and grind the roots and mix with water to make a tannin-rich soaking solution. The leaves of this genus are also rich in oxalic acid. Even the dried seeds have mordant qualities and can, for example, assist the take-up of eucalyptus dyes on linen when added to the dye-bath as a simultaneous mordant.

Acorns from any of the *Quercus* species yield both protein mordants from the core of the fruit and tannins from the dark outer skin as well as the acorn cup. Soaking and simmering the parts separately or together will produce a rich mordant liquid.

protein

BLOOD

Proteins can be sourced from a range of substances, both floral and faunal. The use of the blood of pigs, chickens and cows is unexceptional in parts of Asia and Africa, but unless the dyer lives in a rural area or has access to an abattoir, such material could be difficult to locate. Plant, milk and egg proteins are most likely easier to find and use.

GELATINE

Gelatine, derived from the bones and hooves of bovine ruminants processed for meat, is available in powdered or leaf form. It can be dissolved with rather a greater volume of water than is used to make the usual wobbly jelly desserts in order to make a protein-rich solution to soak any cellulose fibre intended for a plant dye-bath.

SOY

The soybean (*Glycine max*) hails from China and is useful as a food (flour, tofu, soymilk) as well as a soil improver, as the roots of the plants produce small nodules, which help to fix nitrogen in the ground. The beans (seeds) can contain up to 44 percent protein and produce soybean oil, used in paints and as a carrier for printing inks.

The most common protein mordant is that made by grinding and crushing soybeans (alternatively, use soy flour), soaking them in water and then straining off the solution. Unfortunately this mixture does have a tendency to ferment quite quickly and in the process becomes somewhat malodorous, so if there is an interruption to the work schedule and the beans are left for a few days it can all get rather nasty. This may be the reason Japanese dyers had a dedicated day for mordanting all of their fabrics for the year.

If you don't wish to go to the trouble of grinding and soaking, using pre-packaged soymilk from the supermarket works just as well. Choose the brand with the fewest additives and dilute the liquid with about five parts of water to one part

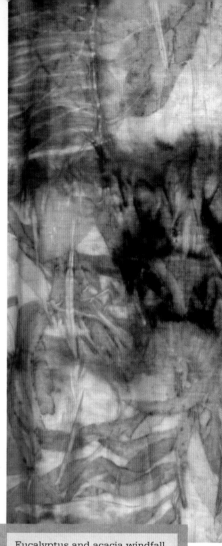

Eucalyptus and acacia windfall eco-prints on merino jersey.

the wee dram

In Scotland, the urine of little boys was reputedly considered the best for woad dyeing, but this is a matter for speculation. It was also rumoured that tub-filling parties were held at the start of the dye season, wherein the refreshments consumed by the men present were subsequently deposited in the woad vat. The substance produced by the male or female of the human species is more likely to be adulterated by individual consumption of liquids, foods and medicines than by minuscule amounts of naturally occurring gender-related hormones. It is unlikely there would be radically differing outcomes in a dye-bath. What is known is that the human body disposes of a relatively constant quantity of soluble substances each day, with the morning emissions containing the strongest concentrations; so the vat parties simply saved the dyer from the exertion of carrying extra buckets of water for the woad bath. Among the animals, herbivores tend to produce less offensively scented emissions; on the other hand, highly ammoniac cat urine may have spectacular effects for those who are prepared to brave the perils of harvest along with the stench.

of soy. The exact proportion comes with experience, as each brand is slightly different. A good way to begin is to half-fill a domestic bucket with water, pour in a 1-litre (32 fl oz) carton of soy and then cram as much cloth into the bucket as will comfortably fit. Turn it a few times over the next 24 hours, whiz the excess liquid out using the spin cycle of the washing machine and hang the fabric to dry.

ACORN FLOUR

Acorn flour can be made by grinding up acorns after the stiff brown husks are removed (use the husks as a source of tannin). If no acorns are available, many grocers stocking Asian foods will have acorn flour available. A little goes a long way, and if weevils appear while the flour is in storage simply sift them out (and feed them to your fowls, if you have any).

RICE FLOUR

Rice flour can be substituted for crushed soybeans or acorn flour. It also makes an excellent resist paste when mixed with a little kaolin (available from pharmacies and, more economically, from potters' suppliers).

EGG WHITE

A mordant traditionally used by the Miao people of China in making their glossy indigo cloth. The egg white is beaten and then spread on to the surface of the blue cloth prior to another over-dyeing. Egg white is also a useful carrier for colour in the event that dyes are to be applied by brush using stencilling or painting techniques.

YOGHURT

Yoghurt can be a good mordant for cotton, linen and other cellulosic fibres. It can be used thick as paint or diluted with water if desired. It is partially 'digested' by the bacteria that are present in the substance, which will make its effect different from that of using fresh milk.

alkalis

ASH

Ash is a common source of alkali. Traditionally, quite specific ashes were made by drying and burning particular plant varieties, such as peach, persimmon and camellia. Different parts of the plants can be dried thoroughly and then burned to make ash. The method of burning — whether, for example, the dried material is incinerated packed into a sealed container (without further available oxygen) or simply placed on a non-combustible surface and ignited — can also affect the quality of the ash.

Ash is usually used suspended in water, but being such a dry substance it is quite resistant to being mixed into a solution. There are a number of ways to make ash-water. Placing the ash in a small

cloth bag and then massaging the bag in a container of water while wearing gloves is useful for small amounts. An alternative is to take a terracotta plant pot and plug the hole in the base with a small amount of straw or dried grass. Place the flower pot over a container, fill the pot about half-way with ash and then pour very hot water onto the ash, preferably using a small watering can with a rose. Be careful not to breathe in any of the ash dust that will rise. The ash-rich liquid will drip through the straw filter into the base of the pot whence it can be collected for use.

AMMONIA

Adding ammonia to a dye solution as a post-mordant often makes substantial differences to the final colour achieved, magically enhancing brightness and richness of colour. Use low-strength household ammonia in a well-ventilated place if you must — however, it is preferable to make your own simply by allowing a bucket of urine to ferment for a couple of days. Clearly this should be

Persimmon (*Diospyros kaki*); the astringent fruit has a long history of use as a mordant.

STAINLESS STEEL   BRASS   IRON   ALUMINUM   COPPER LINED WITH ZINC   COFFEE CAN

SILK

COTTON

WOOL

perforatum collected Dec 2006, frozen
2007
simmering 1 hr
DYING (24 HR)
SPRING'S RAINWATER

BI-CARB soda

ALUM

COPPER SCRAP SOAKED IN VINEGAR From old Red WINE

VINEGAR + ALUMINUM FOIL SCRAPS

NO HORSESHOE (IRON) IN VINEGAR

RUST FLAKES (IRON OXIDE)

CREAM OF TARTAR

GERBER MORDANT AS Hypericum perforatum using solution made for Po...

Multi-fibre swatches from combined pot-as-mordant and Gerber method tests (see page 103) on *Hypericum perforatum*.

solid colour

A dye is considered substantive
if the colour remains unchanged
by washing (that is, does not
run or change shade) or through
'reasonable' exposure to sunlight,
namely the levels of exposure that
might be encountered through daily
wear (admittedly highly variable
between different geographic and
climatic locations).

Remember that *all* textiles
fade if left lying about in the sun,
and some of the worst culprits
are synthetically dyed fashion
disposables such as T-shirts and
dark-coloured bed linen!

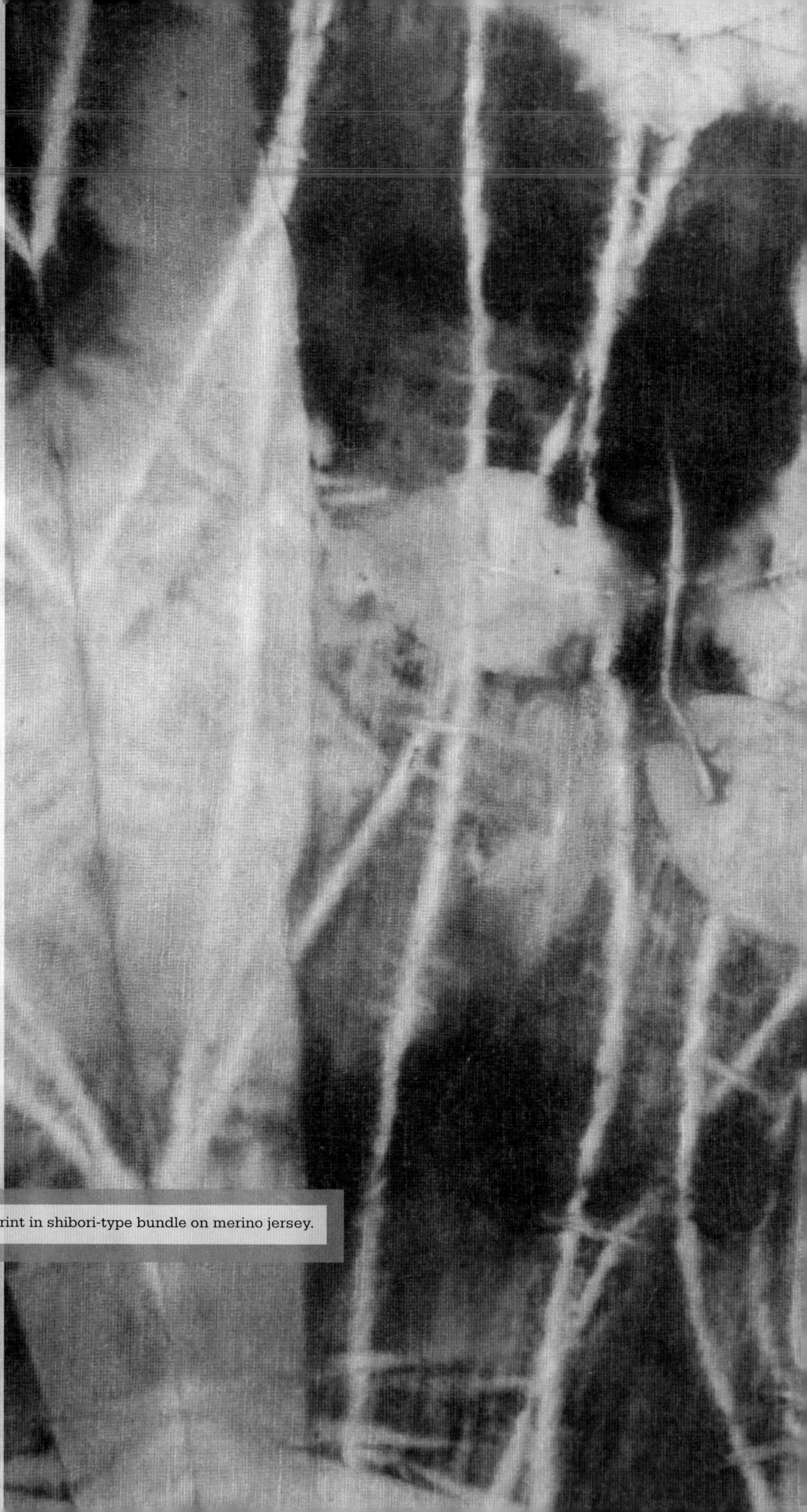

Rose-leaf eco-print in shibori-type bundle on merino jersey.

Sea water is a valuable multi-purpose mordant.

done somewhere that won't be offensive; when choosing the position for such a bucket, keep in mind that the space behind your back shed could be too close for comfort to the neighbour's favourite outdoor eating area. Discretion should be the watch-word. Leftovers can be diluted with water and poured on to the garden.

PLANT SOURCES

There are a number of plants that have alkaline saps and juices. Frequently these can also be poisonous; if in any doubt, don't use them.

Persimmon juice has been used as a mordant both fresh and fermented. Such plants as cucumbers, zucchinis (courgettes) and pumpkins (winter squash) can also provide interesting effects. Many spontaneous plants (more prosaicaly known as weeds) are also inexpensive sources of possible mordants.

The fruit of the plant known variously as the pie, paddy, afghan or wild melon (*Citrullus lanatus*) is extremely alkaline. Cook the fruit in water and strain off the liquid to make a useful pre-mordant.

Quite simply, just as every plant has the potential to give colour in the dye-pot, there is an infinite range of possibilities and permutations for the employment of plant extracts as pre-mordants.

It is important that the user is selective in the choice of plants, bearing in mind rarity, legality of harvest, speed of regeneration, depth of colour, economic management of the dye-bath, user safety (in the case of toxic plants) and ultimate disposal of the solution.

acids

VINEGAR

Household vinegar is a dilute form of acetic acid, usually available commercially at about 3 percent strength by volume. Most of the cold-method red flower and berry dyes (safflower excepted) need an acid environment in order for the fibre to appear red. Such colours do tend to respond to their environment; that is to say, they are not substantive (see box opposite), so care must be taken in laundering or the textile may change colour in the wash.

Fruit vinegars can be made using the peels and cores from various fruits, including pears, apples and plums. Soak the fruit parts in water for a few days. In warm weather, fermentation will set in quite quickly, and when the naturally occurring yeasts have exhausted the sugars present, vinegar will be produced. A commercial pH test kit can be used to determine the strength of the solution.

Cumquats make for
wonderful mordants.

SALICYLIC ACID

In the past, those skilled in the application of herbs knew that a tea made of willow bark could help to ease pain. This is because the willow contains salicylic acid compounds, which are released into the brew; a substance more conventionally obtained in the form of aspirin. Make a tea of willow leaves and bark by pouring hot water onto the plant material and letting it stand for a day or so before use. This will be a more subtle acid than the fruit vinegar described above.

OXALIC ACID

Plants from the *Rumex* genus (dock, sorrel) as well as rhubarb (*Rheum raponticum*) and soursobs (*Oxalis pes-caprae*) contain oxalic acid within their leaves, stems and roots. If brewing rhubarb leaves, which are poisonous, be very careful to keep the solution in a secure container in a safe place out of reach of children and pets.

LEMON JUICE

Lemon juice is not only an acid mordant (citric and ascorbic acids are present), it can also be used as a bleaching assistant to help remove rust stains. Given that lemon juice and salt are the traditional agents for bleaching out rust stains, soaking cloth in sea water before applying lemon juice can be a useful alternative.

metals

DYE-POT AS MORDANT

One method of employing the influence of specific metals on the dye process is to engage the pot as mordant. Immersing the pre-dyed textile in a water bath in a metal dye-pot, or preparing the dye-bath in the pot, will affect the resulting colour. The influence of the metal from which the vessel is made increases with the length of time the textile and the dye solution are allowed to remain in the pot. Iron will generally darken shades; copper has a tendency to enhance greens; aluminium pots tend to brighten shades; stainless steel has little influence. Sometimes, though, an iron pot can turn a red eucalypt dye to purple, while using an aluminium pot can shift *Hypericum perforatum* (St John's wort) from maroon to bright green on wool and silk. The almost unlimited colour variations possible hinge for the most part on the patience of the dyer. While using dye-pot as mordant seems on the surface to be relatively harmless, it must be admitted that *in order for the colour modification to occur* there must of course be some absorption of the substance formed through reaction with the pot material, however minimal. We may assume that similar minor reactions must also occur in the domestic storage of water, cooking and the preserving of foods in metal tins. If these practices are deemed safe, then the use of 'pot as mordant' is, on balance, acceptable.

Aluminium, copper, brass, tin and iron pots may all be employed for this purpose. It is imperative that pots used for dyeing are not subsequently used in the preparation of food (see more information on page 44). Mordants and dyes will have different effects depending on the fibres used (protein, cellulose or synthetic) and on the method of preparation of the substrate.

Try processing a number of samples in the co-mordant pot, and taking them out at intervals, say a day apart. You may well find a range of shades appearing as the pot has increased effect. This is particularly useful in dyeing threads for embroidery.

VERDIGRIS

Verdigris, more properly described as copper acetate, is a green bloom that appears on the surface of the metal where acids are present. It can be encouraged by swabbing copper scrap with wine vinegar, fruit vinegar, lemon juice or simply crushed grapes. Adding a nicely greened copper fragment to a dye-bath can enhance the take-up of green dyes. Wrapping a cloth soaked in vinegar, urine or sea water (to name but three options) around a piece of scrap copper for a few days

can prepare the fabric well for both green and blue dyes.

URINE

Urine is a traditional wool-scouring agent and conditioner and can be used to form the basis of a simple indigo vat. In parts of Asia, water from washing wool is used as a mordant (it contains suint and a proportion of urine as well as dissolved ammonia released when wool is wet) and also in the processing of indigo. It therefore follows that urine in which wool has been washed could be usefully recycled as a mordant. Use urine to soak metal fragments to make mordant teas. Experiment with copper, iron, brass and shredded aluminium foil and use these brews diluted with water as 'after-baths' to brighten or change colours.

Useful things to collect.

Setting up a Gerber mordant test.

Gerber mordant test covered with bubble wrap for warmth — the wrap creates a greenhouse effect to warm the samples using solar energy.

Hypericum perforatum samples warmed over steam.

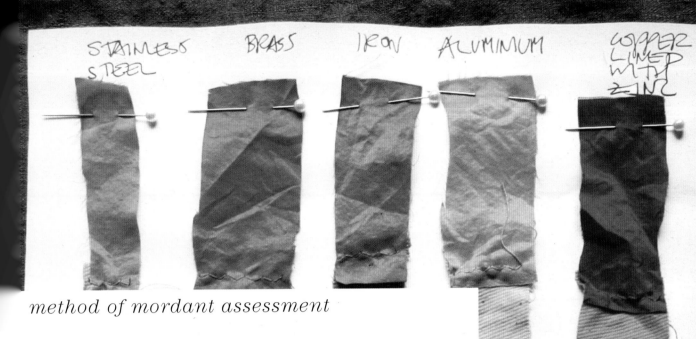

STAINLESS STEEL　　BRASS　　IRON　　ALUMINUM　　COPPER LINED WITH ZINC

method of mordant assessment

This method is attributed to Fred and Willi Gerber, late and legendary dyers of the United States. It is an invaluable technique for finding which might be the most appropriate substance to use as a post-mordant without having to make huge repeat quantities of dyes and thus potentially wasting large quantities of material. The Gerbers' work was groundbreaking at the time, as they discovered that adjunct mordants could be used in far smaller quantities than traditional advice suggested while still having a powerful impact on the colour and longevity of natural dyes.

Make up a dye-bath and process the fibre or textile in it until a satisfactory depth of colour has been achieved. Take out the fibre and set aside for the time being, in a non-reactive vessel of some sort so that no liquid is lost. Meanwhile, set up a series of white porcelain bowls, or glass beakers with a white sheet of paper underneath.

Into each vessel place a small quantity of the dye liquid, and add a small amount of the mordant to be tested; if in a powdered form then ½ teaspoon, if in liquid form about ¼ cup (such liquids being sourced from the list of self-brewed adjuncts mentioned elsewhere in the text; see pages 91–101).

Monitor any colour changes. It's wise to wait for at least 10 minutes before making a decision, as sometimes initial colours are fugacious (fleeting or evanescent) and can be observed to change after a time. Having made a choice of mordant, simply tip the contents of the selected vessel into the main dye-bath, stir the cocktail together and then return the textile to the bath.

You can now choose to return the dye-bath to a heat source, or simply to let it sit and allow time to do the work.

The contents of the test vessels need not be wasted either; use small jars or snap-lock bags and pour the test samples into them together with small fabric pieces or handfuls of embroidery threads. Seal and set aside (see 'Solar dyeing', page 191) until the samples have achieved a colour you like.

extracted by simmering 1 hr
POT-AS-MORDANT (24 HR)
USING 'HOPE SPRINGS' RAINWATER

pre-mordants

PROCESSES FOR MORDANTING CELLULOSIC FIBRES

The cellulosic fibres include cotton, linen, ramie, hemp, nettle and banana. They need special treatment to be able to take up plant dyes efficiently. The logic here is quite undemanding. Plant dyes tend in general to bond well with protein fibres because unlike valencies attract each other. Put very simply, we have a similar situation to that pertaining to magnetism. Like poles reject each other, opposites attract. So the trick is to create a situation in which the plant dyes, which are generally but not exclusively of an acidic nature — indicating the presence of one or more unattached electrons — are able to bond with a substrate exhibiting an available proton. Protein fibres have available protons, as do alkalis.

Soaking the textile in a protein-rich or an alkaline solution creates a surface to which plant dyes can bond. Applying alkaline and protein mordants in succession, building up layers, seems to work even better.

These explanations are admittedly very simplistic; sadly, I did not realise in the heady days of youth just how useful the knowledge of chemistry would become to me, so spent too much time drawing in chemistry class. Therefore the reader will need to seek out more specific and technical explanations elsewhere. What has become clear through reading and practice, though, is that the longer the textile is allowed to rest or cure after the application of the mordant, the better will be the take-up of dye as well as the longevity and intensity of the resultant colour. This is why, in many dye traditions, several years are allowed to elapse between mordant processes and dyeing. Even after dyeing, fabrics may be stored in a cool dry place for one or two years to allow the dye time to mature before the textile is used.

MAKING UP THE ALKALINE SOLUTION

There are many ways to make up the alkaline solution. Ash-water (see pages 95 and 145) is one of the cheapest, made up of a small amount of ash taken either from the fireplace, or from material specifically burned for the purpose. Different leaves, barks, timbers and so forth are all likely to produce different colour variations based on the chemistry of the plant used. Alternatively, use aged or fermented urine, which will have developed ammonia content. It will be a trifle smelly, but the smell won't survive the dye process (unless cats' urine is used, in which case virtually nothing will dispel the aroma). The urine can be used undiluted, or may be diluted with substances including water, old coffee, tea and so on.

---

a mordant method for cotton based on traditional Japanese mordant practice

After scouring, soak the textile in an alkaline solution. Dry in the sun. Repeat the process as many times as you like (traditionally, up to 120 times).

Following the alkaline applications, soak the textile in a protein-based solution. Dry in the sun. Repeat the process as desired (traditionally, up to 30 times).

Alternate the alkaline and protein processes for even better take-up.

Washing soda (sodium carbonate) is a relatively harmless household chemical when used with care, and a dilute solution (a heaped tablespoon to a 10 litre/2 gallon bucket of warm water) makes an excellent pre-mordant.

Consider also making mordants from alkaline plants. Be very careful when working with these, as many plants containing alkaline juices or saps also harbour poisonous alkaloids. The fruit of the plant known as the pie, paddy, afghan or wild melon (*Citrullus lanatus*) is extremely alkaline. Simmer the fruit in water (the proportion of fruit to water will of course affect the colour) and allow the potion to cool. Strain and use as suggested above. Persimmon (*Diospyros kaki*) has been used as a mordant in Asia for hundreds of years. (The strange prickling mouth-feel of the unripe fruit is a clue to the presence of interesting compounds that could affect colour.)

There are hundreds of plants containing alkaloids in varying degrees, such as wolfbane (*Aconitum napellus*), milkweed (*Euphorbia* spp.), and opium poppies (*Papaver somniferum*), many of which are grown as ornamental bedding plants in gardens. Provided they are processed in well-ventilated areas in dedicated vessels not otherwise employed in the family kitchen, and the spent liquids disposed of promptly (they can be safely poured into a composting pit), they may certainly be used as pre-mordants. In fact most traditional medicinal plants, if not dyes themselves, will certainly be useful as mordants. Be sure to wear rubber gloves and a mask when working with toxic vegetation and do not use them as pre-mordants if making objects to be used by babies and young children — just in case.

MAKING UP THE PROTEIN SOLUTION

The simplest source of protein substances is the pantry. Eggs are a rich source of protein; they may be used whole or separated into whites and yolks, immediately giving three options. Beat them well in water to make a soaking solution.

Milk from animal sources (cow, sheep, goat) or from plant sources (soy, acorn, almond and so forth) can be used. Make the nut and seed milks by grinding a handful of the chosen substance and soaking it in water overnight. Strain through a cloth before immersing the textile. Using acorns has the added benefit of introducing tannins into the mix.

Powdered or bottled milk should be diluted with water before use. Commercially prepared soymilk solutions may also be used, but be aware that those with added chemicals will contain extra and not necessarily predictable magic. Usually a litre (32 fl oz) carton of soymilk mixed with a 10 litre (2 gallon) bucket of water makes enough mordant for about 5 metres (5½ yards) of fabric (depending on the weight and absorbency of the fibre).

other useful mordants for cellulosic textiles include:

Tea (rich in tannins)
Wattle (*Acacia* spp.) bark
Eucalyptus barks
Mud
Blood
Cow dung
Oakgalls
Rhubarb and *Rumex* species (oxalic acids)
and any plants traditionally used in tanning leather

PROCESSING PLANT DYES

The traditional approach to extracting plant dyes was by vigorous boiling. The plant material was placed in a pot, covered with water, brought to a sustained boil and when there was adequate visible colour, the liquid was strained off. The wetted pre-mordanted fabric or fibre was then immersed and boiled in the liquid while being kept in motion to ensure an even colour take-up.

When the cloth was considered sufficiently coloured it was removed from the pot, thoroughly rinsed in cold water and hung to dry. In the case of wool, the pre-mordant was generally a heavy-handed mixture of alum and cream of tartar, also applied through a boiling process. Certainly the stirring for even colour take-up has validity, but the rest of the process has serious flaws.

Firstly, boiling the plant material is only necessary when dealing with the eucalypts. The chemicals in the tough leaves from this genus seem to undergo some sort of transformation with intense heat, so that brilliant colour is released for application to protein fibres. Other traditionally boiled plants will, however, benefit from being processed at much reduced heat, when they will exhibit brighter colours. Many flowers are best processed cold, as their colours are fugacious and dissipate entirely under heat. Lichens and indigo species require quite different processing using fermentation at controlled temperatures. Ecologically sustainable practice excludes the lichens, as similar colours may be obtained from other faster-growing and more easily available plants, therefore lichen dyes will only be mentioned in passing in this book. The contemporary 'short-cut' applications of blue from indigo have also been barred from the text, as the chemical adjuncts required are toxic. This section introduces a range of processing options; more specific details in relation to certain plants will be found deeper in the book (see pages 116–117 and 120–145).

There are other disadvantages to the traditional boiling method, particularly as regards the cloth or fibre being dyed. Removing the sample from a hot pot and giving it a cold rinse not only distresses the fibre, it also

Berberis thunbergii leaves being processed.

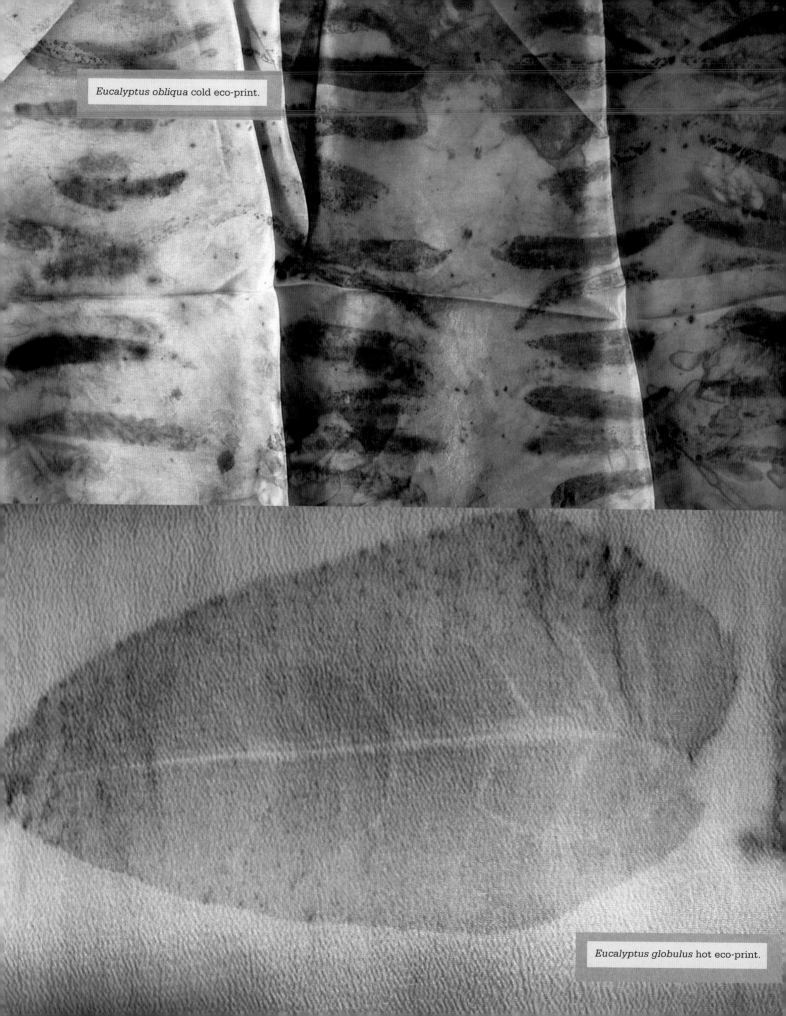

Eucalyptus obliqua cold eco-print.

Eucalyptus globulus hot eco-print.

Dried leaves of *Eucalyptus cinerea*.

Cloth and leaf material can be wrapped around a 44-gallon drum.

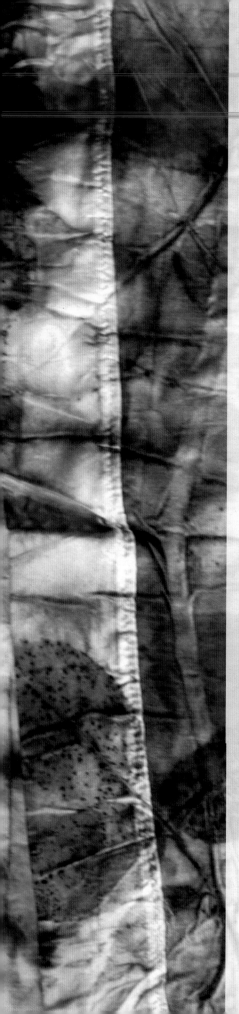

helps wash away a lot of colour before it has had time to properly bond to the substrate. This is especially so in the case of woollen fabrics and yarns. Wool fibres have tiny scales along them, just as fish do. When the wool is wetted the scales lift from their usual smoothed state, so in a wet, warm bath dye particles can actually bond deep within the surface of the fibre. Extracting wool from a bath and giving it a thorough wash will weaken the resulting colour as well as shocking the fibre (which may lead to felting).

dye application processes

It might be possible to spend a lifetime investigating the possible colours from only one plant species by experimenting with the wealth of possibilities afforded by the time of year the material is harvested, how it is dried and stored, how it is processed, how it is applied and what mordants are used at which stage of the process. In summary, dyes can be applied hot, warm or cold, in either capacious dye-baths or small containers such as snap-lock bags. They can be poured or sprayed on, injected into a bundle using a syringe, or the bundles left to stand partially immersed in solutions so that colour is sucked up by capillary action.

Some dye methods require months, whereas others such as the hot-bundled eco-print (see page 161) are more speedily achieved. The various methods summarised here give a range of possibilities that can be expanded exponentially by overdyeing sequentially with or without the introduction of resists. Pre-mordanting, co-mordanting (using pot as mordant) and post-mordanting offer further variables.

HOT EXTRACTION – HOT PROCESSING

Simmer and steep

In general, making a dye from plants is quite simple. Chop leaves and twigs or grind the seeds and bark so that as much surface area as possible is presented to the liquid (in most cases, water) that will make up the brew. Place the plant material in the pot of your choice, cover with water or other liquid (see 'Mordants', pages 87–101) and place a lid on the pot. If the material is dry, allow it to soak overnight before applying any heat. (The soaking liquid, whether water or a mordant, becomes the dye-bath.)

The next step is to apply heat. Gentle simmering or, better still, steeping the mixture overnight is by far the best approach. Time is of the essence here as some plants will release colour quite quickly, while others seemingly take forever. When the brew has attained a colour that pleases you, strain off the liquid. This is best done using a colander lined with a moistened piece of muslin. (There is nothing more tedious than picking tiny pieces of plant material out of a piece of fine felt when one has too hurriedly strained a dye sample!) Make sure the vessel receiving the liquid is constructed of either the same metal as the extraction pot or from a non-reactive substance such as glass, ceramic or stainless steel, otherwise you will find yourself inadvertently adding a mordant.

Return the liquid to the dye-pot, making sure there are no little bits left in the bottom of the pot. Immerse the textile in the solution and then steep for as long as possible. Ideally the liquor should be steaming slightly, but the surface of the liquid should not be moving. When the desired shade has been attained, the pot is removed from the heat and the whole allowed to cool (preferably overnight) before the sample is removed. Where the pot is acting as the mordant, the whole should be left undisturbed for several days so that the full benefit can be enjoyed.

After the pot has cooled, remove the sample, gently squeeze the excess liquid back into the pot and allow the sample to dry in the shade. This will help to lock in the colour. Only then should one consider rinsing. Many traditional recipes suggest putting the work away in a darkened storage space for a while (sometimes years), as some colours become more intense with time. This is 'slow dyeing' indeed!

Note that when dyeing wool tops for felting, there is no need for rinsing as the felting process ultimately gives the fibre a very thorough scouring.

Multiple extractions

Traditionally in most European cultures, plant dyes have been extracted by boiling the plant material in a pot with water, much as though one were making a soup. Most recipes suggest boiling the plant material for an hour or so and straining off the liquid for use. While this is of course effective in making a coloured solution for use, often much of the full colour potential is wasted and discarded without further thought.

Eastern traditions, however, have for centuries made use of multiple extraction processes, whereby the plant material is chopped into small pieces and firmly packed into a pot (choose one with a well-fitting lid). Water is added to a depth of about one-third of the height of the pot, the lid affixed and the pot heated to boiling point for about 20 minutes. The close-fitting lid is vital to retain steam which, being hotter than boiling water, is of great value in the extraction process.

This method can be used to achieve a range of shades from the one batch of plant material or simply to extract the most possible colour. The material is chopped into small pieces, packed into a large pot and water added. The water does not need to cover all of the material but it does

dilution of dye-baths

The usual assumption is that the more water is added to the dye-bath, the more it will be diluted. Whilst this is technically correct in terms of the quantity of dye in relation to the volume of water, it does not mean that increased quantities of fibres can be added and the same colour depth achieved. The depth of colour of piece of dyed cloth of a given size will be determined not by the quantity of water in the dye vessel but by the amount of dye available in the solution. Thus a measure of dye, whether supported by one or one hundred measures of water, will ultimately have the same effect on our set piece of cloth (it may just take longer for the dye to find the cloth in the bigger bath).

TESTING FOR ACIDS AND ALKALIS

The reactive colorant in litmus paper was traditionally derived from the lichen *Rocella tinctoria*. To do this, the lichens were coarsely ground with certain varieties of ash, and soaked for weeks in wooden vessels in a mixture of urine, lime and potash or soda. The mixture was stirred regularly. Eventually the mass became red and then blue. It was reputed to have a scent similar to that of violets and indigo. Neutral paper was dipped in blue colour to make the tester for acids, whereas some of the blue was apparently mixed with a little sulphuric acid to turn it red before application as a tester for alkalis.

Given the modern testing kits available from chemists, it is not recommended to plunder *Rocella tinctoria* stocks for such purposes. On the other hand, a cheap and simple test kit can be made using the somewhat fugacious colour available from red cabbage (*Brassica oleracea*). Use the darker leaves from the outside of the plant. Chop them finely (or shred them) and pack them firmly into a small glass jar. Cover with methylated spirits and leave in a well-ventilated place to stand until the liquid is a deep purplish-red colour.

Soak the ends of cheap cotton tips in the liquid; allow to dry, then store in an airtight container until needed. Whilst the devices cannot be precisely calibrated, dipping the ends into the liquid to be tested will at least give an indication of whether it is acidic or alkaline: acids will turn the dipper red; alkalis will turn it blue.

Distilled water can be used instead of methylated spirits, but the colour will not be as intense and it does require heating (in a stainless-steel vessel) to extract the colour from the shredded cabbage.

mixing colours and over-dyeing

Each colour in plant dyeing has its own particular chemistry depending on the plant from which it was sourced and the mordant that may have been used. This means that traditional colour theory will not necessarily apply when trying to create colour blends or when over-dyeing. Blue and yellow will not always lead to green, particularly if the blue is a slightly alkaline ice-flower dye being applied over a yellow from soursobs (*Oxalis pes-caprae*). Soursob flowers respond to alkalinity by turning a deep orange, so that the dyer will find in this instance yellow plus blue equals surprising toasty tones!

need to be deep enough that the pot won't boil dry. At least a hand width of water is a good depth to aim for. Place a lid on the pot to retain the steam and simmer gently. After 20 minutes, strain the liquid from the vegetable matter and reserve. A fresh quantity of water is then admitted to the pot and the process repeated at least three times. If there is still colour being produced, repeat until the extract becomes too weak to be useful. The extracts can be kept separate or combined to make a larger volume of dye. Keeping them as individual solutions can offer a range of different shades of the same colour and (somewhat surprisingly) with some plants the first and last extract can actually be different colours. Dye plants rich in colour will yield at least three extracts — some traditional Japanese dye plants yield no fewer than seven useful extracts.

While shades can also be produced by either successive introductions of fibre into the dye-bath or successive extractions of fibre from the dye-bath, the multiple extraction method does in general seem to yield the brightest colours. Note however that this method is not advisable for the eucalypts, as they release a substance called kino after excessive boiling, resulting in dark browns as well as a slightly crusty 'handle' being achieved.

Single extractions by boiling

As noted previously, the eucalypts require boiling to make colour available as a dye. Other materials that could benefit from high temperatures include barks, sticks and tough fruits such as acorns, especially when the latter are being processed to be utilised as a mordant. It is helpful to pre-soak all such tough materials to soften the fibres somewhat and reduce boiling time.

Concentrated tinctures

Very concentrated dye-baths can be made by compressing the plant materials into a container, really packing the stuff in, and then adding just

Dark-leaved *Prunus blireiana* are particularly rewarding under multiple extraction.

enough rain water to cover. Let this soak at least overnight, preferably 24 hours. It helps if the dye material has been chopped or ground as small as possible. Then set the pot on very low heat or at the back of the Aga if you have one. A crock pot is ideal for this, or else if you wish to keep the pot warm overnight without leaving the stove on, pack it into a box surrounded by towels or pieces of felt for insulation. Such extended heating is perfect and makes for a highly concentrated dye solution. After pouring off the first extract, continue as for the multiple extraction method (see page 111) so as not to waste any potential colour.

A true tincture is made by soaking or steeping plant material in alcohol, and was traditionally used to make medicinal remedies. It is certainly another very interesting option for processing plant dyes and a good use for those ghastly bottles of wine which invariably find their way into the house during large parties. Wine that is 'over the hill' can also successfully be used to make tinctures. Simply place the macerated plant material in a ceramic or dark glass container, pour the wine on top and seal. Leave for a month or so, strain and trial the solution! Further experiments may be made by using other liquids as the base for 'tinctures'. The section on alternative mordants (see pages 91–101) outlines a few possibilities, including sea water, urine (with or without the addition of scrap metals), vinegar and so on. Some of these potions may become a trifle malodorous, so it is wise to store them

assorted dye applications

Hot extraction — hot processing	Extraction by simmering — application in hot liquid over heat source
Hot extraction — cold processing	Solar dyeing — plant material plus fibre combined in dye vessel (lidded or open) and left in sunny position. May take months; if open container, will need topping up
Hot extraction — cold processing	Snap-lock bag as dye vessel. Fibre and dye extract are placed together in snap-lock bag, with or without added found metals etc Material can be folded and clamped using *shibori-zome* techniques (see page 183) with or without added metals
Cold extraction — cold processing	Compost dyeing — fibre bundled with dye material and buried in compost heap (be aware that wool does not respond well to such 'archaeological' conditions) Ice-flower dyeing (see page 138) Cold-bundling (see page 154) Direct application through *hapa-zome* beating technique (see page 165)
Cold extraction — hot processing	Steaming in bundles — cloth is bundled or rolled around plant material, steamed and then left as long as patience will allow before unwrapping Dye is extracted from dried plant material by long soaking in cold water before applying through steeping Dye extraction by fermentation with adjunct chemicals before hot processing (i.e. orchil lichen processing)

leafing well alone

Don't discard the 'spent' leaf material immediately; it can be used in cold-bundling, or layered on cloth in compost dyeing. The latter is best done during a moist time of year as dry leaves will not make much of an impression on cloth.

Linen, ramie, hemp and cotton textiles can all survive a couple of months buried in the compost heap. Soak them in the mordant solution of your choice before rolling or layering them in the heap. Cover well, keep moist and exhume when you're ready.

Cloth and plant material bundled around scrap metal and left to 'sit'.

summarising extraction and processing methods

dye extraction methods

Hot extraction in water

Drying materials before extraction

Fermenting materials in water

Hot extraction using simultaneous
    pot-as-mordant

Cold extraction in water

Freezing materials before extraction

Fermenting materials in other liquids

Fermenting material using pot-as-mordant

The range of colour outcomes will be determined by the sequence and combinations of the methods noted above.

Hot-bundled eco-prints using *Rosa* species.

nomadic dyeing

When travelling I like to use a small metal teapot for my extractions. It has a built-in strainer and is sturdily constructed of copper, so the metal also acts as a co-mordant. I then combine found metals and scraps from the street with found cloth fragments, bundle them together in snap-lock bags and pour on the slightly cooled solutions. The bags are allowed to sit somewhere warm, such as on a windowsill, or in the shower alcove during my ablutions, until the next stage of the journey. Depending on how the colour is working the samples are extracted and allowed to dry, or the remaining liquid is simply poured away so no runny disasters happen in my suitcase.

It's a delightful way of collecting travel souvenirs, literally soaked in the essence of the place one has been visiting!

away from usual family thoroughfares. Keeping notes is important, in case you have a truly gorgeous result that you wish to replicate later.

PLANTS FOR MULTIPLE EXTRACTION PROCESSES

Try plants such as the purple-leaved ornamental plum trees (various *Prunus* species), goldenrod (*Solidago canadensis*, a wild plant of North America which has become a weed in many countries), the skins of brown and red onions, elderberries (*Sambucus nigra*) and barberries (*Berberis darwinii*).

Eucalyptus and acacia barks can be most rewarding, as can the heps of *Rosa canina* and *Rosa eglanteria*. *Hypericum perforatum* (St John's wort) and *Hypericum tetrapterum* (St Peter's wort) both contain a number of different colours, including reds, yellows and greens. Dipping a protein fibre (wool or silk) in the first extract will withdraw the dark red dye component, leaving a remnant yellow. The second extract, however, is often a quite different colour from the first.

some curiosities to be derived from sequential extractions

ST JOHN'S WORT

Hypericum perforatum (St John's wort) is a noxious weed in Australia, causing photosensitivity and ultimately death in stock if ingested. Despite this, it is consumed by people self-medicating in the treatment of depression. Whether or not that is a good thing is a matter for debate. I find it a most intriguing dye plant. When the plant material is simmered in water a reddish liquid is produced. Immersion of both protein and cellulose fibres together in the same dye-bath generally produces a deep burgundy on the protein fibre and a yellow on the cellulose. Add a little alum, however, and the liquid turns a remarkable green, dyeing green on both fibre types. Clearly there is magic afoot.

Sequential immersion is also amusing. Gather the yellow flowers on a hot day in mid-summer when they are at the peak of flowering. Prepare the brew of flowers with water in a stainless-steel vessel using the multiple extraction method. Introduce yarn or cloth that has been pre-mordanted with alum. It is important that the alum has been allowed to bond well with the fibre, has enjoyed a curing period and has subsequently been thoroughly rinsed so that as few alum molecules as possible escape into the liquid. In a very short space of time the yarn will be bright green. Remove it immediately and set aside. Next, immerse some un-mordanted yarn and steep it in the brew. After some time it will become a deep maroon shade. Remove and set aside.

Take another skein of un-mordanted yarn, place it in the dye vessel, steep for a short while and then leave it to soak in the gradually cooling solution overnight. In the morning it should be a darkish brown. Remove that one as well and immerse the final skein, pre-mordanted with alum. Slowly raise the temperature to a simmer and then steep for an hour or two. This final skein should be yellow in colour.

SAFFLOWER

The safflower (*Carthamus tinctorius*) contains two different yellow dyes as well as a red dye. The flowers are placed in a net bag and the first yellow colour rinsed away under running water, and the red then coaxed out of the flowers by soaking them in a slightly alkaline solution. Too much alkali will spoil the dye. The flowers are allowed to stand in the alkaline solution for about six hours.

Next, take some well-scoured cool damp cotton and work it in the dye-bath for a little while. Take it out and put it to one side, then adjust the dye-bath again by adding a quantity of acid such as vinegar or lemon juice. Stir well and return the cloth to the dye. After a time of immersion (preferably overnight) it should come out a rich deep pink.

Dyeing silk pink using this plant is rather more complicated, as the dye remaining after the first yellow extract, although visually bright red, still contains yet another yellow component that will bond only with silk; if the silk is immersed in the solution as it stands, it will take on coral or orange shades. The red dye must be withdrawn from the solution by absorption in cotton (leaving the other yellow behind for separate application to silk if required), then released from the cotton by a further extended soaking in an alkaline solution.

This solution is then re-acidified, the silk immersed and allowed to soak overnight. The silk will be bright pink. On the other hand, dyeing a skein of silk/cotton embroidery thread in the red residue after the first flower-petal wash will result in an exquisite red and orange filament.

EUCALYPTUS

Oddly enough, most eucalyptus baths will also yield a range of shades with successive immersions. In the case of *Eucalyptus cinerea*, the delightful silver-leafed variety so popular with florists the world over, the first steeping produces a deep iron-oxide-coloured red. Subsequent immersions become steadily browner and less bright red in tone.

out with the bath water

The traditional recipe for safflower dye described here seems frightfully wasteful. Why wash all that yellow dye down the drain? It would make rather more sense to place the flowers in a small cloth bag and allow this to soak in water for at least an hour. Then, wearing rubber gloves, squeeze the bag in the liquid until no more yellow-coloured liquid comes out. Reserve this as a dye in its own right.

Eucalyptus cinerea showing juvenile leaves; *Allium cepa* flower head in foreground.

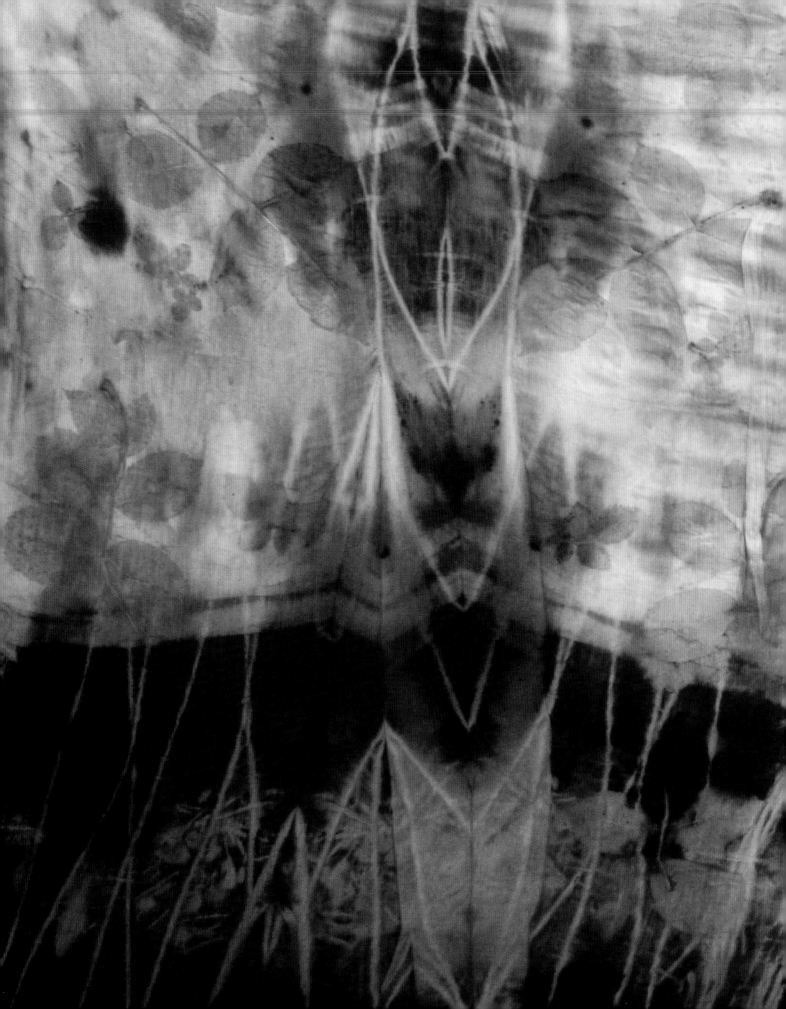

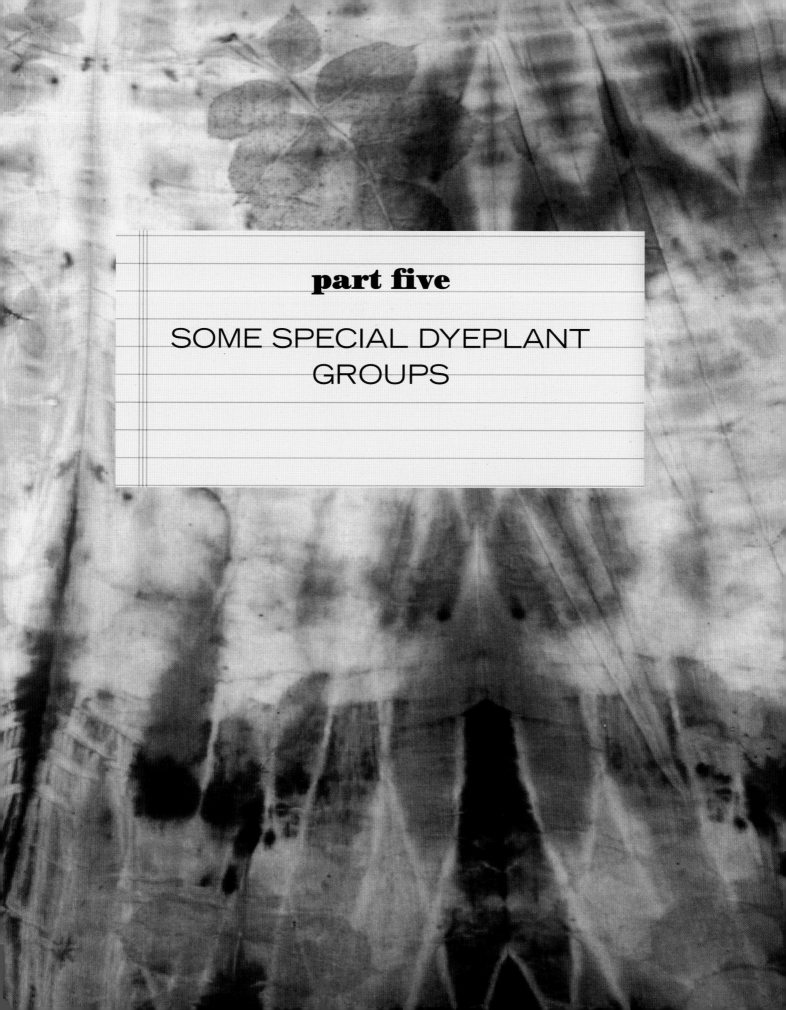

part five

SOME SPECIAL DYEPLANT
GROUPS

EUCALYPTUS DYES

The eucalypts are an evergreen hardwood genus endemic to the Australasian region and embracing an estimated 1,200 species and sub-species that have been identified. Eucalypts are represented across the Australian continent in all but the harshest of the arid interior regions, although they can be found in desert areas marking the positions of soaks and watercourses. Their natural range extends to 9° N (Philippines) and as far south as 44° in Tasmania, with the greatest variety of species concentrated in the temperate zones.

Eucalypts have successfully colonised many other parts of the world, including southern Europe, Asia, South America and west-coast U.S.A., and are still being established in large plantations as timber, a source of fibre for pulp, and as carbon sinks. This hardy genus enjoys the extremes of being regarded as a useful pioneer plant when rehabilitating severely degraded land areas, and conversely also cursed as a vigorous invader.

The eucalypts are distinguished by the rich and spicy scent of their leaves. Australians travelling abroad find their noses twitching happily when encountering the familiar scent far from home. Voyagers in the days of sailing ships, when the air was unpolluted by coal or oil exhausts, would report the distinctive aroma filling their nostrils well before land was sighted. The eucalypt seems to inspire passionate collectors, both real and imaginary. Author Murray Bail wrote a modern fairytale, *Eucalyptus*, in which a 'princess' can only be won by the man who can identify each eucalyptus species in a fictional arboretum in the far west of New South Wales. Thirty or forty years ago, the late John Giles of South Australia planted a living collection of river red gums, grown from seed sourced from five hundred different watercourses across the nation, near Lake Alexandrina in South Australia. More recently, in the late 1990s, noted eucalyptologist Deane Nicholle established his expansive eucalypt collection at Currency Creek, also in South Australia. The latter is meticulously planned and mapped, with the provenance of each seed source noted using a GPS device and taxonomic samples stored at the

Inset: *Eucalyptus citriodora*. Background: Printed fabric from the author's fashion label 'prophet of bloom'.

Above: *Eucalyptus leucoxylon* rosea flowers can be used in a cool dye-bath.
Below: Eco-print from *Eriococcus* infested dried eucalyptus windfalls.

Adelaide Botanic Gardens and State Herbarium. Mr Nicholle kindly allowed me access to his collection for my research on the eco-print.

Dyes from the genus are substantive on protein fibres, meaning that colour can be fixed on wool, silk and other fibres of animal origin without the use of added chemical mordants. The dyes are colourfast and have excellent light-fastness. Dramatic colour shifts can be induced by pre-mordanting with other plant material, the addition of scrap metals to the dye-bath or the use of dye vessel as mordant. The genus shares an interesting feature with a number of other dyeplant families, including *Isatis*, *Indigofera* and *Polygonum*, in that the potential dye colours are not immediately apparent upon visual inspection of the plant, although unlike the other varieties mentioned it requires no special treatment other than the application of heat to conjure colour.

Eucalyptus cinerea (one of the varieties beloved of florists worldwide) for example, bears blue-grey leaves. Upon immersion in hot water, these almost immediately become emerald in colour; after 10 minutes' simmering, they turn khaki and begin to release visible colour into the solution. It should be noted, however, that the colour of the dye-bath prepared from fresh leaves (golden brown) does not necessarily indicate the colour of the dyed textile, which ranges from green (five minutes) through gold and orange (about 25 minutes) and eventually deep chestnut red (45 minutes). Leaves from eucalypts will give different colours depending on whether they are used fresh (picked green), used dried (picked and dried) or collected from the ground beneath the tree (here again there will be different results depending on the residual colour in the leaf). Leaves picked from different sides of the same tree can often give different results.

All parts of the eucalyptus will give colour in the dye-bath, but extracting colour from the heartwood is not really worth the effort, especially as the prerequisite is the destruction of the tree. Colour is obtainable from the leaves, bark, flowers and fruit. The latter can also be tied into cloth to make a contact print. One of the fascinating things about the eucalyptus is that each leaf (even when picked from the one tree) will contain a mixture of colours in slightly different proportions; no two leaves will have exactly the same ratio of components. This means that when a batch of leaves is processed in water in a large pot, the resultant dye-bath is actually a cocktail of colours. These colours seem to be affected by the prevailing weather (dry climates are often productive of more intense colours; on the other hand, rain in the days preceding harvest can induce radical shifts in colour from dark red to pale green) and by the geological growing conditions of the plant. *Eucalyptus globulus* may yield a khaki dye when processed in water, but eco-prints using leaves from the same batch will show orange,

Above: Adult leaves of *Eucalyptus cinerea*.

tan and lime-green coloured spots. The steamed eco-print will reveal what colours are present in the leaf being tested and will help the dyer make an educated guess about the likely dye outcome when a batch of leaves is processed in pure water.

Despite the abundance of this genus, it was not until the late 1800s that any formal experimentation began in terms of their dye potential. Even Baron Ferdinand von Mueller — noted eucalyptologist, discoverer of *Eucalyptus cinerea* (source of one of the brightest plant dyes) and founder of Melbourne's Royal Botanic Gardens — ignored the eucalypt when making dye samples for the 1866 Intercolonial Exhibition in Melbourne, choosing instead to make samples using species from the genus *Acacia*. The eucalypts hid their colour potential well. The Powerhouse Museum in Sydney has early eucalyptus dye samples from J. H. Maiden, who announced in 1887 that he had isolated a yellow colourant from the leaves of *Eucalyptus macrorhyncha*. His work was expanded by Henry Smith in 1896–97. Mr Smith believed that eucalyptus dyes would be of great economic benefit to the (then) colony of Australia, but even though he seems to have also experimented with the making of pigments for painting, nothing concrete seemed to come of his interest.

Eucalypts popped up occasionally in literature throughout the mid-1900s in such references as Country Women's Association pamphlets, where they were recommended as offering suitable dyes for the homespun woollen socks being sent to long-suffering soldiers on various war fronts. It was not until the 1970s that the late Jean Carman began to investigate dyes from this genus. Her ground-breaking research work and the resulting book *Dyemaking with Eucalypts* are still important today. Mrs Carman tested some 240 species using samples that were sent to her from all over Australia and even from Papua New Guinea. Despite using the standard mordants of the time and regardless of the fact that introducing a number of differently mordanted sample skeins to the dye-pot in succession, thus progressively polluting and diluting the solution, would have affected results, this book is important because it was the first serious look at the genus in terms of its dye value. Also interesting was that even though the samples came from different geographic locations, all of the dye-baths had one common factor — the water used to make up the mixture. Even though the significance of water quality is not discussed in the book, the fact that all of the samples have this common foundation is important.

During research for my MA thesis in the last years of the twentieth century, I tested a further 203 species using the eco-print, as well as working intensively with eight of the species already assessed by Mrs Carman. The colours from the genus included red, rust, tan, gold, ochre,

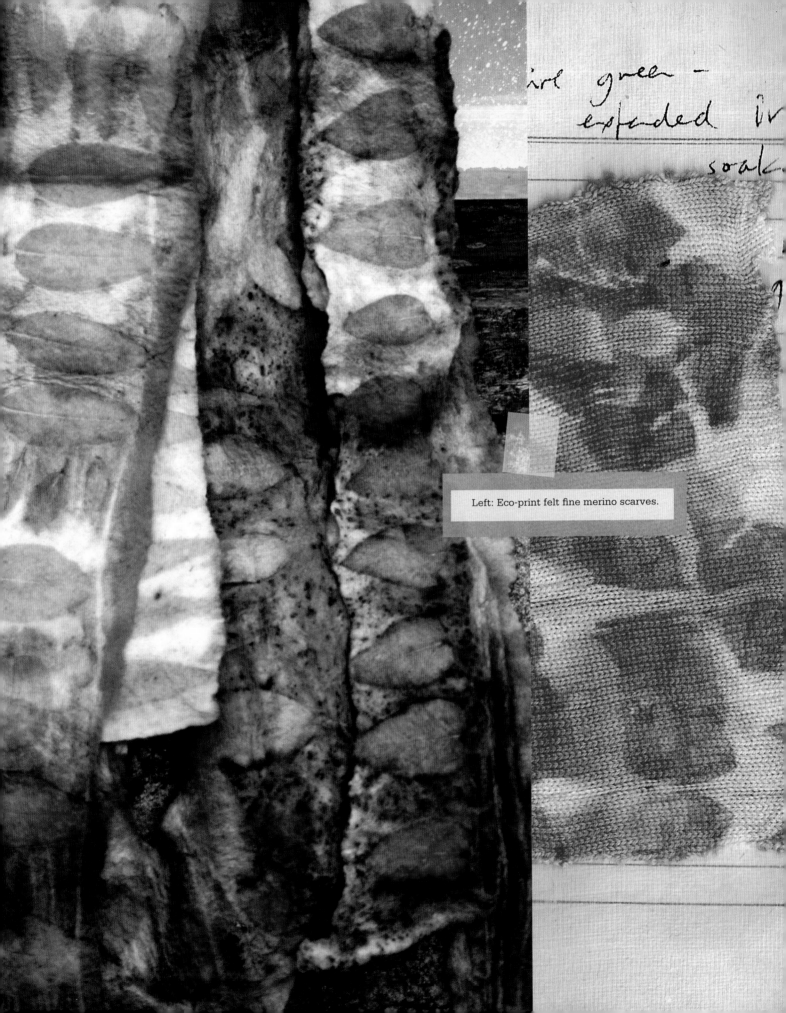

Left: Eco-print felt fine merino scarves.

lemon, green, chocolate, fawn, pink, apricot and beige without any adjunct mordants. Simple addition of pot-as-mordant extended this range to embrace purples, greys and black. Further post-mordanting using the alternative brews and solutions detailed under 'Mordants' (pages 87–105) provided even more interesting colour shifts and enhancements.

There is an insufficiently exploited opportunity for eucalyptus dyes to play a vital role in the Australian textile industry today. Ever-increasing plantations for paper and agro-forestry will offer an abundance of leaf material as a by-product when the timber is eventually harvested. Given the affinity of these dyes for wool, it seems incredibly wasteful not to apply them. The exhausted leaves can be returned to plantations as mulch, the water continually recycled in the dye process and the heating process provided by solar energy. Presently wool is shipped overseas for scouring, spinning and dyeing before returning in the form of expensive clothing. A local textile industry founded in ecologically sustainable practice and without huge transport expenses would seem to be a good thing.

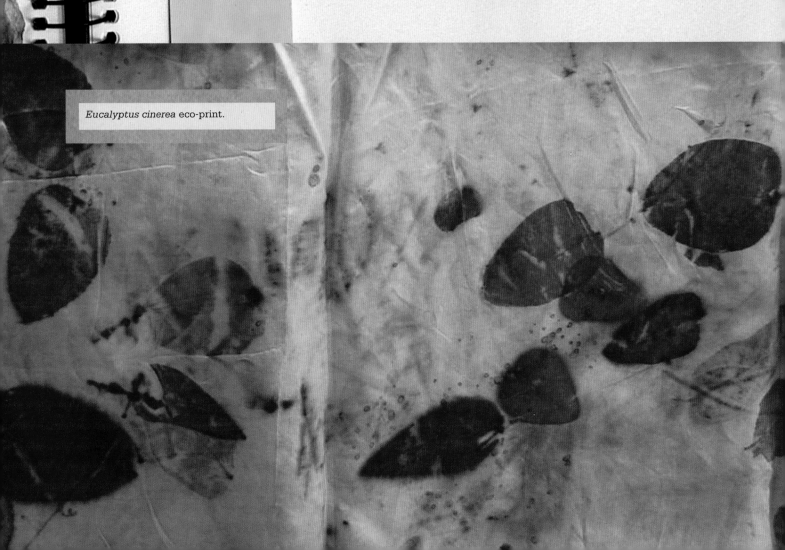

Eucalyptus cinerea eco-print.

mistletoe magic

Some plants benefit from being baked dry in the full sun. The leaves of *Amyema miraculosa*, the mistletoe that makes its home on some species of eucalyptus, will turn a deep red colour if allowed to roast in the sun for a couple of months. This in turn leads to a deep red-coloured dye rather than the greenish gold that would result if the material were used fresh. Curiously, *Amyema miraculosa* will dye both cotton and wool, whereas eucalyptus dyes more readily bond with protein fibres.

Above: *Amyema miraculosa* (mistletoe) detail. Right: Mistletoe-infested eucalypts in the Mount Lofty Ranges, South Australia.

SIMPLE DYEING WITH EUCALYPTUS LEAVES

Take a quantity of eucalyptus leaves (fresh or dried) at least equivalent in weight to the textile you wish to dye. Immerse them in water in a stainless-steel, enamel or aluminium pot of an appropriate size (the pot does not need to be new; purchase a second-hand one from a charity shop and keep it only for dyeing).

The water quality is important for eucalyptus dyes; use rainwater for best results, otherwise neutral to slightly acid reticulated water. Alkaline water will muddy the dyes, while salts in the water will have various surprise effects depending on their constitution. You will soon see if your water is salty, as a murky precipitate will flocculate near the bottom of the dye bath.

STEP 1 Bring the water to the boil and simmer the leaves for at least 45 minutes, but a maximum of one hour. Remove the leaves (either using tongs or by straining the liquid off).

STEP 2 Immerse the textile or fibre to be dyed in the still-warm liquid. Heat the pot for 45 minutes, making sure that the liquid does not boil, or even simmer. The temperature should be such that steam is rising from the surface, but the surface itself is not moving. This is the optimum treatment to maintain fabric life.

STEP 3 Allow the fibre to cool in the dye-bath. The longer it is left, the more intense the colour. After cooling, spin the excess liquid out using the spin cycle on the washing machine, then dry in shade. It is not strictly necessary to rinse out eucalyptus dyes; they smell delightful and will not harm the body if worn next the skin (unlike synthetic dyes).

VARIATIONS Try using pots made from different metals; the colours will change depending on the metal used. For example, *Eucalyptus globulus* processed in a neutral water bath in a stainless-steel pot will generally (this may vary depending on growing location) give a khaki green on silk. However when processed in an iron pot, using slightly acidic water (that is, with a splash of vinegar), the result is frequently closer to purple. If left for a week in an iron pot, black will be achieved. A copper pot, on the other hand, will tend to enhance the golden tones in the dye.

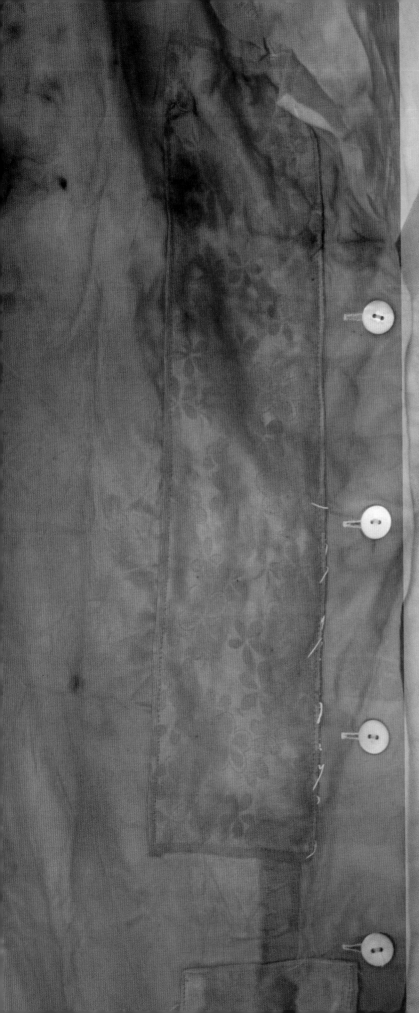

colouring cottons with eucalypts

Applying eucalyptus dyes to a cellulosic substrate (such as cotton, hemp, ramie, nettle, linen and banana) is more difficult. Protein fibres are neutral to slightly alkaline in nature, allowing eucalyptus dyes (slightly acidic when prepared in a neutral aqueous bath) to bond substantively. Cellulose fibres are generally neutral and require pre-treatment in order for dyes to be fixed. Traditional Japanese soy mordants — made by grinding dried soybeans and soaking them in water — work well as precursors to dyeing with eucalypts. After soaking the ground beans, the liquid is strained off. The fibre to be dyed is then soaked in the liquid, squeezed and hung to dry. Bear in mind that the quality of the water (and anything dissolved in it) that is used as carrier for the soy will influence the later colour outcome. Fabric mordanted with soy can be stored for up to a year before being dyed, and in some traditional practices all of the cloth required for a year's dyeing is pre-mordanted annually in one large batch. Commercially prepared brands of soymilk can be just as useful, if somewhat more expensive, obviating the need for grinding equipment, as can the run-off from the production of tofu (useful for smaller applications). The longer the mordanted fabric is allowed to cure, the better the bonding of the dye.

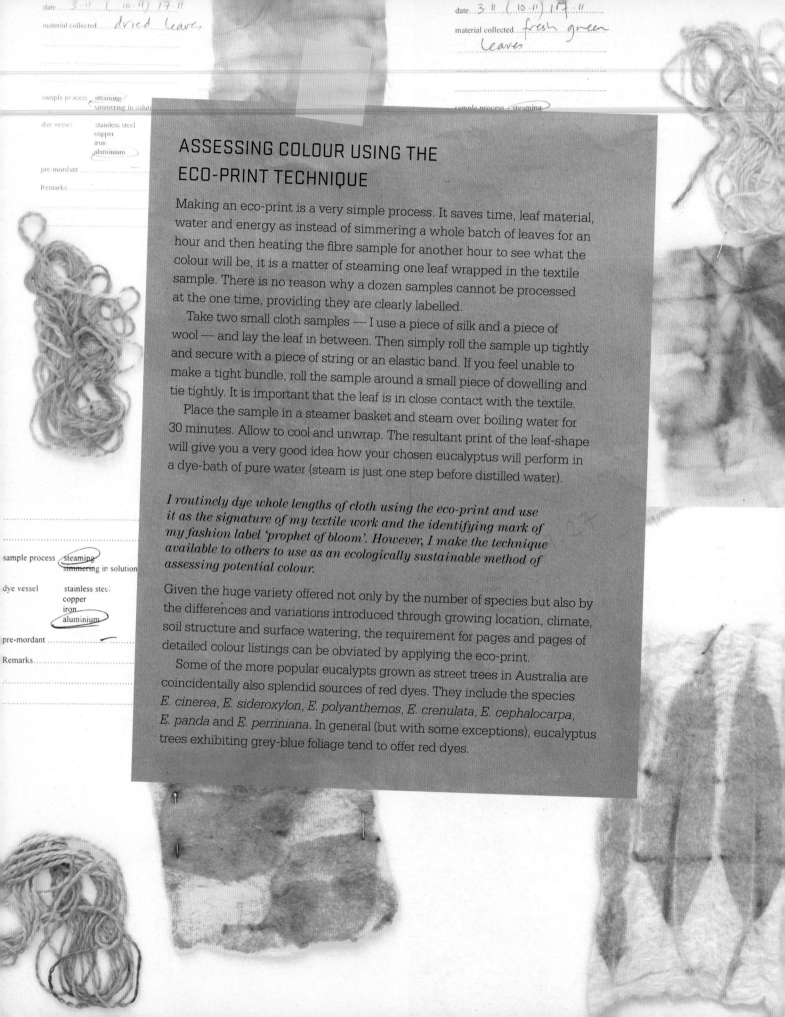

date ...3..11...(..10..11)..17..11

material collected ...*dried leaves*

sample process ...steaming
~~simmering in soluti~~

dye vessel ...stainless steel
copper
iron
aluminium

pre-mordant ....

Remarks............

date ...3..11...(..10..11)..17..11

material collected ...*fresh green leaves*

sample process ...steaming

sample process ...steaming
simmering in solution

dye vessel ...stainless steel
copper
iron
aluminium

pre-mordant ....

Remarks............

ASSESSING COLOUR USING THE ECO-PRINT TECHNIQUE

Making an eco-print is a very simple process. It saves time, leaf material, water and energy as instead of simmering a whole batch of leaves for an hour and then heating the fibre sample for another hour to see what the colour will be, it is a matter of steaming one leaf wrapped in the textile sample. There is no reason why a dozen samples cannot be processed at the one time, providing they are clearly labelled.

Take two small cloth samples — I use a piece of silk and a piece of wool — and lay the leaf in between. Then simply roll the sample up tightly and secure with a piece of string or an elastic band. If you feel unable to make a tight bundle, roll the sample around a small piece of dowelling and tie tightly. It is important that the leaf is in close contact with the textile.

Place the sample in a steamer basket and steam over boiling water for 30 minutes. Allow to cool and unwrap. The resultant print of the leaf-shape will give you a very good idea how your chosen eucalyptus will perform in a dye-bath of pure water (steam is just one step before distilled water).

I routinely dye whole lengths of cloth using the eco-print and use it as the signature of my textile work and the identifying mark of my fashion label 'prophet of bloom'. However, I make the technique available to others to use as an ecologically sustainable method of assessing potential colour.

Given the huge variety offered not only by the number of species but also by the differences and variations introduced through growing location, climate, soil structure and surface watering, the requirement for pages and pages of detailed colour listings can be obviated by applying the eco-print.

Some of the more popular eucalypts grown as street trees in Australia are coincidentally also splendid sources of red dyes. They include the species *E. cinerea, E. sideroxylon, E. polyanthemos, E. crenulata, E. cephalocarpa, E. panda* and *E. perriniana*. In general (but with some exceptions), eucalyptus trees exhibiting grey-blue foliage tend to offer red dyes.

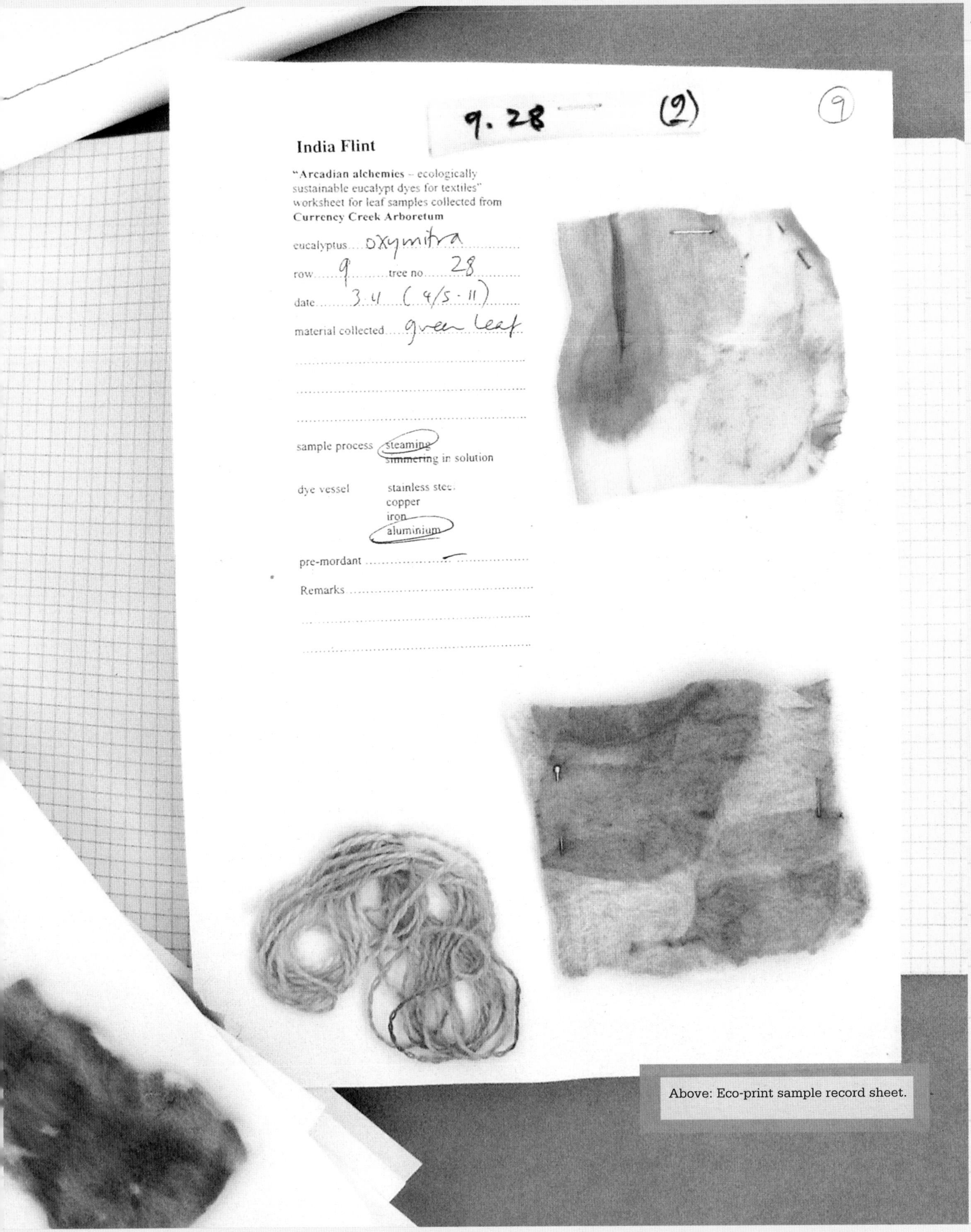

India Flint

"Arcadian alchemies – ecologically
sustainable eucalypt dyes for textiles"
worksheet for leaf samples collected from
Currency Creek Arboretum

eucalyptus...... Oxymitra

row...... 9 ...... tree no...... 28

date...... 3.4 (4/5 · 11)

material collected...... green leaf

....

....

....

sample process ~~steaming~~
~~simmering in solution~~

dye vessel   stainless steel
                copper
                iron
                aluminium

pre-mordant ....

Remarks ....

....

....

Above: Eco-print sample record sheet.

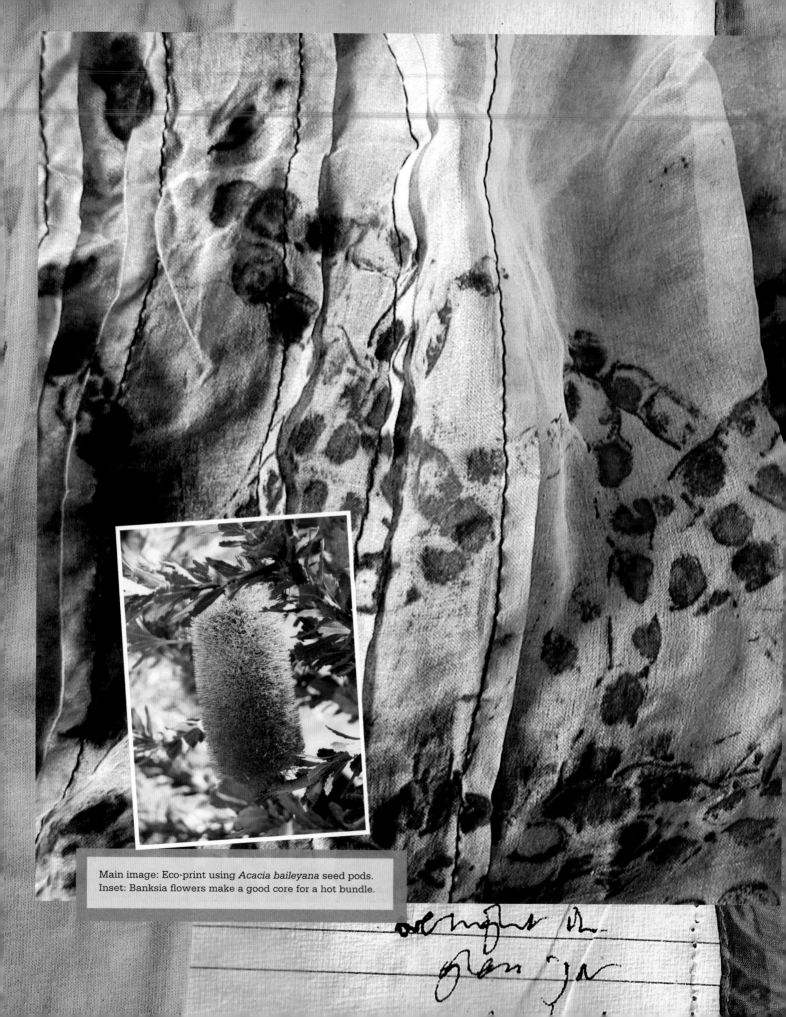

Main image: Eco-print using *Acacia baileyana* seed pods.
Inset: Banksia flowers make a good core for a hot bundle.

BEYOND THE EUCALYPTUS

Australia is rich in dye plants, most yet to be discovered, as is the case for so many other regions in the world. Much of what we know about plant dyes is situated within the context of European practice and closely related to European culinary traditions.

There is so much still to be learned, and meanwhile clear-felling of forests continues, as well as ongoing clearing of farmland as agricultural areas become either exhausted or encrusted with the dog-boxes of suburbia.

It has taken a long time for indigenous plants to be included in gardens in more than a token way. Many generations clung to the notion of the European or exotic garden as a tangible if largely subconscious link with their ancestry. Indigenous plants were considered florally less spectacular and generally had a reputation for being somewhat scruffy. This is rapidly changing as city dwellers find their water allocations dramatically cut.

Interesting research projects are afoot, including the development of eucalypts with enormous and long-lasting blooms for the cut-flower trade. Plant breeders have been enhancing species with decoratively coloured leaves, such as purple-leaved agonis and callistemons. The *Anigozanthos* genus (kangaroo paw) has also been the subject of improvement to produce larger and more colourful blooms on taller, sturdier stalks. The distinctive flower of this plant lends itself beautifully to both the *hapa-zome* (see page 165) and the hot-bundling (see page 161) techniques. When red blooms are beaten into cotton cloth that has previously been washed in any detergent containing washing soda, the prints turn a deep blue within minutes.

Kangaroo paws are interesting because they are a member of the family Haemodoraceae, which also embraces the group *Haemodorum*. This genus of about 20 species is referred to as the 'bloodroots' because of the red colouration of the roots. In contrast to most of the members of the genus, whose flowers are relatively unspectacular, scarlet bloodroot (*Haemodorum coccineum*) features colourful flowers which are quite showy. The flowers produce a bloodlike brownish-red dye and would be well worth cultivating.

HONEY AND BLUES

Indigo can be extracted from fresh leaves by soaking them in fermented urine. Collect about a bucket of urine, cover tightly with a lid and put in a warm place to ferment for six weeks. Then pound about 1 kg (2 lb 2 oz) of fresh indigo leaves, soak them in water until the water turns green (a matter of hours), strain off the liquor and add it to the urine container, stirring well with a stick. Leave the liquid for 3–4 days. Immerse clean, wet cotton or silk fabric and press gently using gloved hands. Avoid introducing oxygen to the brew. Let the fabric rest in the pot for about an hour before lifting it out and carefully squeezing out the excess. Repeat the dipping to deepen the blue. Warm weather is essential to the success of this process.

When you take the cotton out of the pot it will smell absolutely foul and must be washed and rinsed several times until the smell lessens. There was a good reason that production of woad (another indigo dye) was banned from being conducted within 5 miles of any of Queen Elizabeth I's residences or favourite travel routes. Add orange flower water to the final rinse to help sweeten the aroma.

The last edition of the *Encyclopaedia Britannica* to be published in Edinburgh mentions that Italian dyers used lime to dissolve the refined indigo together with honey as the fermentation agent. It also offered the following recipe, which may need to be scaled down for non-industrial applications.

A vat 6 feet in diameter and 7 feet deep is filled with water warmed to 130°F; then 4½ lb (four and a half pounds) of ground indigo, 34 lb (thirty-four pounds) crystals of soda (or instead 16 [sixteen] lb soda ash) and 67 (sixty-seven) lb of bran, and twelve hours afterwards 2 [two] lb slacked lime, are added; in 24 hours the indigo should commence to be dissolved, and a test strip of stuff plunged in the liquid should be speedily dyed, but some hours longer and the gradual addition of 18 or 20 pounds more of lime are required to bring the liquor into its best condition. In this vat, as in the woad vat, the lime controls the fermentation of the bran, and has to be added with care. With each pound of indigo added to replace what has been removed from the vat during a day's dyeing ½ lb (one half pound) of molasses and ½ lb (one half pound) crystals of soda and 3 or 4 pounds lime must be used.

This vat lasts 4–5 months, after which the 'bottoms' are discarded, and the remaining liquor used to make up a new vat.

Encyclopaedia Britannica, 1877, ninth edition, Adam & Charles Black, Edinburgh, vol VII , p 577

In Japan, *Polygonum tinctorium* is harvested twice towards the end of summer and the stems and leaves laid to dry in the sun, before they are piled up to 30 cm thick in a purpose-built fermentation house. Here they are carefully watered and turned for about one hundred days to form a dark compound that must then be fermented in an alkaline solution (from wood ash and water) and 'fed' with starchy substances such as bran. Many repeat immersions (of the textile in the vat) are required to build up the beautiful dark blues traditionally associated with Japanese textiles.

Anigozanthos eco-print

Above, from left: Kangaroo paw eco-print; *Indigofera australis*; kangaroo paw plant.
Right: Bracken (*Pteridium esculentum*) ready for dyeing. Opposite, background: *Hotaru* (firefly) shibori indigo cloth by Nobuko Watanabe Clayton.

The common appellation 'bloodroot' indicates another dye potential. Resist harvesting the roots in the wild, though the thought may be tempting.

Australia also has an endemic *Indigofera* species, aptly named *Indigofera australis*. This somewhat spindly relation of *I. tinctoria* is reputed to grow in all states of the continent and to produce a delightful range of blues depending on the time of harvest and the maturity of the plant. This indigo is best processed using traditional indigo recipes, which can be sourced from the extensive reading list provided at the conclusion to this book.

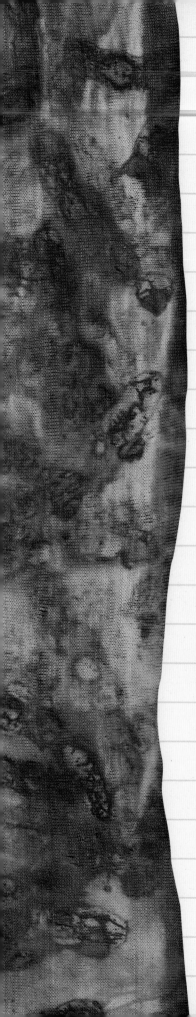

The eucalypts for which this island continent is renowned are afflicted with parasites, including mistletoes of the *Amyema* genus and insects of the *Eriococcus* family. The mistletoes render dyes ranging from greenish gold (fresh leaves processed hot in a copper pot) to deep red (from toasted leaves collected from the forest floor beneath the tree). Intriguingly, if a fibre dyed the greenish gold colour is repeatedly washed in detergent containing washing soda, it too will develop the deep red colour after a few years of repeated washing treatment. While eucalyptus dyes have a specific affinity for protein fibres, the toasted mistletoe leaves will dye any natural fibre. The *Eriococcus* insect must be carefully scraped from the leaves and branches of the host tree using a palette knife. Wear gloves to avoid Lady Macbeth syndrome. Add vinegar or lemon juice as an adjunct mordant and steep silk fabric with the insects for a red colour. They can also produce a rather decorative contact print.

The genus *Acacia*, also known as the wattle, is almost as prolific as the eucalypt, numbering over 800 species. Most of the bright yellow flowers can be used for dyeing. For best results on wool, add a tiny amount of alum as co-mordant, or pre-mordant with alum. For silks, the use of an aluminium vessel coupled with extended steeping should suffice. The bark of these trees and shrubs is rich in tannins and the toasted seed pods, which can be collected in high summer, give a lovely chocolatey red colour on both protein and cellulosic fibres.

Kennedia nigricans is a vigorous strangling climber with black flowers. Although these are small and tedious to harvest, they can be processed using the ice-flower technique (page 138) to make lovely purples on silk.

The bright red flowers of *Callistemon* species also make a nice cold dye. Pack them into a glass jar and pour warm (but not hot) water over them. Let stand overnight and for up to 48 hours before straining off the liquid and immersing silk in the resulting brew. When pulled apart, the individual stamens of the flowers can be beaten into cloth or rolled tightly into silk and steamed. Those of *Grevillea* species can be rewarding as well, when bashed or bundled.

Both the fruit and the leaves of the parasitical plant quandong, or wild peach (*Santalum acuminatum*), yield dyes. In certain mineral-rich well waters the leaves have apparently produced lime greens on silk. Its close cousin the aromatic sandalwood (*Santalum lanceolatum*) also has dye-rich leaves and responds well to extended steeping where the pot is used as the co-mordant. Aluminium encourages gold, copper a greenish brown and iron a darker greyish green depending of course on the quality of the water used. Both of these plants are protected in the wild in some states of Australia and should therefore be accessed only from cultivated sources.

Above, from left: *Callistemon* species growing near Springhead, South Australia; Hot-bundled sample using *Callistemon*; *Acacia baileyana* seed pods soaking in water.

Bracken fern (*Pteridium esculentum*) gives a lovely green when used in an aluminium pot or with an alum mordant. Pre-, co- and post-mordanting may result in different shades. Soak the fronds in water for a couple of days before steeping to extract the colour. Using iron vessels will deepen shades.

The root bark of *Morinda citrifolia*, sometimes known as the dyer's mulberry, was used by indigenous Australians to make a red dye for basketry fibres in the far north by grinding and pasting with and without the addition of ash. This plant is widespread across Southeast Asia and the Indian subcontinent as well as northern Australia.

Beloved of florists in the 1970s, the leaves and stems of the rich green aromatic bushy shrub *Thryptomene calycina* will give a warm orange gold when an alum adjunct is used.

From this brief summary, it can be seen that all of the colours of the rainbow could be made using indigenous sources. Interestingly, few of these dyes were used by indigenous Australians, possibly as their culinary traditions involved barbecuing and roasting rather than steaming and boiling; colour was more usually applied as a surface stain using ground mineral pastes. Clearly there is much work yet to be done in analysing the endemic species of this island continent.

shade shifting

While the eucalyptus eco-print gives an accurate picture of the dye colours contained within the leaves, the same cannot be said of eco-prints made with other flora. In the latter case the print will differ significantly from the brewed dye as well as being affected by laundering — fading and/or dramatic colour changing may occur.

ICE-FLOWER DYES

Many would-be dyers have applied the traditional boiling methods to brilliantly coloured flower petals and discovered that the colour in the petals dissipates with rising temperatures. The method described here was discovered as a happy accident due to the storage of flowers by freezing. It works to best advantage on silk.

I had realised some time ago that the only way of getting satisfactory colour from such plants as violas, delphiniums, iris, pelargoniums and petunias was to extract it by squeezing the flower petals in cold water and then adding small quantities of safe mordants (such as ash, alum or vinegar) depending on the desired outcome. Spectacular results in a range of blue shades led me to plant large numbers of lovely velvety black violas. Unable to process all of the abundant harvest, I stored the flowers in snap-lock food storage bags in the freezer. Needing blue dye in a hurry one day, I placed frozen flowers in a netting bag and immersed them in lukewarm water without waiting for them to thaw and discovered to my amazement that the temperature shock of immersion assisted in the rapid release of colour. Freezing plant material has the added benefit of breaking up the structure of the plant, as the moisture contained within the cells expands while becoming solid. All of this works nicely in the dyer's favour.

The addition of ash or alum (potassium aluminium sulphate) will tend to promote blues, whereas the addition of vinegar will enhance reds. The addition of washing soda (sodium carbonate) can sometimes result in a greenish blue. Remember, though, that the water used to make up the dye-bath will also directly affect the colour outcome, which is dependent not only on the pH but also on any dissolved impurities carried in the liquid.

process

Pick the flowers and freeze them at least overnight (but preferably longer) in a jar, snap-lock bag, recycled yoghurt pot or other freezer-proof container. It is important the container is airtight so that the material does

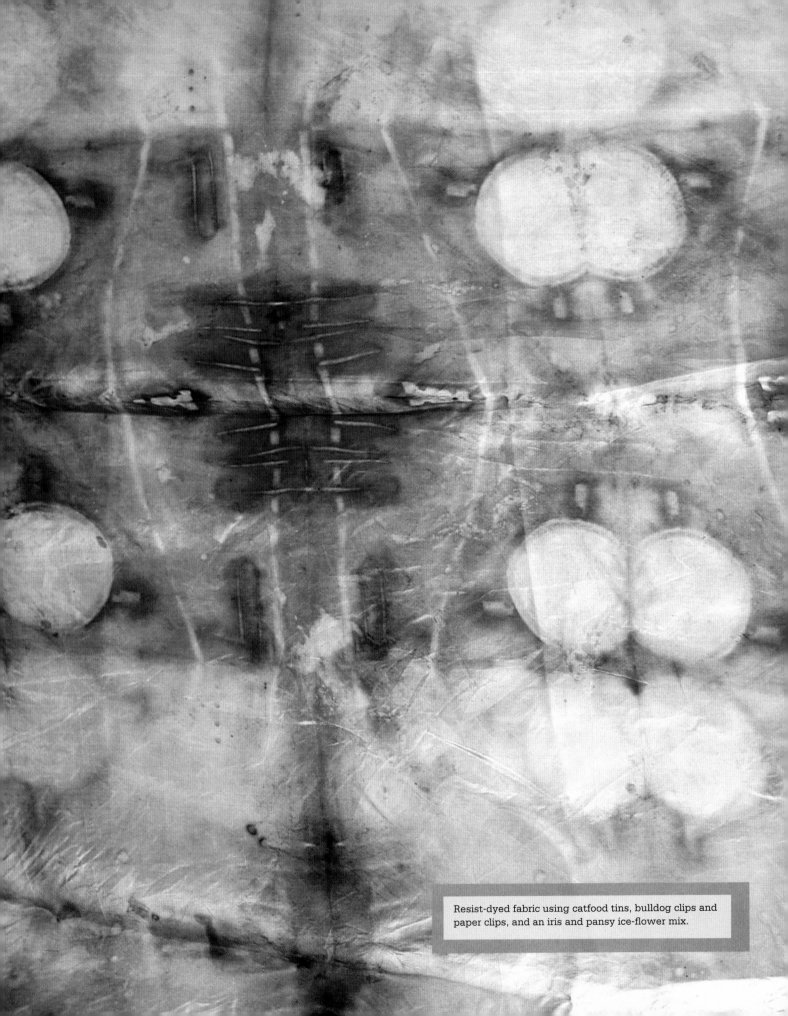

Resist-dyed fabric using catfood tins, bulldog clips and paper clips, and an iris and pansy ice-flower mix.

Below: Soursob (*Oxalis pes-caprae*) flowers.
Opposite: Rose-leaf on silk sample.

Above: Top made from redeployed cotton corduroy overdyed with ice-flowers. Right: Ice-flowers prepared for freezing.

Above, from left: Petunia flowers; Silk velvet and silkwool voile that have been pre-dyed in *Solidago canadensis* being overdyed using a pansy ice-flower brew; Delphinium flowers.

not become desiccated if stored for any length of time. Place frozen flowers in a netting bag (an old sock or stocking will do nicely), tie up the opening with an elastic band or a piece of string and immerse the bag in a large bowl or small bucket of lukewarm water (the size depends of course on the length of fabric you want to dye). As a rule, about 2 cups of frozen violas (pansies) will dye at least 5 metres (5½ yards) of light silk fabric.

Wearing gloves (to avoid blue hands), squeeze the bundle in the water until the liquid is well coloured. Add the desired mordant (a half teaspoon of alum or ash, or half a cup of vinegar to 4 or 5 litres/1–1¼ gallons of water), stir well to dissolve thoroughly and then immerse the cloth, leaving it to soak for 24 to 48 hours (turning occasionally to distribute the dye). If ash is used, it is best to tie it into a small cloth bundle, holding it in the solution and squeezing it to release alkalinity, otherwise it tends to float about on the surface.

variations

Make up a strong dye solution (using less water) and pour the mixture over the cloth in a bowl — whether the cloth is dry or has been pre-wetted will affect the dye take-up and the patterns formed.

Fold the cloth using shibori techniques (see page 183), clamp using either found metals or non-reactive objects and then soak in the dye according to instructions.

Experiment by very gradually raising the temperature of the dye-bath after it has been made up and the cloth soaked. You will find that an iris bath will change colour from purple to blue with added alum mordant, then from blue to teal green when heated slightly. Apply too much heat, however, and the dye-bath eventually yields only grey.

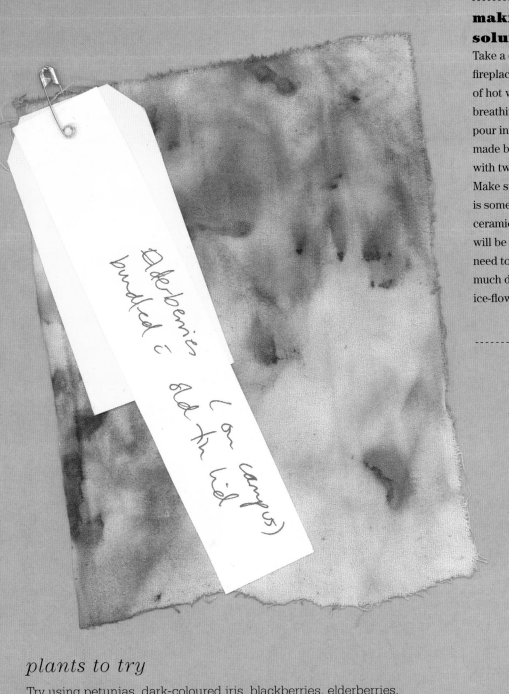

Take a cupful of ash from the fireplace and mix it with a few cups of hot water, being careful to avoid breathing in the dust. Stir well and pour into a double-cloth strainer made by lining a plastic colander with two thicknesses of old sheeting. Make sure the receiving vessel is something inert, such as glass, ceramic or enamel. This solution will be quite alkaline and you will need to experiment to see just how much dilution is required for your ice-flower potion.

plants to try

Try using petunias, dark-coloured iris, blackberries, elderberries, raspberries, cherries, violas (purple, blue and red), violets, delphiniums (the darker the better), petunias (purple and blue), pelargoniums (dark red and purple), *Berberis darwinii* berries (these can also be processed hot) and morning glory flowers. Bear in mind that not all ice-flower dyes will necessarily be substantive and that some may later change colour due to the chemical composition of the detergents applied during the laundering process. On the other hand, it is a cheap, harmless and pleasantly scented method of dyeing cloth.

Left: Recycled cotton knit fabric with clover dye.
Right: Rose petals ready for use in dyeing.

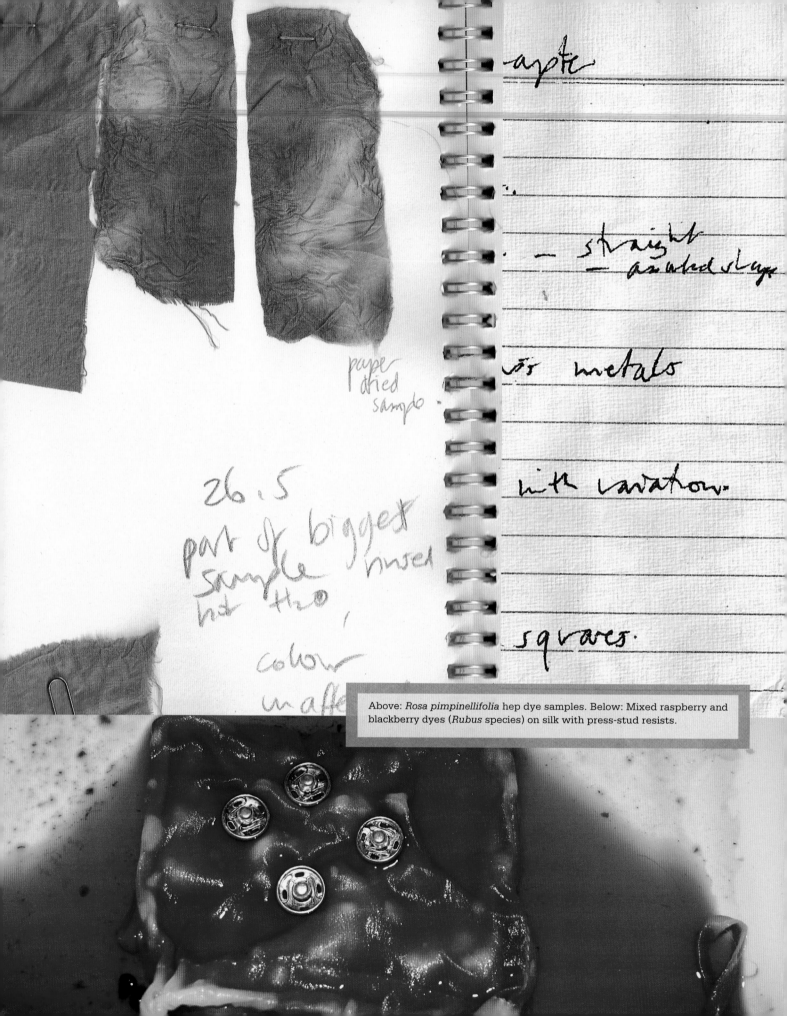

apte

— straight
— assorted shapes

or metals

with variation.

squares.

paper
dried
sample

26.5
part of biggest
sample used
hot H2O,
colour
in afte

Above: *Rosa pimpinellifolia* hep dye samples. Below: Mixed raspberry and
blackberry dyes (*Rubus* species) on silk with press-stud resists.

FRUITS AND BERRIES

Fruits and berries are often brightly coloured when fresh, and yet when boiled tend to lose their brightness and yield reddish brown shades on cloth. The secret to bright colour is to process them cold, beginning with storage in the freezer. The liquids expand during freezing, thus helping to pulp the fruit so that when the mass is thawed it is soft and more easily yields its colour.

Add alkaline substances, such as alum or ash, to encourage blues and purples, or acids, such as vinegar or lemon juice, to produce rich reds.

The fabric is then cold-processed in a bowl or jar for up to three days, before gentle rinsing and drying. The colours achieved might not be substantive, but they will often last up to two years. It's an inexpensive and non-toxic method of colouring cloth; simply repeat it over the life of the object as required.

Experiment by pre-mordanting the fabric in various concoctions until you discover what works best for you, in your region. Try making a concentrated solution of berry juices and painting them onto the pre-mordanted fabric. Consider using paste or mud resists to create interesting patterns.

Cold-processed colours from fruits and berries tend to have most affinity for silk. Cellulose fibres such as cotton, linen, ramie and hemp will absorb them too, but usually not as brightly. To apply cold colours to wool, the woollen fibres need to be soaked in water for at least 24 hours before immersion in the dye. It is a curiosity of wool that is naturally hydrophobic (that is, it repels water) but at the same time it can absorb at least 18 per cent of its dry weight in water without actually feeling damp to the touch. (Other extraordinary properties of this fibre include the ability to self-extinguish in the unlikely event that it catches fire. This happens because wool is rich in nitrogen, which, when released by heat, appears as a foam on the surface of the fibre, blocking the oxygen available to the flames.) Trial and error will determine the best method for wool fibres, as it is difficult to make general predictions. Fine wools will receive colour to a different intensity than stronger wools.

Very satisfying patterned textiles can be produced by wrapping berries and other plant materials together with the cloth to be dyed around pieces of found or scrap metals, making a bundle and applying a mordant solution. Let the bundle sit for several weeks before investigating the contents.

The following are but a few of the possibilities for making cold berry dyes:
    Raspberries
    Mulberries
    Elderberries
    Blueberries
    Cherries
    Blackberries
    Berberis darwinii berries
    Solanum nigrum

Consult your local weed list for other berried plants to experiment with, or investigate the rubbish available at your local greengrocer. When travelling, visit local markets to sample regional produce. Not all berries give colour, nor are all those colours necessarily substantive, but half the fun is in the trying and the rewards can occasionally be spectacular. While you may find that cloth dyed in this way can change colour during laundering and that berry colours do exhibit variable fading (depending on the plant source), the colours are nonetheless beautiful, mostly non-toxic (remember to research and read about what you use) and easily re-dyed.

Silk bag dyed with frozen berries.

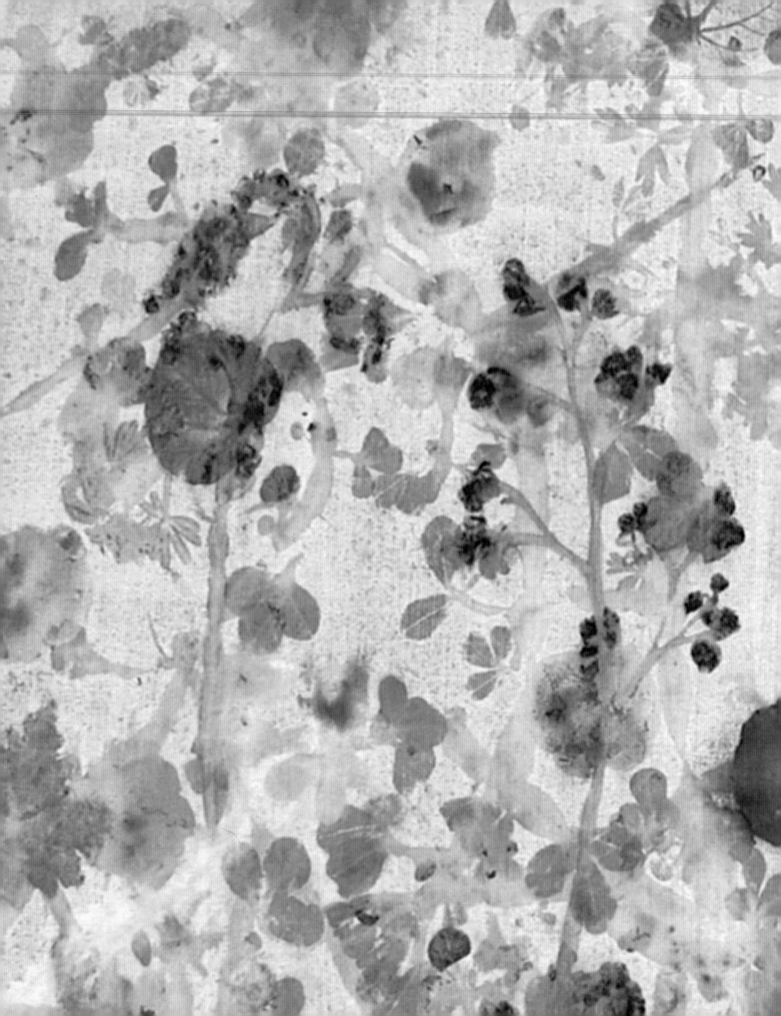

part six

SPECIAL EFFECTS

COLD-BUNDLED ECO-PRINTS

While fresh green eucalyptus leaves give richly coloured eco-prints on wool and silk, many other leaves, especially the dried leaves that collect under trees, can also be used to make beautiful prints on cloth. In the cold-bundle dye process, colour and pattern are achieved without the need for preparatory dye extraction or the use of a dye-pot.

This technique gives delightful results, especially on silk. It's a wonderful method of applying colour to small scraps that can then be used in larger projects. The essential ingredient in this process is time, together with a little moisture. For this method you will require a piece of cloth (any natural fibre will do, but smoothly woven silk responds very well), some plant material, a hand-mister and string or rubber bands to secure the bundle.

The toasted dark-coloured pods from *Acacia* species are a good source of colour. The leaves from *Eucalyptus* trees are very rewarding, as are those of the mistletoe plants (*Amyema* spp.) often found growing on them. In both cases, use the deeply coloured leaves that form a litter under the tree. Onion skins (red and brown) work extremely well, as do beetroot peelings, dark-coloured strips of bark, tea leaves, coffee grounds, wilted cut flowers, slices cut from citrus fruit and the pulp left from making blackberry jelly. Spray the leaves with a hand-mister, lay out on a dampened cloth, roll up the cloth tightly (if large) and tie firmly with string. Alternatively, fold the work a few times, place flat under a sheet of glass or metal and weight down well.

In general, tougher leaves seem to give better results if they are slightly dried first, and exquisite images can be made on cloth by pressing leaves first in a telephone book and then when nearly dried enfolding them in the cloth, so that each leaf is in full contact. Proceed with the moistening spray as described above. You can also apply left-over liquid from other dye-baths to achieve even more variations in colour.

Try pre-mordanting the fabric and allowing it to cure for a while before creating the bundle.

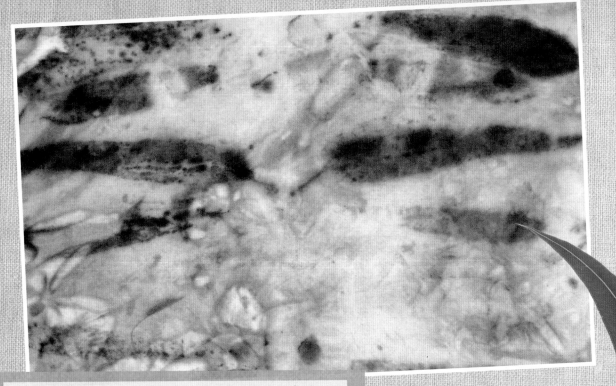

Long, cool and slow dyeing of silks yields lovely results.

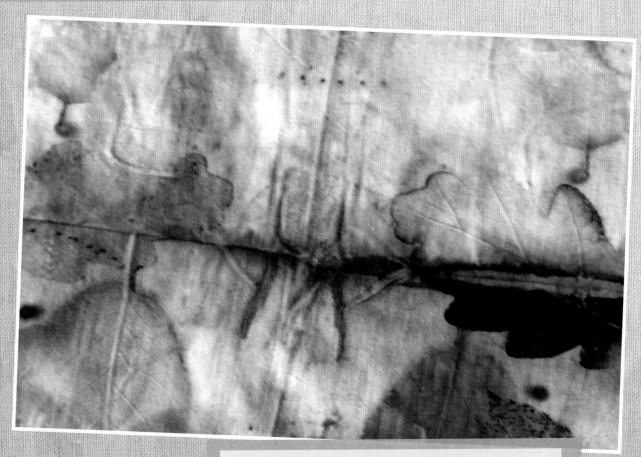

Cloth dyed using oak leaves, which are rich in tannins.

MAGIC MARBLED CLOTH USING ONION SKINS

| Collect a quantity of skins from brown and red (Spanish) onions. Have ready a piece of silk — habutai or crêpe de chine works well.

| Lay the silk flat on the work surface and spread the onion skins over the silk. Moisten using a hand-mister filled with vinegar (or any of the non-toxic home-made mordants). Starting at one edge, roll the silk with the onion skins inside.

| When you have a sausage shape, roll that up as well. Tie tightly with string or fasten with rubber bands. Moisten the outside with a little more liquid, bundle in a plastic bag (or place in a jar with lid), and set aside for at least a week, preferably one month.

| If mould appears, place the object in a snap-lock bag and freeze for a few days. Alternatively, steam it over boiling water for 30 minutes.

| Unwrap, shaking off the plant material (this is best done outside in the garden if you have one).

| Allow to dry, then press with a steam iron (use a pressing cloth). Allow to rest at least a few days before first rinsing.

| The most difficult thing about this method is resisting opening the bundle to check on the colour!

| Post-mordant in an iron-rich solution (or spray on using the hand-mister) and observe the colours change to olive greens and browns.

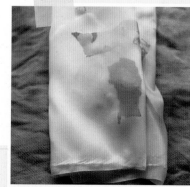

fixing the colour

When your curiosity can no longer be restrained, open the bundle and shake out the plant material. If the cloth is still damp, hang it somewhere in a shady spot to dry. When it is quite dry, inspect it to make sure there is no residual plant matter adhering and then press with a steam iron using a pressing cloth. While some colours will be found to be fugitive, in general the rule is that the longer the cloth is left to cure before washing, the more substantive will be the pattern.

Variations in colour can be achieved by using a range of mordants to dampen the cloth, such as tea, undrinkable wine, vinegar, ash-water, urine and so on — refer to the alternative mordant tables (page 92–101) or see the recipes for treating cellulose fibres (pages 104–105) for guidance.

If pre-mordanting the cloth, experiment by using a range of mordants, or applying resists to some areas using shibori techniques (page 183). Colour will be taken up differently in mordanted and un-mordanted areas of the cloth.

Try the option of collecting leaves, such as richly coloured autumn foliage, pressing them lightly until almost dry, and then misting them lightly with water (or a mordant solution) before rolling the bundle. The pre-drying process helps to weaken the cell structure so that the colour is more easily released into the cloth. The more colourful the leaf, the richer the print pattern is likely to be. Trees such as *Prunus blireiana*, *Prunus pissardii* 'Nigra', *Acer palmatum*, *Acer saccharum*, *Acer rubrum* and other deciduous trees can be used. Each autumn, the trees transfer their waste products to the leaves in readiness to shed them as winter approaches. This gives rise to the exquisite display of reds and golds, which can in turn be imparted to cloth using the cold-bundling technique.

Other variants include adding a small amount of moisture to the bundle using a hand-mister or syringe. This could be water or remnants of dye-pots or even mordant test samples left over from the Gerber testing method (see page 103).

seasonal palimpsests

Not all colours will be substantive *but* they will be unique! One could have a garment that changed with the seasons, in which stains are considered the pre-mordant for another colour. The whole could be progressively patched and embellished, a palimpsest in the form of an ever-changing garment.

Above: Onion skins ready for dyeing. Left: Onion skins in dye-bath.
Opposite page: Onion skins and onion slices colouring merino jersey.

what next?

Don't despair if your first attempt results in soft pale colours; just consider that to be a pre-mordant for the next layer. Do not wash the fabric at this point; it will be loaded with plant acids and if slightly re-dampened will accept prints from found metals such as barbed wire. You may also find that very pale colours will 'develop' if the cloth is placed into a post-mordant solution. A dilute alum solution often turns pale beige into a bright yellow, whereas a copper–urine or copper–seawater solution is likely to enhance any greens present.

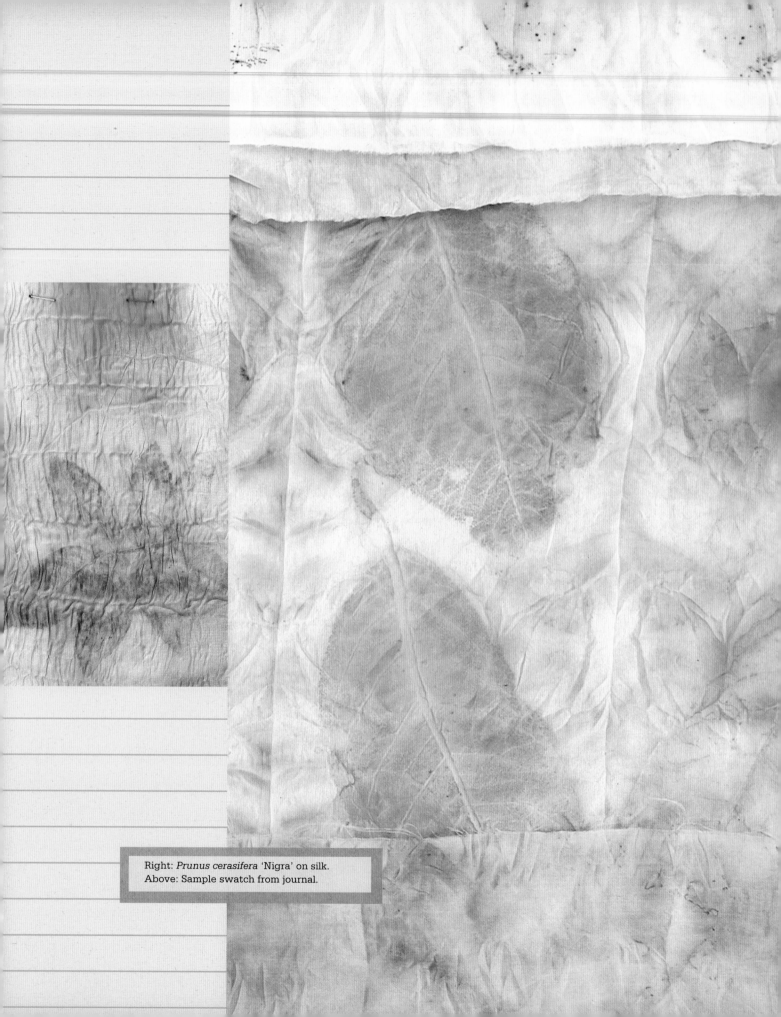

Right: *Prunus cerasifera* 'Nigra' on silk.
Above: Sample swatch from journal.

NON-EUCALYPTUS ECO-PRINTS
USING HOT-BUNDLING

The eco-print (a steam contact process described in the section on eucalypts, page 120) reveals that eucalypt leaves may contain a multiplicity of colours. Because the process uses steam — that is, heated pure water — it offers rapid assessment of potential colour.

The colour assessment is only true in the case of the eucalypt; nonetheless the eco-print also offers a relatively fast means of printing using other plants as well. Bear in mind, though, that while the eucalypts are substantive and their colour remains stable once applied and fixed, this does not necessarily hold true for other plants.

The important thing to remember when preparing to make an eco-print is that there must be very firm contact between the leaf material and the cloth so that at the moment when the dye is released due to the presence of heat and moisture in the form of steam, the cloth is there waiting to accept the dye. It is this direct contact which makes for a much brighter and more concentrated application than if the dye particles were swimming about in solution.

The other important factor is that the steam that is reaching the centre of the bundle is of course pure water, so no dissolved pollutants are interfering with the process.

I suppose I can't really claim to have discovered this technique as I grew up with its being practised annually in the dyeing of Easter eggs (see overleaf). It was more precisely a matter of putting two and two together and realising that what made such glorious patterns on the surface of the eggs would without doubt translate happily to cloth, as it has done.

The method works very well with un-mordanted silk and fine wool. Cellulose fibres must be pre-mordanted (see instructions on pages 104–105). Make up a tightly rolled bundle of cloth and plant material and bind it firmly with string or rubber bands. Place the bundle on a steamer rack over boiling water in a large pot, cover with a well-fitting lid (a pressure cooker is ideal for this) and steam for an hour. Allow to cool completely before opening. If you have the patience to leave the bundle for a few weeks before opening

blue prints

Oddly enough, *Isatis tinctoria* (woad), the plant that is customarily fermented with urine to give a lovely sky blue, makes particularly charming eco-prints, which vary across the leaf print from maroon through to green and turquoise blue.

it, you will be rewarded by the development of unexpected colours due to the action of micro-flora and micro-fauna and to the chemical changes that occur as plant material breaks down. It can be amusing to pour small quantities of dye remnants on to the bundle as well.

Experiment by pre-mordanting the cloth by soaking it in the sea, or post-mordanting with various brews, to watch colours change and develop. At the conclusion of the dye process, squeeze out the excess moisture and allow the textile to dry in the shade. Press using a steam iron and pressing cloth and allow the dyed textile to cure for at least two days before washing.

DYEING EASTER EGGS IN THE LATVIAN MANNER

Latvia is a small and beautiful country situated on the Baltic Sea, renowned for its delicious food, exquisite amber and its textile crafts. The tradition of decorating the first eggs of the season pre-dates Christianity and celebrates the coming of spring after the long, cold and dark winter. These days, dyeing Easter eggs is a pleasant family activity reserved for Easter Eve (the Saturday immediately preceding Easter Sunday).

Given the delightful colours that can be coaxed from Nature, anyone who persists with dipping hard-boiled eggs into toxic synthetic dyes and then actually eating them probably needs counselling! Try this method instead.

You will need

A dozen fresh eggs (choose eggs that have pale shells for the best effect), and a large saucepan.

Gather together a collection of small leaves of interesting shapes: clover, strawberry, dill, dandelion, basil (purple and green), thyme, marjoram.

Find small flowers as well.

Have ready a bag of onion skins, of both the purple and the brown varieties, and thread for wrapping and tying. I use silk embroidery thread for re-use later in stitch work. You may also have some old stockings on hand, or fragments of silk. These can be used to help wrap the onion skins around the eggs, becoming beautifully patterned in the process.

What to do

Moisten your stock of onion skins slightly; this will make it easier to fold them about the eggs.

Take some of the larger pieces and spread them in your hand to make a kind of cradle. Lay some of the small leaves and flowers in the onion skins.

Place an egg in the middle and carefully fold the onion skins around the egg. Wrap the egg-bundle with long lengths of silk or string. Alternatively, slip it into an old stocking or wrap it in a piece of silk and secure.

Place the wrapped egg in the saucepan, on a thick bed of onion skins. Continue wrapping and stacking eggs until all are done. Cover the egg-and-onion-skin pile in the saucepan with water and bring it to the boil. Simmer for 10 minutes, then allow the eggs to cool in the solution (if you have the patience). At least try to wait until the brew is only lukewarm.

Each egg will be unique and beautiful and a joy to unwrap. Save the pieces of thread and silk to use later. Use the remnant dye-bath to dye other fibres, perhaps just in a glass jar in the sun.

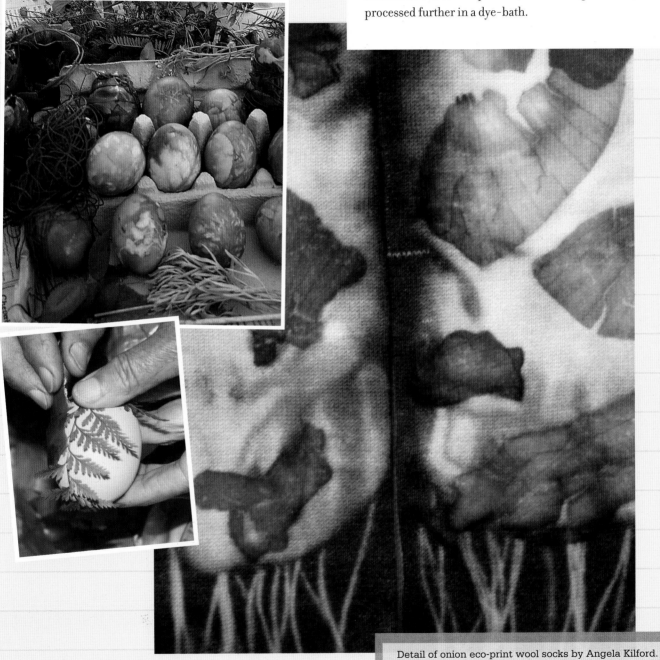

COLOURFUL CORES

If making a sock or stocking tea-bag, consider using it as the foundation of a hot bundle and wrapping a piece of cloth or hank of yarn tightly around it so that an intense area of colour is applied when the bundle is heated and steam penetrates the core. This will only extract a small amount of the colour present; the 'tea-bag' can then be processed further in a dye-bath.

Detail of onion eco-print wool socks by Angela Kilford.

Experimenting with *hapa-zome* can achieve some wonderful results.

Rich dark prints from petunias and geraniums.

HAPA-ZOME — BEATING
COLOUR INTO CLOTH

This is an almost ridiculously simple method of introducing colour into cloth by beating. It works very well on linen, ramie, cotton and hemp, and it also works on some of the denser silk weaves. On loose weaves such as pajeant silk or butter muslin, the colour tends to spread, while on heavily textured weaves it is difficult to make a precise impression of the leaf. Wool fabrics respond best to hot-bundling treatments for leaf prints.

While the name *hapa-zome* (literally 'leaf-dye' in Japanese) might be seen as a piece of cheeky cultural misappropriation by some, I gave the name to the process having perfected the technique during a short stay in Japan while having to think of a way to rapidly colour a floor cloth for a floating stage using plant materials. There was no pot available that was large enough to dye 36 square metres (40 yards) of cloth, and had the cloth been dyed in sections even subtle differences in colour would have been glaringly obvious when the whole was pieced together. So I hit upon the solution of applying colour directly by thumping it on with a small hammer.

All that is required are some leaves, a small hammer or mallet, some cloth of fairly dense weave and thin cardboard or thick paper to protect the cloth from the hammer and from the surface it is being beaten on.

First, place some thick paper or card on the work surface, preferably an uncarpeted floor or very sturdy bench. The leaves are placed on the cloth, covered with another piece (fold over another part of the cloth you are working on), protected by another piece of card or paper and careful strokes of the hammer applied. It does take a little practice to get the pressure right, so that a perfect print of the leaf is made without the leaf itself disintegrating into green porridge and sticking so firmly to the cloth that it becomes impossible to remove. Different plant species will require slightly different pressures as well. It is a case of practice making perfect. Beginners are advised to use a rubber mallet for their first efforts as the elasticity in the rubber will generally prevent the plant material from being pulped into the cloth surface by over-exuberant beating. It is best to experiment on scraps of fabric from the rag bag before attempting a large work.

garden garments

Lovely summer T-shirts can be printed using the *hapa-zome* method. As the prints gradually fade they can be replaced by others, making the T a truly trans-seasonal garment that reflects the abundance of the garden. Change the colour scheme to suit your mood.

Alternatively, have a series of small panels or pockets that button on to a larger garment. Apply colour to the panels using the *hapa-zome* or combinations of other techniques. The panels can be further enhanced with embroidery and beading; make them reversible if you like. This is a simple and amusing way of adding small changeable colour details to a simple outfit — great for travelling, as those pockets can also become your souvenirs, picking up colour along the journey.

Plants for *hapa-zome* at Edith Cowan University, Perth.

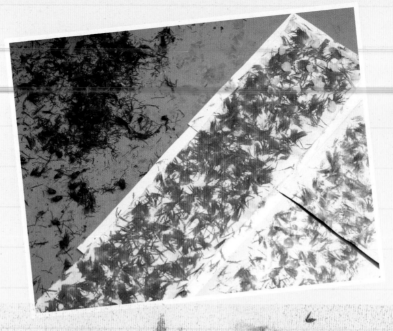

Left: Intense colour applied from shredded red flowers. Note how the colour has changed where the print has been taken up by the paper cover sheet — this is due to the paper having been finished with kaolin clay to make it smooth to write on.

Left: The leaves of the Japanese maple (*Acer palmatum*) are particularly beautiful, with their fine red edges.

Once the cloth is sufficiently decorated, allow it to dry thoroughly and then press with a steam iron, or better still in a heat press. This helps to set the colour on the cloth. Although this is not the most permanent of printing methods, most prints will survive at least a couple of years if only carefully hand-washed from time to time.

Pre-soaking the cloth in a mordant solution and allowing it to dry thoroughly before printing can also be useful. If using recycled textiles, one can sometimes witness quite radical colour shifts as the sap of the plant reacts with the remnants of washing detergents attached to the fibres. All detergents will act as mordants; certainly most of them contain sodium carbonate in addition to a host of other chemicals. The longer that *hapa-zome* prints are allowed to cure on the cloth before initial laundering, the better will be their staying power. Leaf prints generally last a lot longer than flower prints.

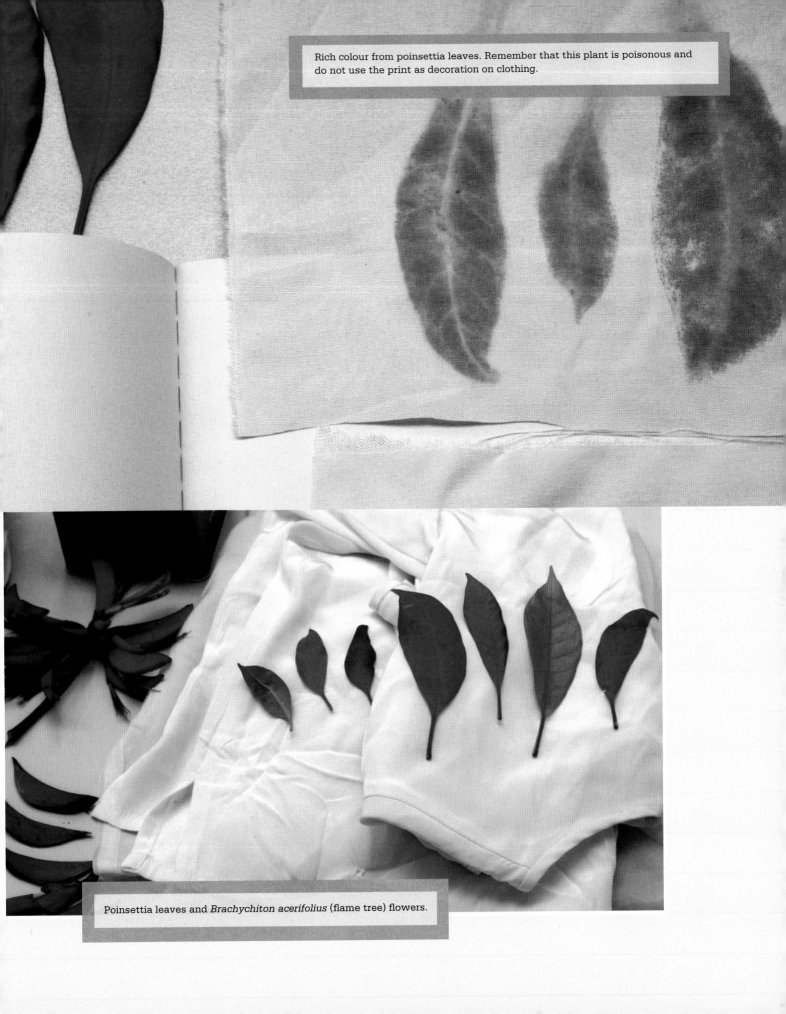

Rich colour from poinsettia leaves. Remember that this plant is poisonous and do not use the print as decoration on clothing.

Poinsettia leaves and *Brachychiton acerifolius* (flame tree) flowers.

DYEING WOOL YARN
AND SLIVER

The most important thing to remember when dyeing any sort of wool is that heat and moisture — two of the conditions necessary for felting and shrinkage — are already present, so the trick is to make sure to avoid introducing friction if possible. The other absolutely vital thing to avoid is any sudden change in temperature of more than 5° C (9° F) in immersion baths, otherwise the fibre will simply be shocked into shrinking.

If the sliver or yarn is required to be of an even colour, then pre-wetting will be necessary, as will some movement in the dye-bath to ensure uniform take-up of dye. Therefore dyeing wool does require a degree of care.

basic procedure

Prepare the dye solution and strain it well through a cloth, as any small pieces of vegetable matter will inevitably lodge themselves in the fibres. Place the un-dyed wool in a colander.

Prepare a water bath in which the colander will stand comfortably. Immerse the wool, still supported by the colander, in the soaking bath and allow it to rest in the water for at least half an hour. If two colanders are available the wool can be sandwiched between them so the excess water may be gently pressed out.

The wetted fibre is then immersed in the dye-bath. If the colander is heat-proof, of a non-reactive substance and fits inside the pot, so much the better. If the colander won't fit into the dye vessel, carefully remove the wool and lower it into the dye-bath. Place the whole on the heating device and very slowly raise the temperature to the point at which the liquid just begins to steam. Don't let it boil or even simmer. Maintain this for a couple of hours, turn the heat off and then allow the whole to cool overnight.

If the wool has been dyed resting in the colander, it can be very easily lifted from the bath and the excess liquid allowed to drain back into the pot. Repeat the gentle squeezing process if a second colander is available. Allow the wool to dry in the colander in a shady spot. Drying the wool before

Above: Wool sliver soaking in an *Oxalis pes-caprae* (soursob) bath in a copper pot. Bottom left: A skein of wool wound around a piece of dowel resting across the top of the pot. The wool can be gently wound by twisting the stick, so that the skein can be variably dyed. Bottom right: Variably dyed silk yarn.

Dyed wool sliver ready for spinning or felting.

rinsing the last of the dye off will generally ensure a richer and longer-lasting colour. If the substance being dyed is sliver for felting, no rinsing will be needed. If it is yarn, it may need to be rinsed (still in the colander) using a hose or other spray device.

dyeing multicoloured yarns and sliver in a microwave oven

While there is no way I would prepare food in such an oven, much less knowingly eat it, I certainly concede that a contrivance which introduces heat into a substance without visibly moving it can be a handy thing (agitation does occur but it is at molecular level). The sliver or yarn laid flat on a microwave-safe receptacle can be dampened with cool water (here again oven bags can be useful; just don't seal them or they'll explode), cool concentrated dye solution(s) applied and the whole heated and re-heated at intervals as required. The beauty of this method is that the process can be continued over a number of days. For some reason I don't understand, certain greens are brighter when applied using the microwave oven.

The disadvantage of using a microwave is that firstly it is impossible to tell if the machine leaks, which is a frightening thought. Secondly, no metals can be used, so that the interesting possibilities offered by introducing scrap metals in contact dye processes cannot be exploited.

multicoloured yarns using scrap metals and plant dyes

Delightful effects can be achieved by wrapping hanks of wool yarn around pieces of metal, such as old horse-shoes, scraps of copper pipe, old tent pegs or railway dog-spikes. The bundle can be secured with a rubber band or two, or a piece of string — this will introduce un-dyed areas to which other colours can be applied later if desired.

Immerse the bundle in a fairly concentrated dye-bath and heat gently. Allow to cool and then remove the bundle. The longer the bundle is allowed to rest before it is opened the greater will be the effect of the metal on the yarn.

Pre-soaking the yarn in a mordant solution increases the colour possibilities, especially if parts of the yarn have been covered by a resist in the ikat technique (see opposite).

ikat dyeing

Ikat is the name given to the weaving technique originating in Malaysia and Indonesia where patterns are introduced to the warp and sometimes also the weft by tying off areas before the yarn is immersed in a dye-bath. Tying off the complex patterns requires great skill and dexterity.

The technique has been adopted throughout Southeast Asia. In Pochampally, India, strips of recycled bicycle tubing are used to exclude dye from the thread.

Silk and wool can be dyed without pre-mordant; however cotton, linen and other cellulose fibres should be pre-mordanted first for efficient dye take-up.

Above left: Ikat dyed silks at Pochampally, India. Above right: Silk before immersion in dye, with the areas that are to remain white tied off using slices of old bicycle inner tubing. Below right: Hot processing wool yarn in eucalyptus dye.

to heat or not to heat

Some plants give different colours at different temperatures. Eucalypts, for example, give the brightest and richest colours from the still-hot first extract; cooling and re-heating the dye-bath will change the hue. If dyeing wool with eucalypts, strain the solution through a cloth into the dye vessel and return it to the heat source to keep it warm. If you have a thermometer handy, take note of the temperature. Prepare a water bath of similar temperature to the dye-bath and immerse the wool (resting in a colander) in the bath to wet it. If it is a cold day you may need to heat the water bath while the wool is soaking in order to maintain the temperature. When the wool is thoroughly wetted, extract it from the water bath (as described above) and immerse it in the dye.

Should this exercise seem unspeakably tedious, simply immerse the dry yarn or sliver in the dye-bath and accept the lovely accidental mottling that will occur.

A vat of remnant dye holds skeins of yarn as well as T-shirts being pre-soaked in preparation for compost dyeing.

MULTICOLOURED YARNS

*Multicoloured yarns for knitting and embroidery can be very expensive
to purchase and quite simple to dye. Silk, in particular, has an affinity for
plant dyes, and colours beautifully.*

method 1

A simple way of dyeing multicoloured yarns for craft uses is to take a
hank of yarn (I usually use silk) and lay it out in a flat food storage box.

Then take small quantities of concentrated dye solutions and carefully
apply these to chosen areas, making sure there are distinct colour areas.
Where dye solutions meet there will be interesting blends and new colours
may form as a result of chance cocktails. When all of the silk has some
colour applied, seal the storage box and let time work its magic. Leave it for
at least a few days, preferably for a week. If you plan to leave it for longer
periods of time, monitor the contents regularly! Once the dye begins to
decompose (which can happen quite quickly in warm weather depending
on the dyes — eucalyptus dyes can be left for months, whereas ice-flower
dyes have a much earlier use-by date), things can get a bit smelly and this
is best avoided. It is good practice to freeze the entire box from time to time
if you want to leave the dye in contact for an extended period.

Pre-mordanting the skein of silk may help dye take-up and will influence
the intensity and shade of colour achieved.

When the depth of colour is to your satisfaction, place the hank or skein
in a strainer and gently spray with water using a hose. When the water runs
clear, squeeze out excess moisture and hang the skein in the shade to dry.

method 2

Using string, rubber bands or slices of recycled bicycle tubing, create
areas of resist around a skein of silk or wool. Immerse the hank in a dye or
mordant bath and process as desired. When dried, remove the resists and
then continue the process following Method 1.

method 3

Immerse the skein of silk or wool entirely in a dye-bath. After processing as desired, and when the skein is dry, tie off areas using the resists described above and immerse in another dye-bath. Continue these processes with successive overdyes as desired. A final rinse in a dilute vinegar-and-water solution will restore soft handle to the fibre.

If the skein is partially pre-mordanted with various substances, the diversity of colour will be even greater.

method 4

Try wrapping the thread around an object such as a piece of metal, a tea-bag or a richly coloured piece of bark, then continue with Method 1.

See also 'Dyeing wool yarn and sliver' (page 170) for other possibilities.

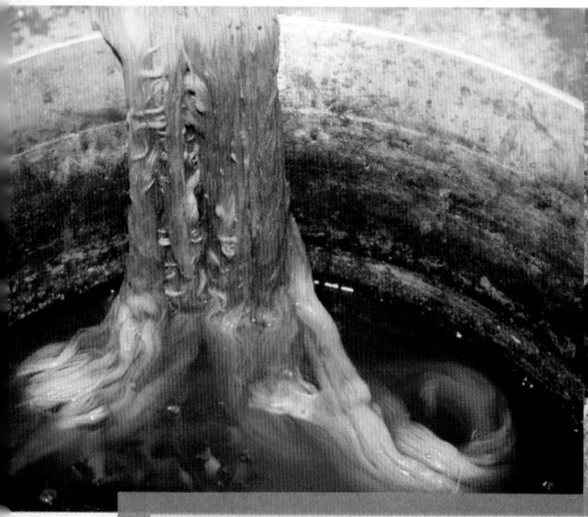

Plant vs protein

Silk and wool can be dyed without pre-mordant; however, cotton, linen and other cellulose fibres should be pre-mordanted first for efficient dye take-up.

Above left: Pre-dipping in a nearly exhausted dye-bath. Above centre: Applying colour with a syringe. Above right: 'Cooking' in the sun in a plastic bag.

A hank of silk yarn, pre-soaked in a nearly exhausted yellow dye-bath (made up of a cocktail of various yellow remnants).

These images show the various stages in a folded and clamped *shibori-zome* dye procedure. The clamps prevent the dye from being taken up by applying pressure to the cloth. Repeat folding and overdyeing can be used to develop cloth of great complexity. Above: The hexagon pattern is created by first concertina folding and then folding again with folds at 60° angles in a triangular format. Top right: Unfolding the triangles. Above right: Clamping for a tartan-like pattern.

Left and below left: Opening out the bundle.
Below: The unfolded complex cloth.

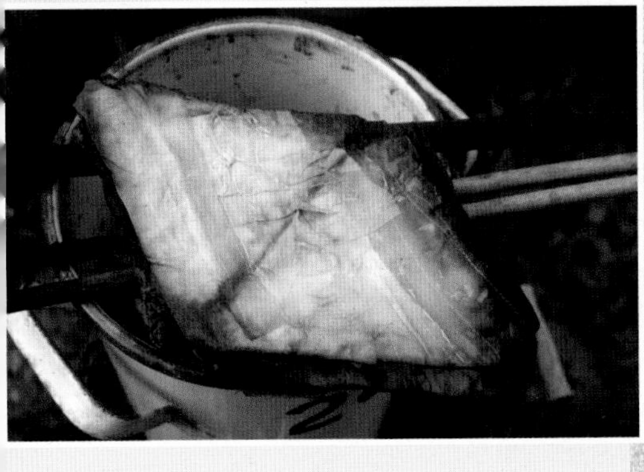

PRINTING WITH PLANT DYES

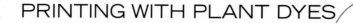

These days, newspapers are often printed using an ink made of soya oil as the carrier for the pigment. While I am personally of the opinion that few designs can surpass the beautiful imprints made by the plants themselves, it is nonetheless sometimes necessary to print information such as care instructions, composition or the name of the maker directly on to a piece of work.

Asian countries have a long and complex history of cloth printing using plant dyes, stencils made of paper and blocks made of metal or wood.

To generate a printed mark that harmonises with the dyed cloth, it is necessary to select a printing medium of sufficient density that bleeding is prevented, yet also conversely no crust is formed on the surface.

While some texts recommend the use of Manutex (a derivative of seaweed), other substances such as gelatine, egg white and cooked starch pastes are also suitable as carriers. The dye itself will need to be fairly concentrated. This is best done by placing the selected liquid in an open heatproof container in a warm place, such as next to a slow combustion stove or in a sunny breezy spot (the latter will take longer). Vigorous boiling to reduce the amount of water present will tend to dull the colour. When the solution has attained the required consistency it should be mixed with the carrier.

For silk-screen printing, it will be important to ensure that the mixture has been sieved and ground meticulously to prevent clogging of the screen. For block printing, the dye mixture is best worked thoroughly on a glass plate using a roller or paintbrush before picking up with the block.

Prepare a padded surface to support the cloth being printed by spreading out a few layers of old blanket followed by a layer of clean sheeting or calico. Pin the padding down firmly at the edges using drawing pins or blue tacks. Stretch the (pre-mordanted) cloth over the print pad and pin it to prevent wrinkling. Proceed with printing, moving the cloth as required.

When the printing has been completed, allow the cloth to dry thoroughly.

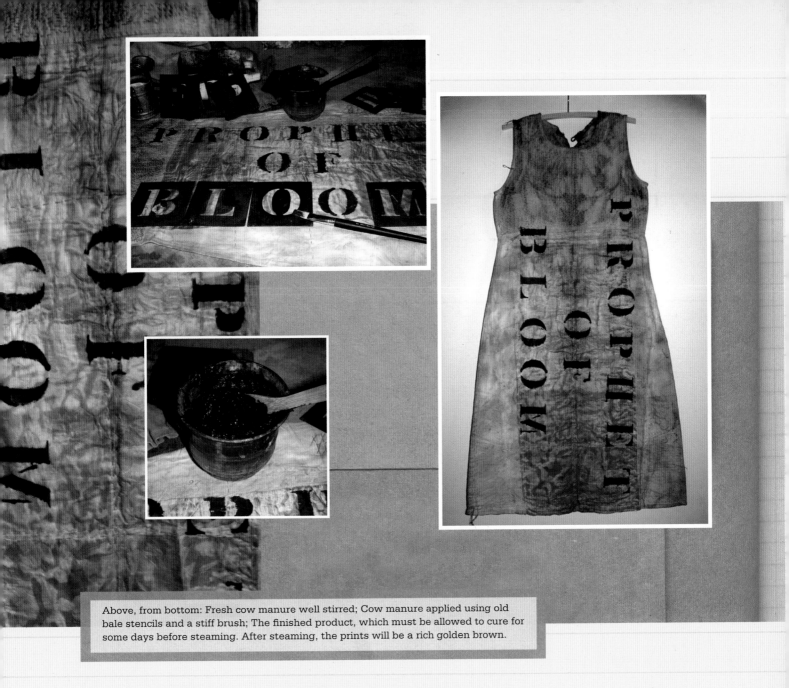

Above, from bottom: Fresh cow manure well stirred; Cow manure applied using old bale stencils and a stiff brush; The finished product, which must be allowed to cure for some days before steaming. After steaming, the prints will be a rich golden brown.

The next step, that of heat fixing, will depend on the chosen dye. If an extract from ice-flowers has been used, then all that is required is a few days' curing time before pressing with a warm iron. The longer the cure, the more enduring will be the print. If eucalyptus dyes have been used, then the fabric must be steamed. Whether it is rolled with layers of paper in between to keep patterns separate, or simply crumpled into the top of a steamer in the hope that magic will happen, is entirely up to the individual. Steam over boiling water for at least 30 minutes and allow complete cooling in the basket before rinsing.

Post-print dipping in one or more mordant brews may prove amusing.

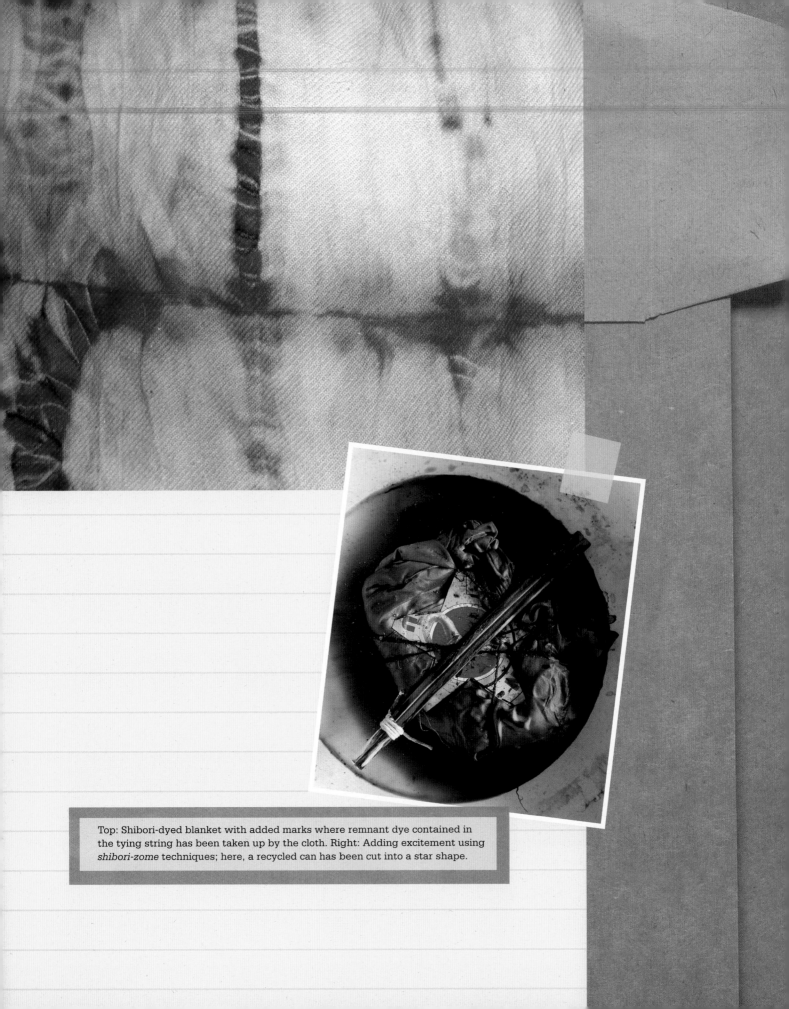

Top: Shibori-dyed blanket with added marks where remnant dye contained in the tying string has been taken up by the cloth. Right: Adding excitement using *shibori-zome* techniques; here, a recycled can has been cut into a star shape.

USING SHIBORI TECHNIQUES AND LAYERED DYEING

Plant dyes seem to love silk and wool and, when applied using the traditional Japanese resist technique known in the West as shibori (which literally means 'to squeeze'), can produce exquisite patterns on cloth with relatively little effort. Repeated overdyeing can be used to build up layers of colour. Properly the technique is known as shibori-zome, zome *being the Japanese word for 'dyeing'.*

Clamping or stitching resist patterns can be a most satisfactory method of introducing designs onto the surface of a piece of cloth. The manipulated fabric can be immersed directly in the selected dye-bath, or alternatively in a pre-mordant solution. Once dry, the resist can be removed and the cloth subsequently dyed. Such partially mordanted cloth can result in two different colours (or two shades of one colour) from the one dye-bath, depending on the plant material and mordant selected. Sometimes, where there is sufficient compression, the dye will actually be filtered as it is absorbed into the parcel, resulting in coloured areas with different coloured edges.

This method can be repeated as often as desired, whether using dye solutions or mordant after-baths, re-setting the resists in between treatments to develop a quite complex textile. There are many works available discussing traditional *shibori-zome* patterns and how to apply them. The purpose of this book is to lead the reader into experimental zones using the technique.

Experiment using stitching to exclude areas of dye or simply by folding the cloth, sandwiching between two resist objects and tying or clamping the bundle together. Whereas traditional practice would involve the use of wooden resist blocks that would not react with the dye, it can be most exciting to use other things such as tin lids, old CDs or ice-block sticks as resists, as well as clamps, bulldog clips, paper clips and copper electrical clamping jaws. Found scrap metals can add interesting patterns to the work. Look out for interestingly patterned objects such as discarded cheese graters and pieces of mesh.

hexagonal or honeycomb patterns

Take a piece of woven silk or wool and first fold it in half, lengthwise. Marking the desired pattern onto the cloth beforehand (using chalk) can be helpful.

Then make small triangular folds, concertina-fashion. A warm iron is a useful tool in encouraging the fabric to stay where you want it. The sample should then be tied using objects that might act as a resist and some string. Rubber bands are quite useful also. It is important to tie firmly, as the pattern is made by excluding dye from chosen areas. You can also use a needle and thread to stitch layers of cloth together. Where the stitching is firm and tight the dye will not penetrate, so that dye particles will tend to congregate on exposed areas, forming patches of deep colour.

When the bundle is formed, immerse it in a prepared dye-bath and heat gently (just below simmering) for an hour or so. Remove the bundle from the bath, allow to cool, open and enjoy the patterns!

tartan patterns

Folding the cloth concertina fashion in first one direction and then the other before clamping with a bulldog or other strong clip will make a lovely simple pattern on the cloth. After the first immersion, the cloth can be re-folded so that a different area is exposed to the dye. Where the previously dyed areas are exposed to new colour, a new shade will be introduced, so that from two dips there will be three colours. The process can be continued until the whole cloth is covered with an almost tartan interlocking colour grid.

chequerboard patterns

Delightful chequerboard patterns can be made by sandwiching small square metal off-cuts in between the layers of cloth as they are being folded. Apply pieces to the outside of the bundle as well and either tie the whole with string for beautiful crisp un-dyed marks along the deeply dyed edges, or clamp the bundle using bulldog clips.

multicoloured fabrics

Combine elements of the hot-bundling method with shibori techniques and introduce small quantities of plant material into the layers as well. Onion skins are particularly rewarding when used in this way. Where they come in contact with the metal it will have a mordant effect; steel will

layer upon layer
In applying *shibori-zome* processes, remember the bath can be a dye or a mordant. Successive applications will give rise to beautiful and complex patterned textiles. Experiment with combinations of methods, perhaps giving the entire cloth a final dip in an ice-flower or cold berry solution or treating it to a solar-dye process. Your fabrics will be unique.

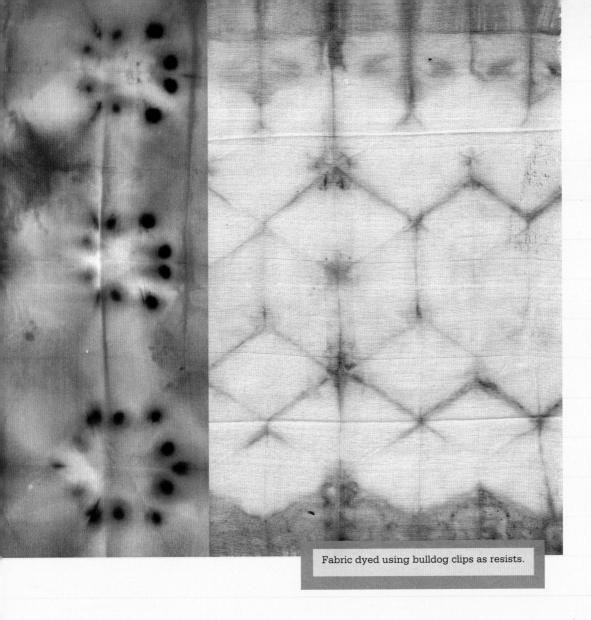

Fabric dyed using bulldog clips as resists.

scrap metal magic

Punch holes in scrap metal using a hammer and nails to create interesting patterns through which the dye can seep on to the cloth. If you do not have access to scraps, cut open tins (of the pet food or drinking chocolate variety) and flatten them by beating before adding your designs.

promote lime and olive green patterns, whereas copper or brass will encourage golden greens and yellows. Elsewhere, in parts where the metallic influence does not reach, direct colour will be absorbed from the onion skin. On the sides of the bundle there will be areas of intense colour from whatever dye-bath is used. Depending on whether string or clamps are used, a further complexity of marks will be seen on the cloth. So it will be seen that many colours can be introduced during a relatively short space of time, by combining a number of processes.

RESISTS

Resists are applied to prevent dyes from reaching selected parts of the fibre being dyed. They can be mechanical (tying, squeezing and clamping) or may be applied in the form of pastes. Traditional batik requires the application of a wax resist.

Almost any type of flour can be used to make paste resists (although the finer the better) — rice flour, cassava, soya, cornflour (cornstarch), whatever you have on hand. The resist can be applied with a paintbrush, printed using blocks or silk screens, or applied with a wee paper cone. Interesting effects may be achieved by applying the resist quite thickly, allowing it time to dry thoroughly and then cracking the paste carefully. One of the best paste resists is a mixture of gum arabic and kaolin, sometimes also containing a little alum. This is best left to cure for a couple of weeks before use (it works well for indigo and other cold dyes).

block printing

Paste resists have long been applied with wooden blocks (lino, sponge, brush and stick applications also work well). To do this, a printing pad must be prepared. Construct it from two layers of cotton cloth laid over a pad made of sponge or blankets and pinned down firmly at the sides. Alternatively, spread the resist on a piece of glass using a brush, working it well from side to side before picking it up with a dip of the block. The paste must be perfectly smooth and the consistency such that the block can 'pick up' without the details becoming clogged. Alternatively, apply the paste to the block using a roller.

batik — wax resist

The two principal forms of wax used are beeswax (soft) and paraffin wax (hard). The latter will give a crackled effect (being quite brittle) whereas the beeswax is soft and more likely to bend with the cloth. Many artists

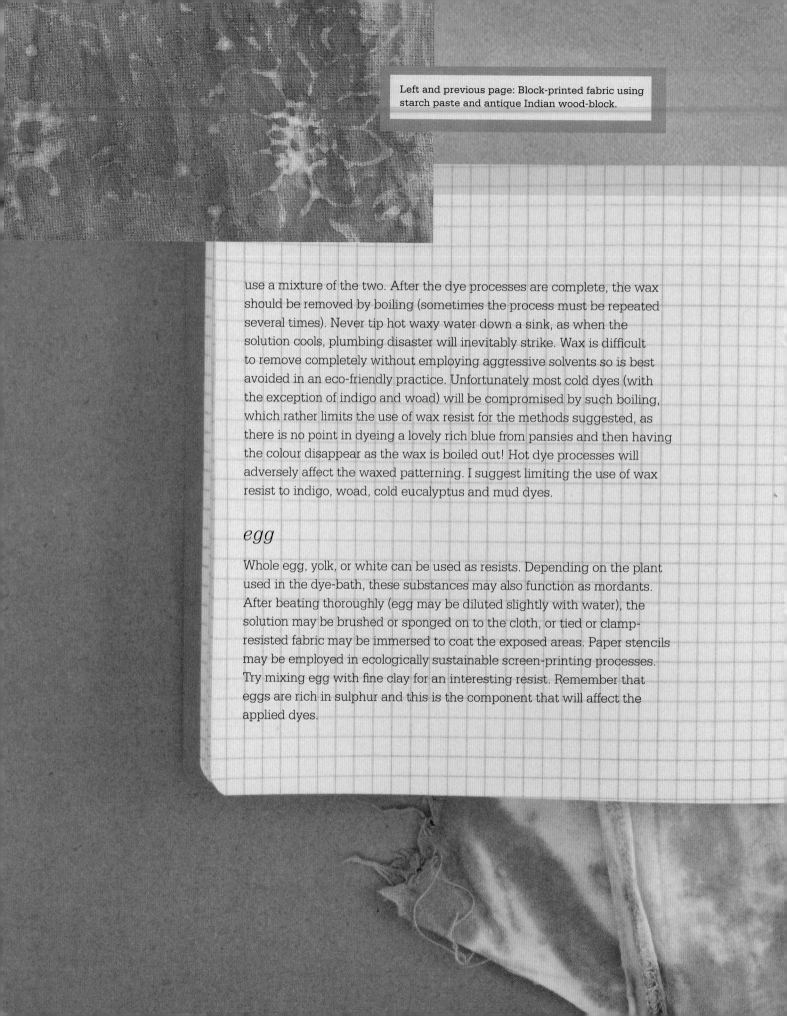

Left and previous page: Block-printed fabric using starch paste and antique Indian wood-block.

use a mixture of the two. After the dye processes are complete, the wax should be removed by boiling (sometimes the process must be repeated several times). Never tip hot waxy water down a sink, as when the solution cools, plumbing disaster will inevitably strike. Wax is difficult to remove completely without employing aggressive solvents so is best avoided in an eco-friendly practice. Unfortunately most cold dyes (with the exception of indigo and woad) will be compromised by such boiling, which rather limits the use of wax resist for the methods suggested, as there is no point in dyeing a lovely rich blue from pansies and then having the colour disappear as the wax is boiled out! Hot dye processes will adversely affect the waxed patterning. I suggest limiting the use of wax resist to indigo, woad, cold eucalyptus and mud dyes.

egg

Whole egg, yolk, or white can be used as resists. Depending on the plant used in the dye-bath, these substances may also function as mordants. After beating thoroughly (egg may be diluted slightly with water), the solution may be brushed or sponged on to the cloth, or tied or clamp-resisted fabric may be immersed to coat the exposed areas. Paper stencils may be employed in ecologically sustainable screen-printing processes. Try mixing egg with fine clay for an interesting resist. Remember that eggs are rich in sulphur and this is the component that will affect the applied dyes.

cotton flannelette -
soy bean mordant
beaten egg + h₂0 resist
onion skin overdye

experimental printing paste recipe

Take a cupful of flour (whatever variety is handy) and a cupful of finely powdered kaolin clay and grind the two together well using a large mortar and pestle. It is important that the ingredients be as fine as possible. If only wet clay is available, then mix the flour with a little water before mixing the two together. When you are satisfied the mixture is very fine and smooth, add a cup of 'gel' medium. This can be gelatine, gum arabic, agar jelly, Manutex gum or even egg white. Stir the ingredients together well, adding extra water if desired so that the consistency is that of thick cream.

While such a paste won't survive extended heating in a warm dye-bath, it is quite adequate for dipping in an indigo bath and is certainly easy to remove from the cloth later.

Fabric solar-dyed pink using purple (Spanish) onion skins with fruit vinegar co-mordant.

Solar dyeing equipment and dye-bath.

SOLAR DYEING

This is an almost ridiculously simple method of dyeing cloth or fibre, which can even be used on greasy wool direct from the sheep. It is a process that requires that most precious of ingredients, time. On the other hand, little intervention is required once the dye-pot has been set up. Be warned, though — the process will test your patience as you burn to investigate the exciting things happening in your containers.

The equipment required is laughably simple; merely as large a collection of jars with lids as you can muster. The beauty of the process is that the jars do not even need to be rinsed in advance, as remnant jams, pickles and sauces can all act as interesting mordant adjuncts. Solar dyeing is another way of using up fabric scraps and ends of dye baths, or small handfuls of dye-stuffs that are not worth boiling up, as well as being a simple path to colour if you don't have time or space for the more complicated dye processes.

process

Place fibre and dye material in a glass jar, pour in liquid (either hot or cold) to cover both, seal and place the jar in a warm sunny spot for at least one month.

When your patience has been exhausted, open the jar. Pour off the liquid (which by this time will retain little if any colour) and rinse the fibre in lukewarm water. If you have a lot of small scraps, place them in a netting washing bag and machine wash on a gentle cycle. Then simply hang the whole bag somewhere in the shade to dry.

If there is visible mould, place the jar (with the lid loosened to allow for the expansion of the contents once frozen) in a plastic bag in the freezer for a week to kill the mould. Then thaw and rinse in the usual way.

The variations on this simple method are limitless. Roll up dried eucalyptus or mistletoe leaves (fallen under the tree) in the cloth itself, stuff into jar and pour water (or left-over tea, or cold coffee, or the liquid from

sealing wax

If planning to leave the jar for an extended time, place a small stone on the fibre being dyed to weight it down so that the contents do not break the surface, and pour a quantity of melted wax into the vessel. This will prevent mould growing on the dye, and even though the wax may melt in the heat of the day it should remain impenetrable to air. (To recycle the wax, empty out the contents when they are cool and the wax is solid.)

Plant-dyed T-shirts for ethical fashion label 'Fully Stoked'.

pickled beetroot) over the top, seal and leave. Try this with any natural fibre, and with almost any plant available (keeping in mind the guidelines for responsible collection).

It is an especially good process for the tougher-leaved varieties (be advised that delicate flowers do have a tendency to rot). The less water, the more interesting and defined the patterns on the cloth will be, resulting in exquisite fragments for use in embroidery and patchwork.

Remnant dyes can be used to dye sliver for felting, threads for stitching, and multi-hued yarns for knitting and weaving.

Use the solar-dye technique to extract colour from flowers by cramming a jar with blooms, covering them with water, sealing the jar and then allowing it to stand somewhere warm until the liquid is a pleasant colour. Strain and use as desired.

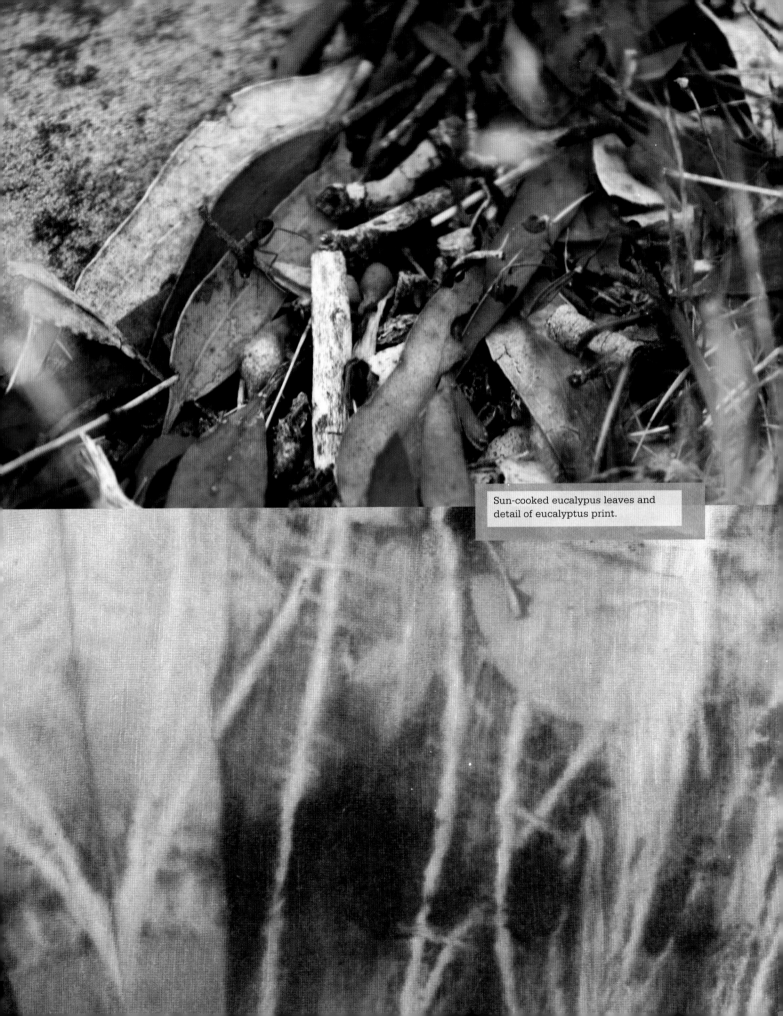

Sun-cooked eucalypus leaves and detail of eucalyptus print.

Opposite: The T-shirt at left has been dyed using *Solidago canadensis* on the resist-tied object, after which it was unbound and dipped into an ice-flower cocktail. That on the right was folded and clamped using the lids from tin cans, which have acted as a resist as well as imparting a grey print. Below: *Rosa pimpinellifolia* journal samples.

paper
dried
sample

sughtar liked sample ar
using hard towel (paper) —
acid? in paper has very slight
reddened the colour

26.5
part of bigget
sample rinsed
hot H2O,

colour
unaffected

lay sample
dried up
in solution
from large
sample
10-2
VW 12-2

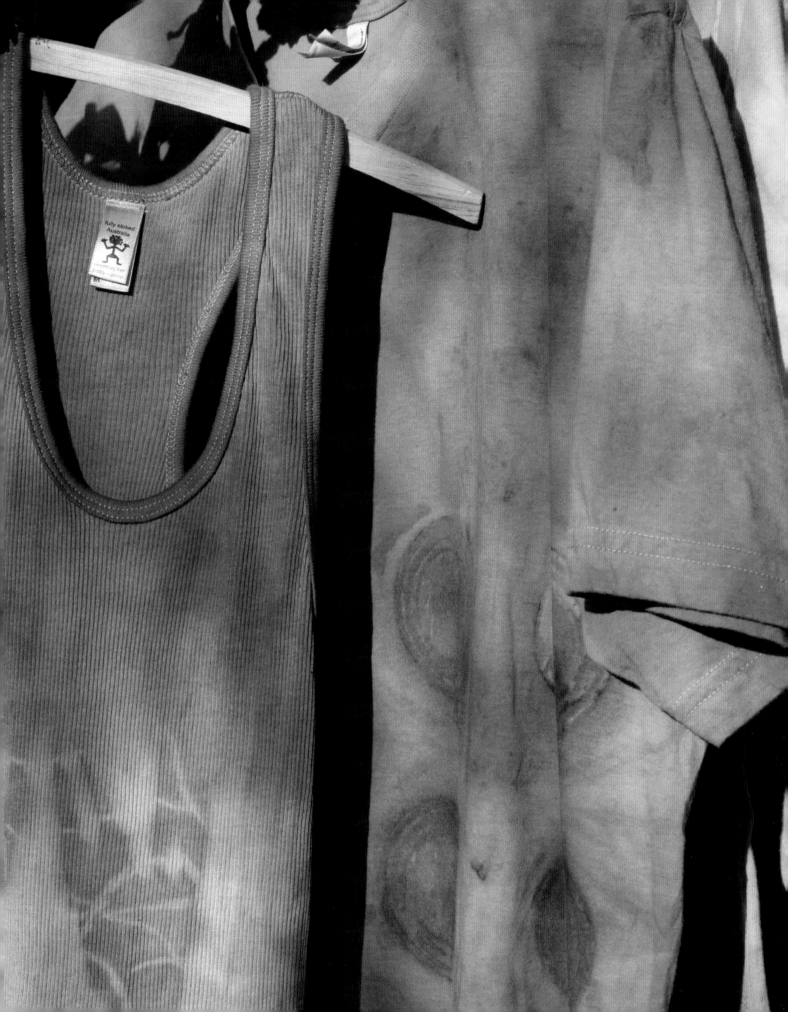

MUD AND COW PATTIES

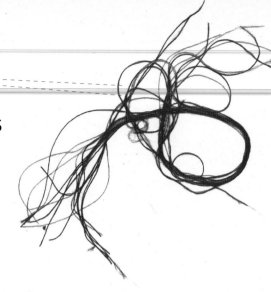

Mud is an almost universally available substance (except in periods of drought). It can be used as a kind of resist, or if mineral concentrations are high, as a dye. Faeces from herbivores are also well worth investigating, again as both dyes and resists.

mud

Mud can offer an applied colour usually giving rise to a stain, rather than a true dye wherein a chemical bond is formed between the cloth and the dye participle. Variations in results will depend very much on the mineral and vegetable content of the mud. Best results are obtained using mud of a very fine consistency. When collecting mud in urban or industrialised areas, be aware of industrial pollutants and avoid collecting any potentially toxic samples. While these may well enhance the ultimate colour of the cloth, introducing substances of unknown chemical provenance to dye practice can be dangerous.

Pre-mordant the cloth to which the mud will be applied using a tannin-rich solution made from tea, acacia bark, acorn husks or oak galls. Soak the cloth for 24 hours, drain and spread in the sun to dry. Follow the tannin soak with a protein-rich solution made from ground soybeans, milk or acorn flour mixed with water. Apply the mud using a paintbrush or small squeeze bag, or print it on to the cloth using a wood block or an interestingly shaped object. Leave to dry and allow to cure on the cloth for as long as possible before removing. An old toothbrush is useful to brush the dried mud off.

The traditional Bogolanfini mud cloth worn by the Bamana people of Mali is famous for its distinctive patterns and is avidly imitated by dyers around the globe. The designs tell stories and offer protection to the wearer, and complex combinations are developed by the maker. The black patterns on the Malian textiles are made by allowing the iron-rich pond mud to ferment for a year after it is collected before applying it to the cloth, which has been pre-mordanted with a solution made from the pounded leaves of the cengura tree. It would appear that vegetable matter present in the mud

Painting black acidic mud collected from a creekbed on to recycled cotton cloth.

contributes to the fermentation by supplying an acidic environment, thus resulting in the black colour. Application of the decoration can take some considerable time, as the entire cloth is covered with hand-painted symbols. After the first treatment, the cloth is washed and the process repeated. Before the work is considered complete, the yellow colour from the leaf solution is bleached out using a caustic soda, peanut and bran solution carefully applied around the black areas. Whether the pond mud is a dye or is acting as a mordant (in which case the leaf solution is the dye) is unclear. What is important is that the two substances when applied in sequence give rich colour to cloth.

Bamana hunters customarily wear stiff long-sleeved cotton hunting coats dyed a rich red with mud and hung with charms and amulets to give power and keep the wearer safe. In such instances, the mud has not been fermented and thus retains the red colour commonly associated with iron oxide.

The Miao people of China use the muddy waters of the rice-paddies as a post-mordant bath. The fibre is first dyed in the leaves of the Chinese tallow tree (*Triadica sebifera*) and then soaked in red muddy water from the rice field. The red colour of the liquid and the subsequent black colour of the fibre would indicate the presence of iron oxides.

cow patties

Excrement and urine from herbivorous animals have been used for hundreds of years as a source of dye, wool conditioner and adjunct mordant. It is a little-known fact that the brown-flecked oatmeal-coloured 'Berber' carpets so popular in the 1970s were woven from crutchings,

sustainable stencils

In some parts of the world, sturdy stencils are made by cutting shapes into banana leaves. Any large-leaved plant from the garden could be used, rather than cutting stencils from plastic or paper. The trimmings and the spent stencil can be disposed of on the compost heap, and what is more, the materials are free.

MUD AND COW PATTIES

197

red dust country

Dust from the Pilbara region in Australia's north-west is also a distinctive rich red and can be successfully applied to cloth to generate rich and lasting patterns. Mixing the dust with a small quantity of flour and water to the consistency of thick cream makes a very workable paste. Applied to silks and fine silk/wool blend fabrics, it leaves solid red colour which resists vigorous laundering even without the benefit of a pre-mordant.

Cellulose fibres benefit from pre-mordanting with tannins as described (page 92) for mud. The protein dip is not strictly necessary.

Experiment by mixing mud and dust with protein-rich carriers such as egg white or yoghurt before applying to the cloth. In cases where the carrier is likely to experience a further change

of state through fermentation, interesting colour surprises are likely to occur.

Mixing a richly coloured mud with a paste resist before applying a separate dye opens up even more possibilities.

There are many locations around the globe where interesting muds and minerals may be found. Collecting coloured earth from the side of a volcano or scooping sulphurous gloop from an exotic boiling mud hole will certainly give you a nicely coloured travel souvenir. On the other hand, simply experimenting with finely ground potting clays or silt from rivers can frequently give delightful results. Many colour-yielding earths are discovered inadvertently — if it accidentally stains your best jeans, it will dye your cloth as well!

Above: Mali hunter's coat (maker unknown), photographed at UNESCO Symposium on plant dyes, Hyderabad, India, 2006.

the stained wool that is trimmed from the rear ends of sheep prior to shearing so that the clip will retain its purity. The stain is from repeated applications of urine and faeces. When washed, such wool is a lovely golden-brown colour naturally dyed without adjunct chemical mordants!

Thick, freshly harvested cow pats are a perfect paint for textiles. They are rich in calcium and sodium phosphates, which contribute to the fixing of the colours produced by the cocktail of greenery consumed by the ruminant. Simply paint the dung on to the cloth (mordanted as described above) and allow to dry. Roll the textile with or without layers of newsprint; steaming the bundle is a good way to further fix the dye.

Alternatively, collect fresh cow pats, dry them in the shade so they don't bleach and then break them into small pieces before soaking in a vat of water. After a day or two the liquid can be strained off through a cloth to make a nice golden-brown dye. Steeping the cow-pat dye in an iron cauldron gives pleasant greys and blacks (the latter require a concentrated brew).

Charolais cow at Hope Springs, South Australia.

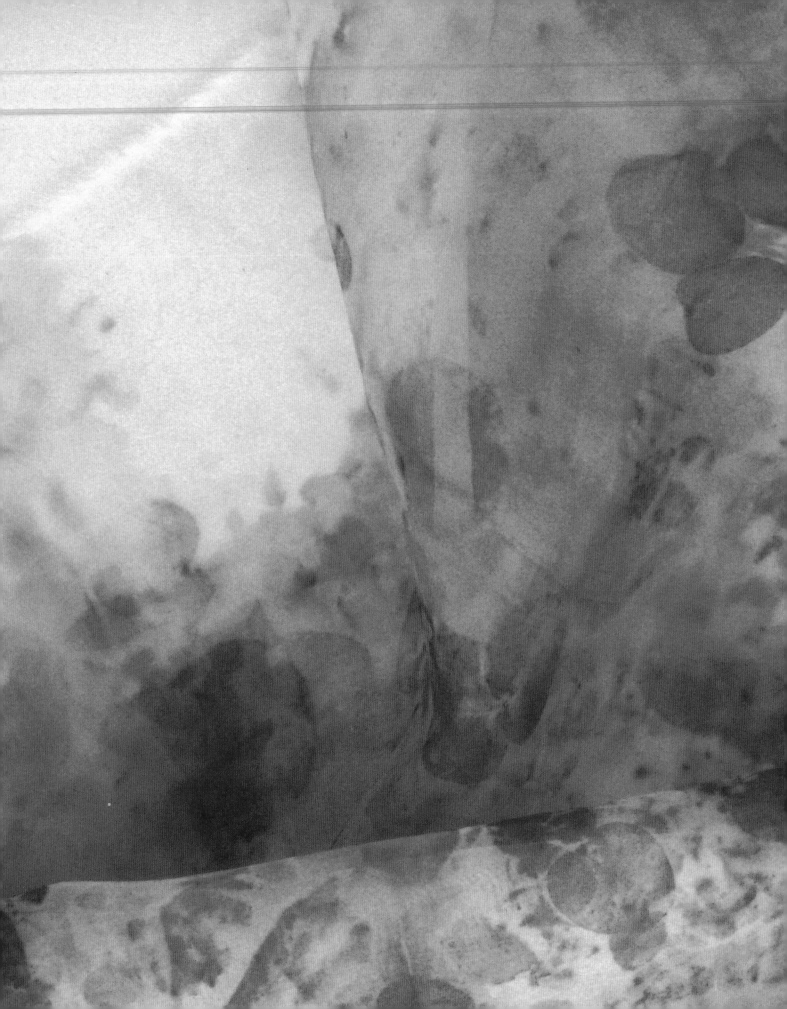

part seven

SOME OTHER CONSIDERATIONS

THE IMPORTANCE OF WATER

Water can be one of the most important mordants. The aqueous substance (used as carrier for dyes) available through reticulated water services around the world varies considerably in pH. Factor in the dissolved salts, minerals and other impurities and water might not be quite as innocuous as it seems. Mordants and dyes will have different effects depending on the fibres used (protein, cellulose or synthetic). The method of preparation of the fibre (wet, dry, scoured, greasy, starched, etc) will also influence the end colour result.

Research indicates that the pH of the water used to establish the dye-bath (as well as possible adulterants in the reticulated service) can have a dramatic effect on the resultant colour. In teaching dye classes across Australia, for example, I have found a variation in the pH of water available in households from 5 (at Geelong, Victoria) to 8 (at Orange, New South Wales; Perth, Western Australia; and Launceston, Tasmania). Add to this the varying proportions of unknown salts and minerals in addition to known chemicals, and results can often surprise. Water sourced from bores and wells can often give surprising colour outcomes and many traditional recipes may actually rely on water from a specific source to replicate suggested results. During periods of drought, some bore waters will exhibit increased concentrations of soluble chemicals. Subterranean reserves in Perth (Western Australia) in the summer of 2007 became so acidic that users were advised not to water gardens with the stuff and to avoid contact with eyes and sensitive skin!

The water in Adelaide is piped from the Murray River (a polluted and salt-compromised traversing the eastern states of Australia) to open-air reservoirs in the Mount Lofty Ranges. Chlorine is added on the way to storage, where 400 tonnes (440 tons) of copper sulphate (added to control algae) annually join the cocktail. Consider the impact of a daily evaporation rate of at least 1 centimetre (½ inch) in concentrating the levels of soluble pollutants, as well as the further impact of fluoridation. In a drought year (such as 2007), little or no rain falls to dilute this mixture.

Water samples collected during world wanderings being tested for their response to volatile viola flowers.

When teaching on an occasion in Adelaide I was much surprised to find that a dye-bath of *Eucalyptus sideroxylon*, where the expected outcome that I had confidently predicted to my students (frequently achieved before in water from the same supply) would be a bright red on protein fibres, was in actual fact a lime green. Among the number of possible variables available my students and I hypothesised that we may have been accessing the supply shortly after the annual copper sulphate addition, a reasonable hypothesis given the tendency toward green when some eucalypts are processed in copper vessels.

Eucalyptus dye-baths can indicate not only alkalinity in water but also the presence of dissolved salts. If the water has a pH greater than 7.5, the eucalyptus dye progressively tends towards murky brown and even becomes slightly sticky. Where dissolved salts are present, a murky precipitate will form in the depths of the dye-pot. Similar effects can be seen in rural dams; if they appear clear on the surface they are likely to be salty, as the tiny mud particles are precipitated out and flocculate in the depths.

Plant dyes are best processed in a neutral to slightly acidic aqueous substrate, so adjusting the pH of the available water using vinegar is advisable if the water is alkaline.

THE IMPORTANCE OF TIME

While a rational observer could reasonably suggest that the craft of plant-based dyeing straddles the disciplines of art and science, requiring at least basic competence in plant identification and a passing understanding of chemistry, some results do defy logic and fall into the realms of magic and witchcraft. When working with plant dyes one thing is certainly clear. Time is (quite literally) of the essence, as the longer the period that materials are given to soak or steep or be absorbed into cloth, the better will be the eventual result.

Temper this advice with the awareness that plant substances are prone to fermentation and decomposition depending on ambient temperatures and the make-up of the material being used. Dyers must make judgements based on recipe research, advice and personal experience.

Slowness should be the watchword. It's hard not to rush the process in the eagerness to discover the next treasure, but well worth the patience to allow soaking before extracting and then long gentle steeping for maximum colour adhesion. Cooling the fibre in the dye-bath rewards the wait.

Teaching dye processes in one-day workshops can be very frustrating, as not only are the real rewards not revealed in so short a time, but so much material barely has its surface skimmed before being poured out in readiness for the end-of-session tidy-up. The only exceptions are the eucalypts, as this truly astonishing genus can give up brilliant colour on protein fibres within only a few hours.

When demonstrating the potential of pot-as-mordant, days are needed for colours to fully develop. Cold-bundling takes anything from a week to a month or more. Good colour from the compost heap generally needs a season before exhumation. Solar dyes can be left for a year, especially when sealed using a layer of wax. The red dyes in Turkish carpets reputedly required twelve years' curing time for the colour to attain the most potency. Plant-dyed embroidery samples kept in the Hermitage Museum in Russia are as fresh and brilliant now as they were on the day the last thread was snipped. Allowing pre-mordants extended periods of curing time indubitably helps make the most of the mordants' potential.

So — just as slow food tastes so much better than the supposedly edible substances of the 'fast' variety, and slowly and carefully crafted clothes tend to last longer than those thrown together in a high-volume sweatshop — slow-brewed plant dyes heedfully applied will give exquisite results that stand the test of time.

Berberis darwinii

berries

Above: *Berberis darwinii* samples.
Opposite page: Rose-leaf eco-print
on merino jersey wrap.

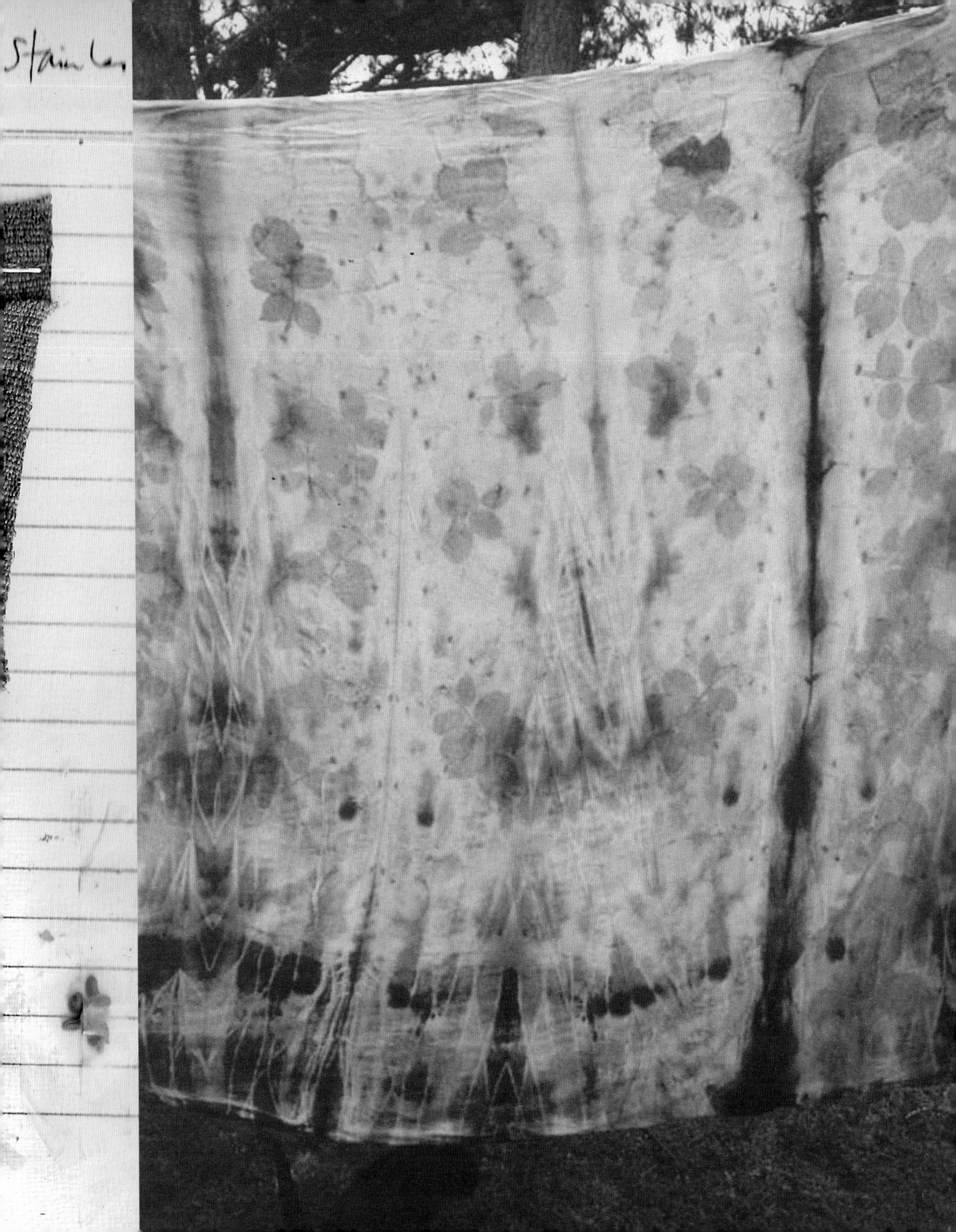

Opposite: Water from different locations will have an effect on the dye-bath due to the unique mixture of chemicals it contains. Above: Detail of eucalyptus print.

1 Redeployed knit top dyed using string resist and *Eucalyptus cinerea*. **2** *Eucalyptus cinerea* swatches. **3** Blue from violas balancing the earthy colours from eucalypts. **4** Eucalyptus-dyed ensemble. **5** *Eucalyptus cinerea* dyed costumes for the West Australian Ballet Company. **6** Detail of silkfelt reconstructed coat en route to the dye-pot. **7** Detail of viola dyes on silk.

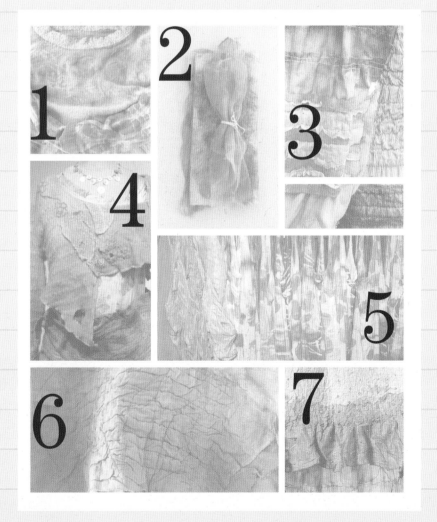

Bundle-dyed silk scarves.

CARING FOR CLOTH

Whether your clothes are plant-dyed or synthetically dyed, they will benefit from proper care.

silk

Too many labels in silk shirts recommend a 'dry clean only' approach. This should be avoided at all costs, as not only do the petrochemicals used in the dry-cleaning process destroy the fabric, progressively dulling the surface of silks with successive applications, they are also extremely toxic to humans.

A good rule to follow is to treat silk textiles as you would treat your own hair; after all, it is made of a very similar substance. Anything woven from silk should be hand-washed in a pH-neutral eco-friendly washing liquid (if nothing else is to hand, use shampoo), rinsed thoroughly and then have its pH balance restored by a final rinse in water with a tablespoon of vinegar added, much as one would apply conditioner to hair.

Why condition your cloth after dyeing? Even the best-quality detergents are usually slightly alkaline, making the fabric feel slightly rough to the touch. The slight acidity of the water-and-vinegar rinse acts as a neutraliser and restores smooth handle to the cloth.

Gently squeeze out the excess moisture by rolling the wet object in a towel, but never wring.

Always dry plant-dyed clothes in shade to avoid bleaching. Silk, in particular, is highly susceptible to destruction by solar radiation when wet and if left out in the sun can become quite brittle.

wool

Like silk, wool is a protein fibre and responds best if treated in a similar manner. Remember not to vary the temperature of the wash and rinse waters by more than 5° C (9° F) or felting may begin.

cotton, linen, ramie and hemp

Cloth made from plant fibres can be treated rather more brutally than that constructed from protein fibres and there is no reason why it should not be vigorously washed in a machine — unless it has been plant dyed. To preserve the intensity of colour on plant-dyed items it is advisable to launder them with care as well. Use a gentle wash cycle and an eco-friendly detergent.

On the other hand, when preparing the cloth for dyeing, traditional bleaching by spreading the damp cloth in the sun is highly effective and preferable by far to using the modern laundry chemicals.

Plant-dyed cloth should nonetheless be dried in the shade.

Squeezing ice-flower dye on to a nuno-felt wrap.

Inset: 'Flannel flower' top made from redeployed silk and cotton, dyed using *Eucalyptus maculata*.

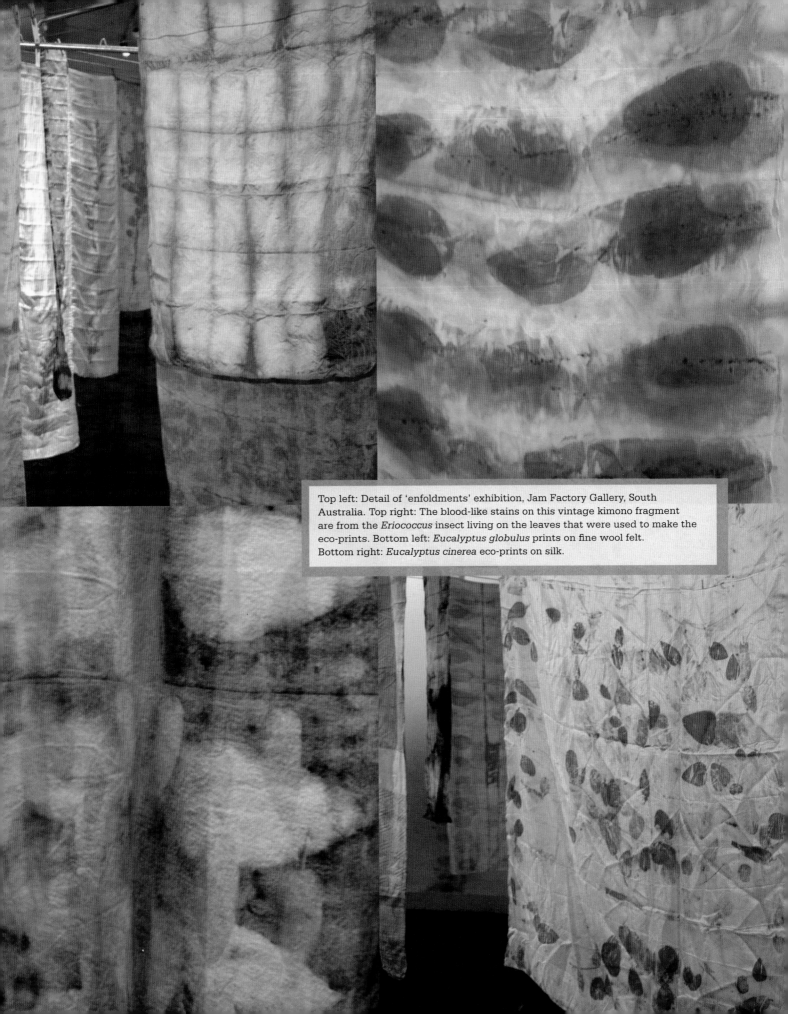

Top left: Detail of 'enfoldments' exhibition, Jam Factory Gallery, South Australia. Top right: The blood-like stains on this vintage kimono fragment are from the *Eriococcus* insect living on the leaves that were used to make the eco-prints. Bottom left: *Eucalyptus globulus* prints on fine wool felt. Bottom right: *Eucalyptus cinerea* eco-prints on silk.

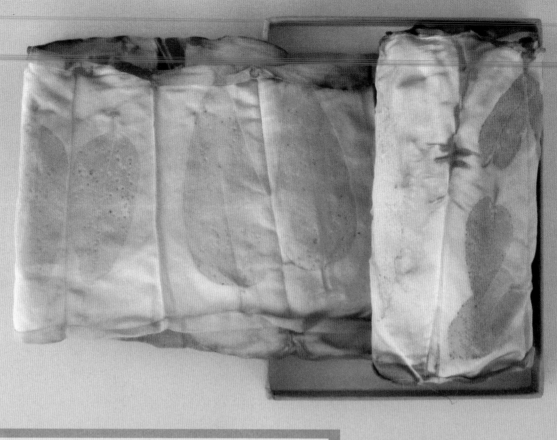

Above: Eco-print samples on hempsilk fabric. Below: Eucalyptus eco-prints act as resists when overdyed with ice-flower dyes.

Silkfelt crinkle scarf dyed brown using *Eucalyptus citriodora*.

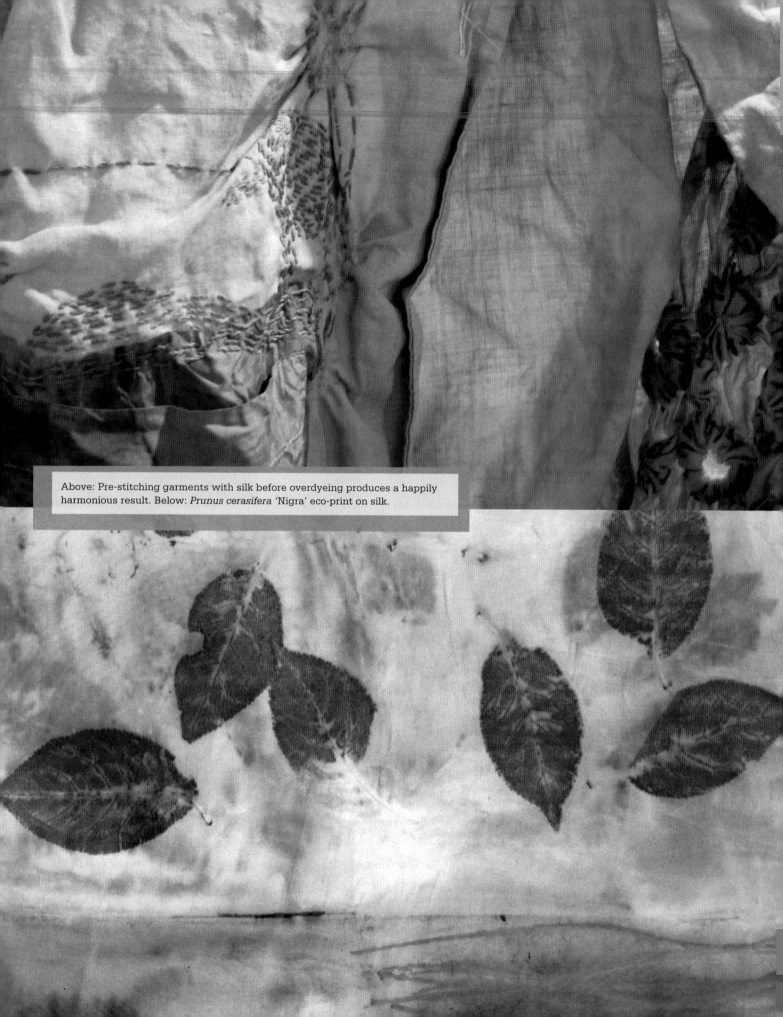

Above: Pre-stitching garments with silk before overdyeing produces a happily harmonious result. Below: *Prunus cerasifera* 'Nigra' eco-print on silk.

Most of the plants in my garden give rich colour.

DISPOSAL OF WASTES

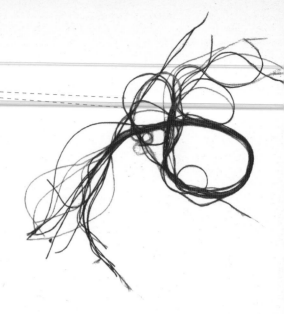

Whatever the process used, there will inevitably be some sort of residue needing disposal.

liquids

If toxic chemical adjuncts such as potassium dichromate or stannous chloride are used to help plant dyes bond with the fibre, then disposal becomes a problem. Liquids must be reduced by evaporation and the residual sludge taken to a commercial waste disposal unit; simply pouring such substances on to the compost heap will ultimately cause a problem. The traditional mordants copper sulphate and ferrous sulphate, while admittedly freely available in hardware stores and also used as agricultural chemicals, are also poisonous. I strongly advise against their use.

If the only adjuncts used are mordant solutions prepared from other plant materials, from scrap metal or from such liquids as vinegar, urine or milk, their disposal by dispersion through the compost heap is simple and safe. Remnant alum-water can be poured on to plants such as hydrangeas if there is no compost heap available, but given that a diet of pure leaf litter will create an unbalanced compost heap, adding the occasional alkali in the form of alum, ash or washing soda can actually do a lot of good.

When sea water is used as part of the mordant cocktail it does tend to complicate the issue, as pouring salt on the soil in any quantity is not advisable. If, however, one has made a mordant 'tea' using scrap metals and sea water and then uses only a small amount of this substance in a dye procedure, it is likely that most of the salts in the solution will have bonded with the fibre as part of the process. This would imply that the remnant solution could probably compare quite favourably with urine or soup in terms of salinity; my recommendation is either to recycle the base solution as part of the next dye-bath or to dispose of the liquid via the sewerage system.

There has been some debate as to the use of pot-as-mordant and what the levels of metal toxicities might be in such cases. The simple answer is that the levels are difficult to control or assess, but that it is clear that increased time in such a dye-bath correlates to increased effect on the cloth of the metal of the pot; the longer the bath sits, the stronger the solution will be. Consider re-using the remnant solution in a non-reactive pot to get the most benefit from it. Otherwise, dispose of iron-influenced solutions by pouring on the roots of citrus trees, and copper solutions by diluting heavily with water in a watering can and sprinkling over the fallow part of the vegetable patch, where in both instances they will do some good.

vegetable matter

If you live in a small apartment and wish to work with plant dyes, do not despair. Left-over leaves, bark, seeds and twigs can be used as mulch and if chopped into small pieces can be discreetly disposed of in public parks and gardens. During my travels I inevitably succumb to the lure of experimenting with some newly discovered treasure (usually weeds or windfalls when I am residing in hotels). Snap-lock bags become portable dye vessels, and metal scraps found in the street along with the dregs of the wine from the evening meal act as mordants. Processed and exhausted plant material is ripped into small shreds and judiciously applied to the flower beds of the public gardens I enjoy during my morning constitutional.

Dyers with gardens of their own will benefit from the abundance of mulch produced by the enjoyment of plant dyes. Alternatively, try bundling the processed material in cloth and layering or burying it in the compost heap for a cold-dye process (bearing in mind that the compost heap can actually get quite hot at times). Include a few pieces of scrap metal and keep the compost heap moist. Monitor the pile regularly, as micro-fauna can make holes in cloth quite quickly and compost heaps provide the ideal environment.

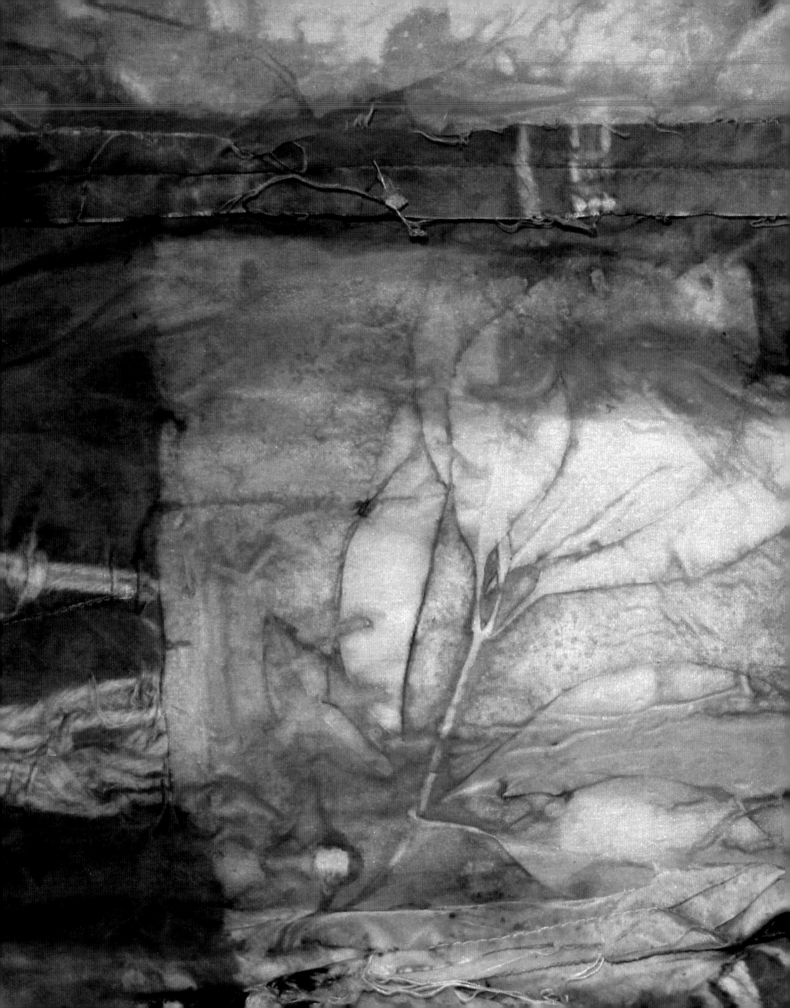

part eight

REFERENCES

FURTHER READING

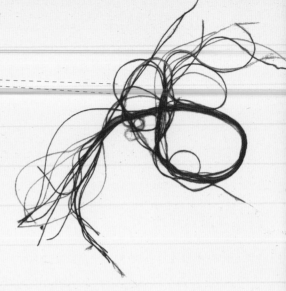

ADROSKO Rita, 1971, *Natural Plants and Home Dyeing*, Dover, New York

ANDERSON Beryl, 1971, *Creative Spinning, Weaving and Plant-dyeing*, Angus & Robertson, Australia

AULD B.A. & MEDD R. W., 1992, *Weeds: an Illustrated Botanical Guide to the Weeds of Australia*, Inkata Press, Melbourne & Sydney

BÄCHI-NUSSBAUMER Erna, 1980, *So Färbt man mit Pflanzen*, Verlag Paul Haupt, Bern & Stuttgart

BACK Philippa & LOEWENFELD Claire, 1976, *The Complete Book of Herbs and Spices*, Reed, New Zealand

BAKER Patricia L., 1995, *Islamic Textiles*, British Museum Press, London

BALFOUR PAUL Jenny, 1998, *Indigo*, British Museum Press, London

BARBER E. J. W., 1991, *Prehistoric Textiles*, Princeton University Press, Princeton

BARBER Elizabeth Wayland, 1994, *Women's Work, the First 20,000 Years*, Norton, New York & London

BARBER Elizabeth Wayland, 1999, *The Mummies of Ürümchi*, Macmillan, London

BARTON Jane, KELLOGG RICE Mary & WADA Yoshiko Iwamoto, 1999, *Shibori*, Kodansha International

BEMISS Elijah, 1973, *The Dyer's Companion*, Dover, New York

BINDON Peter, 1998, *Useful Bush Plants*, West Australian Museum, Perth, Australia

BÖHMER Harald, 2002, *Koekboya*, REMHÖB Verlag, Ganderkesee, Germany

BOLTON Eileen, 1972, *Lichens for Vegetable Dyeing*, Studio Vista Publications, UK

BONNEY Neville, 1997, *Economic Trees and Shrubs for South Australia*, Greening Australia

BOSENCE Susan, 1985, *Hand Block Printing and Resist Dyeing*, David & Charles, Newton Abbot & London

BOUGHER Neale L. & SYME Katrina, 1998, *Fungi of Southern Australia*, University of Western Australia Press, Nedlands, WA

BRANDON Reiko Mochinaga, 1986, *Country Textiles of Japan — The Art of Tsutsugaki*, Weatherhill, Tokyo & New York

BROOKLYN BOTANIC GARDENS, 1973, 'Dye Plants & Dyeing', special printing of 'Plants and Gardens' Vol 20 No 3

BROOKLYN BOTANIC GARDENS, 1978, 'Natural Plant Dyeing', Brooklyn Botanic Gardens Record (Plants and Gardens) Vol 29 No 2

BRYANT Kate & RODD Tony, 2005, *The Ultimate Plant Book*, CSIRO Publishing, Australia

BUCHANAN Rita, 1995, *A Dyer's Garden*, Interweave Press, Colorado

BUCKINGHAM Peggy & SYME Katrina, 1998, *Western Australian Fungi for Textile Dyes: a Preliminary Survey*, Claremont & Denmark, WA

BURNETT Sarah, 1990, *Passion for Colour*, Conran Octopus, London

CANNON John & Margaret, 1994, *Dye Plants and Dyeing*, The Herbert Press in association with the Royal Botanic Gardens, Kew

CARMAN Jean, 1978, *Dyemaking with Eucalypts*, Rigby, Australia

CASSELMAN Karen Diadick, 1997, *Natural Dyes of the Asia Pacific*, Studio Vista Publications, Nova Scotia, Canada

CASSELMAN Karen Diadick, 2000, *Ethical and Ecological Dyes: a workbook for the Natural Dyer*, Studio Vista Publications, Nova Scotia, Canada

CASSELMAN Karen Leigh, 1993, *Craft of the Dyer*, Dover, New York

CHRISTMAS Liz & DALBY Gill, 1984, *Spinning & Dyeing, an Introductory Manual*, David & Charles, Newton Abbot (London), North Pomfret (Vermont)

COATS Alice M, 1956, *Flowers and their Histories*, Hulton Press, London

CONWAY S, 1992, *Thai Textiles*, British Museum Press, London

DEAN Jenny, 1994, *The Craft of Natural Dyeing*, Search Press, UK

DEAN Jenny, 1996, *Dyeing without Chemicals*, Dean, Shefford, UK

DEAN Jenny, 1999, *Wild Colour*, Mitchell Beazley, UK

De BOER Janet, 1987, *Dyeing for Fibres and Fabrics*, Kangaroo Press, Australia

FLINT India, 2001, 'Arcadian Alchemy – Ecologically Sustainable Dyes for Textiles from the Eucalypt Forest', MA Thesis, University of South Australia, Adelaide

FOY Nicky & PHILLIPS Roger, 1990, *Herbs*, Pan Books, London

GLASSON Ian & GLASSON Mikki, 1980, *A Eucalypt Dyer's Handbook*, Glasson, Carcoar

GRAE Ida, 1974, *Nature's Colors* Macmillan Publishing, New York

GRIERSON Su, 1989, *The Colour Cauldron*, Mill Books, Scotland

HALLET Judith V., 1993, *Natural Plant Dyes*, Kangaroo Press, Australia

HANDWEAVERS & SPINNERS GUILD OF VICTORIA, 1974, *Dyemaking with Australian Flora*, Rigby, Australia

HARRIS Thistle Y, 1979, *Wild Flowers of Australia*, Angus & Robertson, Australia

HARVEY Janet, 1997, *Traditional Textiles of Central Asia*, Thames & Hudson, London

HOCHBERG Bette, 1993, *Fibre Facts*, Hochberg, Santa Cruz

HUH Dong-hwa & ROBERTS Claire, 1998, *Rapt in Colour*, Powerhouse Publishing, Sydney

HULBERT Mollie & PETTER Frieda, 1989, *Australian Plant Dyes and Knitting Patterns for Woolly Jumpers*, Kangaroo Press, Australia

KOEHLER Horst, 1976, *Horst Koehler's Buntes Blumenbuch*, Mosaik Verlag, München, Germany

LILES J. N., 1990, *The Art and Craft of Natural Dyeing*, University of Tennessee Press, Knoxville, USA

LLOYD Joyce, undated, *Dyes from Plants*, Lloyd, New Zealand

LLOYD Joyce, 1971, *Dyes from Plants of Australia and New Zealand*, Reed, Auckland

LOW Tim, 1991, *Bush Medicine: a Pharmacopoeia of Natural Remedies*, Angus & Robertson, Australia

MAIDEN J. H., 1889, *The Useful Native Plants of Australia (including Tasmania)*, Trubner & Henderson, Sydney

MAXWELL Robyn, 2003, *Sari to Sarong*, National Gallery of Australia, ACT

MILNER Ann, 1980, *Natural Wool Dyes and Recipes*, John McEndoe, Dunedin, New Zealand

MILNER Ann, 1992, *The Ashford Book of Dyeing*, Lothian, Victoria

NICOLLE Dean, 1997, *Eucalypts of South Australia*, Nicolle, South Australia

PAVORD Anna, 2005, *The Naming of Names*, Bloomsbury Publishing, London

PHILLIPS Roger & RIX Martyn, 1988, *Roses*, Pan Books, London

PHILLIPS Roger & RIX Martyn, 1993, *Vegetables*, Pan Books, London

POLAKOFF C, 1980, *Into Indigo*, Anchor Books

ROBERTSON S, 1973, *Dyes from Plants*, Van Nostrand Reinhold Ltd, New York

SANDBERG Gösta, 1994, *The Red Dyes*, Lark Books, Asheville, NC

SCHOESER Mary, 2003, *World Textiles, a Concise History*, Thames & Hudson, London & New York

SCHULTZ Kathleen, 1975, *Create your own Natural Dyes*, Sterling Publishing Co., New York

SOUTH AUSTRALIAN COUNTRY WOMEN'S ASSOCIATION, 1939 (reprint May & November 1947), *Handicrafts for Countrywomen*, Adelaide

STORER Joyce, 1978, *Dyes and Fabrics*, Thames and Hudson, London & New York

SUMNER Christina, 1999, *Beyond the Silk Road*, Powerhouse Publishing, Sydney

TALALAJ S. D. & J., 1991, *The Strangest Plants*, Hill of Content, Melbourne

THEROUX Alexander, 1994, *The Primary Colours*, Henry Holt & Company, New York

THEROUX Alexander, 1996, *The Secondary Colours*, Owl Books, USA

THURSTAN Violetta, 1970, *The Use of Vegetable Dyes*, The Dryad Press, Bristol, Great Britain

TODD Carol, 1995, *Earth Tones – Colours from Western Dye Plants*, Rowland Press, California

TORIMARU Sadae & TORIMARU Tomoko, 2004, *Imprints on Cloth*, Akishige Tada, Japan

TROTMAN E. R., 1970, *Dyeing and Chemical Technology of Textile Fibres*, Charles Griffin & Co. Ltd, London & High Wycombe

URBAN Anne, 1990, *Wildflowers and Plants of Inland Australia*, Portside Editions, Australia

VAN STRALEN Trudy, 1993, *Indigo, Madder and Marigold*, Interweave Press, Colorado

WEISS Walter M, 1998, *The Bazaar, Markets and Merchants of the Islamic World*, Thames & Hudson, London

WICKENS Hetty, 1983, *Natural Dyes for Spinners and Weavers*, B. T. Batsford, London

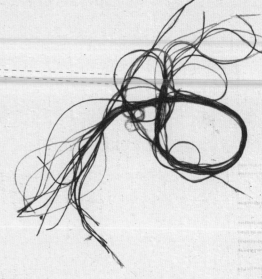

WEBSITES

Following is a list of interesting website addresses specific to fabric dyeing, dyes and cloth.

http://ace.acadiau.ca/arts/classics/COURSES/2233/Nomenc/Nomenc_.htm
Taxonomy of plants — history and explanation

http://en.wikipedia.org/wiki/Dye
About dyes

http://groups.yahoo.com/group/NaturalDyes
A natural dyes discussion list

http://groups.yahoo.com/group
NaturalDyes/links
The links page from the natural dye list

http://marjory.salles.monsite.wanadoo.fr/page1.html
Colourist working with madder and red

http://stainsfile.info/StainsFile/theory/mordant.htm
About mordants

http://woad.weebly.com
The woad pages

http://www.avani-kumaon.org
NGO working in India using plant dyes and ecologically sustainable energy methods

http://www.azulmaya.com.sv
An indigo hacienda in El Salvador

http://www.bacterio.cict.fr/trueper.html
A site about the naming of bacteria, but with helpful tips

http://www.bleu-de-lectoure.com
Company in France working with woad in the traditional way

http://www.csdl.tamu.edu/FLORA/Wilson/tfp/car/nomenclatures01.htm
Taxonomy of plants — lecture notes kindly posted on the web by Hugh D. Wilson

http://www.chm.bris.ac.uk/webprojects2002/price/azo.htm
http://en.wikipedia.org/wiki/Azo_compound
http://en.wikipedia.org/wiki/Category:Azo_dyes
Information on Azo dyes

http://www.couleurs-de-plantes.com
Company specialising in the production of plant pigments

http://www.couleurgarance.com
French resource for plant dyes

http://www.earthnetwork.info
Japanese sustainable plant dye network

http://www.johnmarshall.to
Informative site by a North American master dyer

http://www.kakishibui.com
A site about persimmons

http://www.mnh.si.edu/africanvoices/mudcloth/index_flash.html
Amusing and educational site about mudcloth

http://www.mukogawa-u.ac.jp/~ushida/e_ai_exp.htm
About Japanese indigo

http://www.pfaf.org/database/search_use.php?K%5B%5D=Dye
Plant database

http://www.rubiapigmentanaturalia.nl
A site about madder

http://www.wildcolours.ik.com
Teresinha Roberts' site

www.beautifulsilks.com.au
A source of ethically produced silks

www.fullystoked.com
**Ethical fair-trade source of un-dyed T-shorts
(on both cotton and superfine merino wool)
for dye experiments**

www.indiaflint.com
The author's own site

www.woolontheweb.com.au
**Site detailing the latest developments in
Australian merino**

http://www.library.cornell.edu/africana/about/mudcloth.html
Site about mudcloth

visit www.earthisland.org
Information on shatoosh

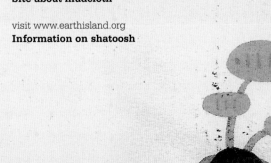

INDEX

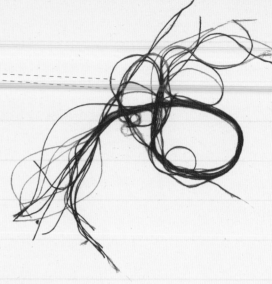

onion-skin hot bundle print

About the author

Designer, artist, writer, sheep farmer and occasional ragbag princess India Flint was born in Melbourne and has lived in diverse localities from the Andamooka opal fields to rural Austria and metropolitan Montreal. This gypsy life enriches a textile practice embracing art, theatre and fashion.

Presently based on a rural property on the eastern escarpment of the Mount Lofty Ranges, South Australia, she is known for the development of the highly distinctive eco-print, an ecologically sustainable plant-based printing process giving brilliant colour to cloth.

India's work is represented in collections and museums in Australia, Latvia and Germany. She produces and sporadically exhibits a range of hand-worked salvage clothing under the label 'prophet of bloom', as well as designing and sewing plant-dyed costumes for theatre and dance.

Acknowledgements

I could never hope to thank all of the people who have helped to shape this book, but I would like to make an attempt. Be grateful, dear reader, that this is not an Oscar acceptance speech, as at least you are spared the sight of me snivelling into a microphone as I read from my 'just-in-case' list. I wish to thank my family for putting up with chaos during the writing of this book. In particular I thank my daughter Anna-Louisa, whose delicious cooking has nourished us all while I wrote and brewed dyes, my son Christian, the ever-patient in-house IT consultant, and my daughter Rosie for making killer fudge, and all three of them for making beautiful music to soothe the inner beast. For verifying my allusions to chemistry I thank Jack Nisbet.

I fondly remember Bob Blows, David Thomson and Karoly Szabo, three exceptional plantsmen who nurtured my love and knowledge of green things and let me work in their nurseries. The list of green thumbs to honour includes also my parents Peter and Ārija Schwerdtfeger who instilled in me a love of scholarship and have generously provided a farm for me to live (and play) on. They also taught me that any day on which you wake up breathing is a jolly good one. And thanks, Ma, for the proofreading.

I thank Diana Hill and Janine Flew, my mentors at Murdoch; and Gayna Murphy for her clear vision in designing the book.

I am deeply grateful to John Kelley, the patient and gifted musician who guides my fingers on the tenor sax and thus helps to keep me calm, relatively sane and musically satisfied; and to Janet de Boer, who has offered joyful and entertaining encouragement throughout my career.

Last but by no means least I thank my many students around the world, through whose adventurous experiments in workshops my practice has been enriched.

First published in the United States by
Interweave Press LLC
201 East Fourth Street
Loveland, CO 80537
interweavestore.com
All rights reserved.

Text © India Flint 2008
Design © Murdoch Books Pty Limited 2008
Photography © India Flint 2008 with the exception of the following: page 29 (indigo hacienda, cakes of indigo): Grace Guirola Seassal; page 39 (woad): Getty Images; page 98 (wool parting): Chris Shannon; page 199 (Charolais cow): Peter Schwerdtfeger; page 135 (*Indigofera australis*): Murdoch Books Photo Library, photographer Sue Stubbs.

Captions

Cover: Motif adapted from lupin eco-print. Front jacket and endpapers: Complex shibori and eco-print silk taffeta with ice-flower over-bath. Pages 18–19: Assorted vintage kimono fragments felted onto merino wool, shibori dyed with *Eucalyptus cinerea*. Pages 34–35: *Prunus cerasifera* 'Nigra' hot-bundle-dyed on vintage silk kimono fragment. Pages 46–47: Cocktail of blue ice-flower dyes over *Eucalyptus maculata* eco-print. Pages 74–75: Cold mixed eucalyptus eco-print on cotton, a process that took six months. Pages 118–119: Rose-leaf eco-print on merino jersey, using *Eucalyptus citriodora* as the dye-bath for the bundle. Pages 152–153: *Hapa-zome* direct print plant sample on cotton fabric, produced by students in a workshop in the textiles department at Edith Cowan University, Western Australia. Pages 200–201: *Eucalyptus cinerea* eco-print on a silk organza costume for Leigh Warren & Dancers. Pages 224–225: Eucalyptus and found metal magic on a redeployed silk coat.

All rights reserved. No part of this publication may be reproduced, stored in a retrieval system or transmitted in any form or by any means, electronic, mechanical, photocopying, recording or otherwise, without the prior written permission of the publisher.

Cataloguing-in-Publication Data available from the Library of Congress.
ISBN 978-1-59668-330-3

Colour separation by Colour Chiefs, Australia.
PRINTED IN CHINA by Asia Pacific Offset, Ltd.
This book is printed on 100% recycled paper (both white and brown papers), using soya-based inks.

DISCOVER EVEN MORE IDEAS AND DESIGNS FOR
FABRIC ART WITH THESE INSPIRING RESOURCES
FROM INTERWEAVE.

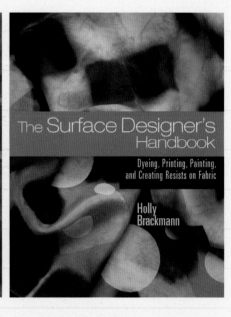

The Complete Guide to Natural Dyeing
Techniques and Recipes for Dyeing
Fabrics, Yarns, and Fibers at Home
Eva Lambert and Tracy Kendall
ISBN 978-1-59668-181-1
$24.95

Art Cloth
A Guide to Surface Design for Fabric
Jane Dunnewold
ISBN 978-1-59668-195-8
$26.95

The Surface Designer's Handbook
Dyeing, Printing, Painting, and Creating
Resists on Fabric
Holly Brackmann
ISBN 978-1-931499-90-3
$29.95

INTERWEAVE.
interweavestore.com

Quilting Arts
MAGAZINE®

Whether you consider yourself a contemporary
quilter, fiber artist, art quilter, embellished
quilter, or wearable-art artist, *Quilting Arts*
strives to meet your creative needs.
Quiltingarts.com

QuiltingArts.com

Quiltingarts.com, the online contemporary
quilting community, offers free patterns, expert
tips and techniques, e-newsletters, blogs,
forums, videos, special offers, and more!
Quiltingarts.com

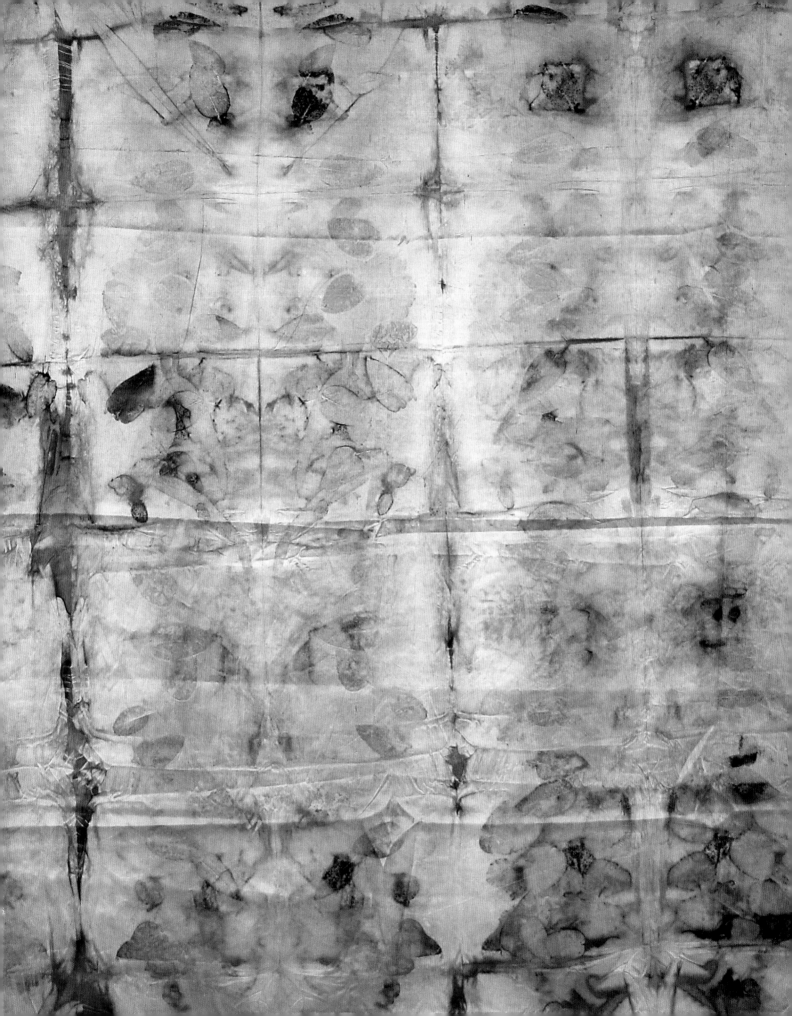

DISCARD